ISD

INHIBITED SEXUAL DESIRE

Dr. Jennifer Knopf and Dr. Michael Seiler
with Susan Meltsner

Produced by The Philip Lief Group, Inc.

WARNER BOOKS

D0109883

A Time Warner Company

Warner Books Edition

Copyright ©1990 by Philip Lief Group, Inc. and Jennifer Knopf
and Michael Seiler
This Warner Books edition is published by arrangement with
William Morrow and Company, Inc. 105 Madison Avenue, New York, NY 10016

Warner Books, Inc., 666 Fifth Avenue, New York, NY 10103
Ⓦ A Time Warner Company

Printed in the United States of America
First Warner Books Printing: March 1991

10 9 8 7 6 5 4 3 2 1

Library of Congress Cataloging in Publication Data
Knopf, Jennifer.
    ISD : inhibited sexual desire / Jennifer Knopf and Michael Seiler,
with Susan Meltsner.
        p. cm.
    "Produced by the Philip Lief Group, Inc."
    Includes bibliographical references.
    ISBN 0-446-39235-9
    1. Sex instruction. 2. Lust. 3. Sex in marriage. I. Seiler,
Michael. II. Meltsner, Susan. III. Philip Lief Group. IV. Title.
HQ31.K67   1991
613.9'6—dc20   90-48054
                                                                    CIP

Cover design by Anne Twomey

ARE YOU SUFFERING FROM INHIBITED SEXUAL DESIRE? TAKE THIS SEXUAL DESIRE SELF-TEST AND FIND OUT:

Do you think most couples have sex more often than you do?

Do you think you should be having sex more often?

Do you and your partner disagree on how often to have sex?

Do you or your partner engage in sexual activity even when you're not really interested in having sex?

Do you or your partner have or enjoy sex less often than you once did?

Is your relationship or your life in general different from what it was—before your sex life took a turn for the worse?

Do you find you're more interested in sex when your partner is not around or when you're thinking of some past or fantasy partner?

If you answered "yes" to any of these questions, then Dr. Knopf and Dr. Seiler have information that can dramatically change your sex life.

INHIBITED SEXUAL DESIRE

"RECOMMENDED."
—Library Journal

To my father, Leonard, and my brother, Rennie
—J.K.
To Marcy, Jessica, and my family
—M.S.

ACKNOWLEDGMENTS

WHILE OUR NAMES APPEAR on the cover of this book, it could not have been developed without the contributions and support of many other people. First, we would like to thank those at the Philip Lief Group. Cathy Hemming's encouragement and enthusiastic support helped us to undertake this project. Susan Meltsner converted our rather technical language into English and brought our ideas more to life. Nancy Kalish guided us when we got off track, helped us reconcile our creative differences, and provided us with expert editorial support. Nancy did all of this and more with a gentle hand and a wonderful spirit. In addition, we would like to thank our advocates at William Morrow—Jim Landis, who believed in our project from the beginning, and Liza Dawson, whose editorial skill greatly benefited it.

In a less direct but equally important manner, many others contributed to the completion of this book. Alicia Trujillo, the program coordinator of the Sex Therapy and Education Program at Northwestern University Medical School, typed our often illegible writing, tolerated our moodiness, and repeatedly went well beyond the reasonable expectations of a colleague in supporting us throughout this project. Our colleague Karen Abram also provided significant support in numerous ways, bringing laughter and energy into days that were often quite long. Lawrence Weiner listened and frequently offered me

(J.K.) a calm, patient, commonsense perspective. Marcy Seiler listened, encouraged, and loved me (M.S.) throughout this effort.

We would be remiss if we did not acknowledge the many professionals whose ideas and work we learned from and used as a foundation for this book. Specifically, the classic work of Helen Singer Kaplan, Lonnie Barbach, David Scharff, and Bernie Zilbergeld has influenced our own understanding and ideas about sexual desires and sexual desire disorders. We would also like to acknowledge in general our many colleagues at Northwestern University and the University of Chicago who have contributed to our own professional development.

Finally, we would like to acknowledge the many individuals and couples who have worked with us in treatment; their willingness to share their internal and interpersonal struggles has helped us to understand the causes and appreciate the pain of sexual difficulties. Our hope is that we have learned well enough from them and the others we have studied with so we may help you and yours enjoy your sexuality.

CONTENTS

INTRODUCTION

WE ALL REFUSE OR put off sex occasionally. Too tired, too tense, too distracted by other concerns, or simply not in the mood, we cannot arouse sexual desire on demand and so we exercise our right to say, "No, thank you. Not tonight."

But what if your response to sexual activity is "not tonight or tomorrow night or the next night either" for weeks, months, or even years on end? What if your lack of interest in sex leads to marital or relationship problems, or causes you such great despair that you isolate yourself from people and social situations? What if you, your partner, or both of you feel alarmed, angry, hurt, frightened, or frustrated because you are having sex less often than you think is normal or feeling less sexual satisfaction than you think you should?

Then you may be experiencing inhibited sexual desire (ISD)—a lack of interest in sex, or an inability to feel sexual or get sexually aroused—or there may be desire discrepancies—which can result in dramatic personal or relationship conflicts when you and your partner have naturally different levels of sex drive and cannot negotiate compromises about when, how, or how often to have sex. These are complex sexual problems, but also very common ones.

Most sex therapists—ourselves included—will tell you that they see far more patients with ISD and desire discrepancy disorders than any other type of sexual disorder and that these conditions are clearly on the rise nationwide. According to recent research and surveys of the general population, as many as half of all married or cohabiting adults (both male and female) mention their own or their partners' lack of sexual interest when asked about difficulties in their sex lives or relationships.

NOT TONIGHT, DEAR

Barbara and Dan

Smiling dreamily, Barbara slips into her new negligee. Feeling its silky fabric against her skin, she imagines the look her husband, Dan, will get on his face when he sees it. That look will say he wants her. It is a look she hasn't seen in a long, long time.

Barbara inspects her reflection in the full-length mirror and decides that, at forty, she is still a very attractive woman. Dan, however, appears not to notice. In pajamas and a flannel bathrobe, he reclines on the bed and watches the evening news. Barbara circles to his side of the bed, takes the remote control device from the nightstand, and turns off the television. She looks at him seductively, her intentions abundantly clear. He looks away and pretends not to notice Barbara's unspoken sexual overture.

Dan's sigh may be apologetic, but it does nothing to ease Barbara's feelings of exasperation, rejection, disgust. "Not tonight, Barbara," he says and takes the remote control from her hand.

Andrea and Paul

Scribbled across the bottom of a page in Andrea's appointment book is the word "Tonight!!!" Andrea knows the same notation can be found in the daily planner of her husband, Paul. It is a reminder to leave work early so they can have a relaxing dinner together and find time to have sex.

Unfortunately, a call comes in from the west coast at 4 P.M. and the crisis it precipitates keeps Andrea at the office until half-past seven. She frantically rushes home, only to discover that she need not have berated herself for once again allowing business to interfere with romance. Paul's message on their answering machine informs her that a contract is taking longer to negotiate than he anticipated. He will be home as soon as he can.

Andrea eats dinner alone and falls asleep on the sofa. Paul wakes her when he arrives. Affectionately and apologetically, he asks if she still wants to keep their "appointment." She thinks they should. Unable to revive herself by taking a shower, Andrea realizes she isn't up to having sex and hopes Paul won't mind postponing it again. When she returns to the bedroom, she sees she does not have to ask. Paul is undressed, under the covers, and fast asleep. He awakens briefly as she gets in bed. "Not tonight, huh?" he mumbles groggily. She gives him a little kiss on the forehead and replies, "No, not tonight."

Rachel

The man pokes at the olive in his martini as he waits for her answer. Rachel considers the question, weighing the pros and cons. He's good looking, she thinks. That's a plus, and he did buy the drinks and dinner. But according to the guys in the sales office, he's a wild one, picking up a different woman every night when he's on the road. Wondering what else he might have picked up, Rachel asks herself if sleeping with him is worth the risk.

Her thoughts stray. If she leaves now, she can rent a movie and watch it with time to spare before the evening news. Then again, it's been quite a while since she last had sex. Of course, the unopened carton of fudge marble ice cream in the freezer sounds almost as appealing and she does have to get up early to meet her mother at the airport. And what if he turns out to be one of those guys who give women a hard time about having to use a condom?

"So, how about it?" he asks.

Rachel gives him her decision: "Sorry, not tonight."

Not tonight. In all probability, at one time or another you too have uttered those words or listened while someone said them to you. At that moment, you or your partner lacked the time, energy, or desire for sex, and therefore refused a sexual overture, passed up a sexual opportunity, or postponed sexual activity. There is absolutely nothing wrong with that. Sometimes saying no is truly is the most realistic and comfortable response to a sexual invitation. In fact, because the ability to become sexually aroused is influenced by fatigue, stress, the possibility of being interrupted, illness, depression, relationship conflicts, and much more, you can reasonably expect your sexual desire to come and go periodically. Problems arise, however, when it goes but won't come back.

Sexual Desire Self-test

Do you think you are less interested in sex than:

- other people the same age?
- you should be?
- you were in the past?
- you want to be?
- your partner wants you to be?

Is your partner less interested in sex than:

- other people the same age?
- he or she should be?
- he or she was in the past?
- he or she wants to be?
- you want your partner to be?

Do you rarely or never feel interested in sex?

Do you rarely or never initiate sexual overtures?

Do you frequently or always reject or avoid your partner's sexual overtures?

Do you find that you're more interested in sex when your partner is not around or when you're thinking of some past or
fantasy partner?

Do you think most couples have sex more often than you do?

Do you think you should be having sex more often?

Do you and your partner disagree on how often to have sex?

Do you or your partner engage in sexual activity even when
you're not really interested in having sex?

Do you or your partner have or enjoy sex less often than you
once did?

Is your relationship or your life in general different from what
it was before your sex life took a turn for the worse?

    If you answered yes to one or more of these questions, you
may be among a growing number of men and women who, *on
a regular basis,* lack the desire or choose not to have sex despite
ample opportunities to do so. You may have sex infrequently,
if at all; rarely even think about sex; and, in some instances,
completely lose interest in it.

    If you do, in fact, respond to most sexual opportunities
with a lack of interest, or are repeatedly turned down by a
partner who is perpetually turned off, and as a result feel worried or unhappy about the frequency or quality of your sex life,
this book can help you understand what is happening to you
and why. It can make you aware of and show you ways to
overcome ISD—a sexual difficulty that not only robs people of
sexual pleasure, but also wreaks havoc on relationships and
seriously damages emotional health and self-esteem.

    In the simplest terms, ISD is the lack of hunger for or
interest in sex. Your desire for sex and your ability to get sexually aroused diminish or disappear altogether. You feel "sexy"
very rarely or not at all. Although you may occasionally engage
in sexual activity, chances are that you have sex less often than
you once did and find it less pleasurable, more mechanical—
more like work than play.

    Although ISD begins with a noticeable decrease or absence
of interest in sex, it does not end there. You may find yourself

avoiding sex as well as any physical contact or emotional inter-
changes you think might lead to it, arguing with your partner
about it, and feeling guilty, inadequate, or like a "freak" for not
being as enthusiastic about sex as everyone else seems to be.
You may develop other sexual problems like impotence or an
inability to have orgasms. Sometimes the mere thought of having sex will set off a full-fledged anxiety attack.

If you are married or involved in an intimate relationship,
you may see the relationship itself begin to crumble. If you
are not involved in a relationship, you may begin to isolate
yourself from people, staying away from any place or situation
where you could encounter someone who might want to have
sex with you.

In the Sex Therapy and Education Program of Northwestern University Medical School, where Jennifer is program director and Michael is assistant director, and in our private
practices, we see many, many couples and individuals suffering
from ISD, ranging in age from eighteen to the mid-eighties.
They come to us through referrals from physicians, other therapists, and other patients, or by reading about us in the magazine articles in which we have been quoted.

Some of our patients are merely victims of their own misconceptions about what is "normal." They are alarmed because
they do not have sex as frequently as the national average for
people their age. Or they are distressed because their sex lives
seem to be less exciting than the ones they read and hear about
in novels, movies, television shows, and magazines. Yet they
need little more than some accurate information and the encouragement to give up myths about how sex is supposed to be
in order to enjoy a sex life that is normal *for them*.

On the other hand, many of the individuals and couples we
treat have little if any interest in sex. They never think or fantasize about sex and show no reaction to sexual situations or
stimuli that excite other people, or even those that excited them
in the past. Married and physically capable of performing sexually, they may not have engaged in sexual activity for months
or even years, perhaps as long as a decade.

Both of us have been involved in sex and marital therapy

for the last ten years as practicing clinicians, lecturers, researchers, and program administrators. Over that time, we have become experts in the treatment of sexual desire disorders, including ISD, a term that Dr. Harold Lief first coined in 1977.

Since the Northwestern Sex Therapy and Education Program began four years ago, we have achieved success in treating ISD in 70 percent of the individuals and/or couples that remained in treatment. The techniques that we use in our therapy are presented in this book. Our approach is to emphasize an understanding of the cause of a sexual problem and explore all possible influences, including medical factors, family background, present and past relationships, and outside stresses, as you will do in the following chapters. Once the cause has been discovered, we put our patients to work solving the problem with exercises such as those you'll find in Chapters Six, Seven, and Eight.

Most of our patients—and most people with ISD—fall into at least one of the following categories:

- couples with desire differences. Like Barbara—who would gladly have sex every day—and Dan—who is more than satisfied with sex once a month—these couples get trapped in a seemingly endless cycle of invitations and refusals, seductions and rejections. Conflicts about when and whether or not to have sex spill over into their relationship outside the bedroom. Feeling frustrated and inadequate, the individual with more desire may become preoccupied, even obsessed with luring the lower-desire partner into bed. Feeling pressured, misunderstood, and angry, the lower-drive partner's desire often decreases further. It should be noted, however, that not all couples with desire differences include one partner who suffers from ISD. Even if the lower-drive partner does not have ISD, the frustration, pain, and problems the couple experiences are actually very similar and cause the same types of relationship conflicts.
- couples experiencing significant relationship conflict in general. Feelings of anger, emotional pain, and disap-

pointment, along with the tense relationship atmosphere that unproductive fighting creates, make it difficult for partners to draw close to each other and establish either emotional or physical intimacy.

- couples with inhibiting lifestyles. Achievement-oriented, upwardly mobile individuals like Andrea and Paul, who have high-pressure careers and high personal standards, are particularly susceptible to ISD. They are too exhausted, under too much stress, and too preoccupied with other matters to develop interest in sex or find the time and energy for it. When they realize that the frequency and quality of sex as well as their interest in it have decreased dramatically, they often panic. Fueled by their high expectations and drive to succeed at all they do, they try everything they can think of to solve the problem, creating additional stress and anxiety, which only further dampen sexual desire and satisfaction.
- men and women suffering from depression—which, along with a generally apathetic attitude toward once enjoyable activities, leads to a loss of sexual appetite
- single men and women, reacting to their difficulty in finding suitable partners and their fear of disease, as well as other anxieties. Like Rachel, they learn to block out their desire for sex and often distract themselves with work, food, shopping, watching television, exercise, and other nonsexual pursuits.
- men and women who feel pressured to perform sexually, and who may have failed to perform in the past. Fearing that they will not perform well enough and believing that it is best not to enter a race they can't win, they avoid sexual situations and often the social situations that can lead to sexual ones.
- men or women who fear intimacy and try to avoid becoming vulnerable, making a commitment, or risking rejection by suppressing sexual desire altogether or acting upon it only during casual, impersonal sexual encounters
- divorced or widowed men and women of all ages who are still grieving over their loss, who fear that getting

close will once again lead to rejection and pain, or who have difficulty in adapting to being single again

- young married couples from strict religious backgrounds who have no experience with sex and very little information about it. Guilt, fear, and ignorance combine to make sex extremely unpleasant and anxiety provoking, so much so that a couple may not consummate their marriage for years, if at all.

ISD can also develop as the result of stress, illness, reactions to past sexual traumas like rape or incest, and many other physiological or psychological factors.

Intense feelings of guilt, blame, fear, and frustration almost always accompany ISD. At times, often after another series of fights about sex, a temporary improvement does occur. All too often, however, this change is transient, and the pattern of increasing rejection and avoidance evolves again. Too frequently, ISD sufferers are bitterly accused of being "frigid," of "not being a man" or a woman, of having affairs or being homosexual, or of simply not loving their partners. Those accused may shrink back in silence and begin to doubt themselves even more, or may in turn accuse their partners of being pushy, demanding, insensitive "sex fiends." But ISD, as one sex therapist put it, has two victims and no villains.

As you can see, ISD is a complex and varied condition. People experience it in different ways, to different degrees, and for different reasons. Homosexual men and women as well as heterosexuals can and do suffer from it. More young people than old complain of it, and more women than men are likely to admit to it. Many people who have it don't know it, and may initially seek professional help for other sexual difficulties or relationship problems.

Experts themselves don't always agree on who has ISD and who doesn't, sometimes calling the problem hypoactive sexual desire, sexual apathy, or low libido, as well as ISD. As a result, exact figures on how many people suffer from ISD are hard to come by.

If you believe—as most people do—that the vast majority

of today's men and woman are in hot pursuit of sex, enjoy it immensely, and engage in it as often as they reasonably can, experiencing even mild ISD is bound to be extremely disturbing to you. After all, everywhere you look, you see more evidence that you are not "normal." It seems so obvious to you that your sexual activities are less exciting and less frequent than the sex you read or hear about constantly. You don't want sex as much or as often as everyone else seems to. You must be missing something, because you certainly don't enjoy it the way other people do. In fact, you can think of at least a dozen things you'd *rather* do than have sex.

Logically, you conclude that there is something terribly wrong with you, and naturally you make a valiant effort to "fix" the problem—trying harder, scheduling time for sex, having sex because you think you should even though you don't really want to, and carefully critiquing your every move and reaction. Sex becomes a stressful and nerve-racking chore. Not surprisingly, your desire, instead of increasing, decreases further—creating a snowball effect that leaves you and your partner even more confused, angry, frustrated, and frightened.

HOW THIS BOOK CAN HELP YOU

"Why, why, why?" our patients ask us. "Why can't my (or my partner's) sex drive be like 'normal' people's? Why isn't my sex life the way it's supposed to be?"

There are no easy answers to those questions. However, understanding and improvement of any sexual difficulty begins with accurate information. You will find that information here. You can get to the root of the problem and start digging out from under it once you know what may be causing it. The physical, psychological, and relationship factors that can lead to ISD are explored fully in this book. Finally, change for the better is achieved by doing. Consequently, in this book we offer you a multitude of specific suggestions and exercises for overcoming ISD, bridging desire discrepancies, and developing satisfying sexual relationships.

But please, do not think this book is a magic wand. Reading it and doing the exercises will not miraculously transform you into the world's greatest lover or erase all your concerns about sexual frequency and the quality of your sex life. So do not expect to reach the final page, shut the book, and discover that your sexual desire has been restored completely. In fact, reading this book may convince you that you could benefit from sex therapy, and we have included information on where to look for it and what to expect from it.

ISD *is* treatable and curable. The cure begins by opening your mind and putting aside the sexual myths you have been inundated with since childhood and the misconceptions that may be making you miserable. It continues with the development of a healthy relationship that allows sex to flourish. So, before getting to new ideas about sex and sexual desire, let's take a close, clear-eyed look at the ideas and expectations most of us already have—and where we got them.

CHAPTER ONE
What Is Normal— for You?

WENDY IS A TALL, slender woman with long, dark hair and the awkward, halting speech and anxious facial expression we've grown accustomed to seeing in first-time visitors. At forty-six, Wendy is a widow with a six-year-old son. Her husband, Mark, died two years earlier after a grueling battle with cancer. Wendy has come to see us because she is completely uninterested in sex—a relatively recent development.

Unlike the majority of our patients, who are uncertain about the onset of their loss of desire, Wendy can say with certainty that she lost interest in sex six months before her husband's death. Those last six months were "like being in hell," according to Wendy, but at the same time, Wendy and Mark "felt more love for each other and were closer than we ever were before." Wendy accepted Mark's caresses as a gift, but never felt turned on by his kisses and hugs. "Which was just as well," she says, "because he was way past the point of doing anything sexual."

A few months after Mark died, Wendy began to spend a lot of time with Mark's best friend, Bill. They both were still grieving their loss. "At first, we mostly talked about Mark," she explains. "But as time passed, we found that we had a lot in common." Wendy shows no signs of guilt or anxiety when she reports that in many ways she and Bill were more compatible than she and Mark had ever been.

"I don't feel sexually attracted to him, though," she sighs and then she chuckles. "Which is really kind of funny, because I used to think he was just about the sexiest guy I knew. I even used to tease Mark about it, telling him that if I ever left him it would be because I'd run off with Bill. Now I kiss him and it does nothing for me. Sometimes I even feel panicky and nauseous. He's been incredibly understanding so far." Bill recently asked Wendy to marry him. Although she loves him deeply, Wendy believes she will have to turn him down. "How can I marry the guy when I can't imagine making love to him?" she groans.

Wendy admits that she cannot imagine making love with anyone. She no longer has sexual fantasies, and when she does start feeling a little turned on, she makes herself concentrate on something else. This worries her. During the months preceding and immediately following her husband's death, Wendy's loss of sexual desire was a way of adapting to stressful and emotionally disturbing circumstances, and she knew it. She fully expected it to bounce back soon enough. But it didn't.

Wendy wound up in our office because she wanted to get back something she had lost, and something a growing number of other Americans are losing as well—their sexual desire. Sexual desire problems in one form or another are currently considered to be the most prevalent of all sexual problems. A recent survey of 289 sex therapists revealed that the most common complaint they receive—from 31 percent of all patients—concerns desire differences between partners, with individual desire problems coming in second at 28 percent. At our clinic at Northwestern University Medical School, almost 50 percent of our patients are seeking treatment because of problems concerning sexual desire. And research from other sexual therapy clinics around the country confirms that as many as half of all adult men and women are likely to experience desire difficulties to some degree at some time.

Prior to the feminist movement of the 1970s, ISD was often seen as only a female problem and mislabeled "frigidity." But women's liberation and the sexual revolution forced clinicians and researchers to reevaluate their old assumptions about female sexuality. It was then that women's true capacity for sexual pleasure was "discovered" and freed from the oppressiveness of chauvinistic scientific and cultural biases.

While it is true that women seem to be twice as likely to experience a lack of sexual desire, the myth that all men have a constant need and desire for sex has also been dispelled. In fact, in a 1978 study of happily married couples (a group once thought to be resistant to sexual difficulties), 16 percent of the men reported a lack of interest in sex. More recently, a *Psychology Today* magazine survey of fifty-two thousand people revealed that 39 percent of the men who responded admitted to occasional or regular lack of interest in sex and that 30 percent believed sex was a burden, more like work than play. People who suffer from sexual desire problems are from every economic group, homosexual and heterosexual, single and married, and of all ages.

Bobby is a handsome, healthy twenty-year-old pre-med student who came to our office after hearing one of us lecture at the university he attends. Lounging casually in his chair, his long denim-clad legs stretched out in front of him, his blond hair flopping over his forehead and occasionally falling over his deep blue eyes, Bobby is attractive and athletic looking, someone who has probably had numerous sexual opportunities. But Bobby is troubled and badly needs to talk about sex.

"When you talked about ISD, it really got me thinking," he begins, "because I've spent my whole life worrying that I was sick or brain-damaged or something when it came to sex."

Bobby has never had sex with a partner and only on a few isolated occasions during his early teens has he masturbated, an activity that was motivated more by curiosity than by a desire to experience sexual pleasure. "I've never really been interested in sex," he claims, and as far as he knows he has never fantasized about it. Although he does occasionally have "wet dreams," he never remembers the erotic dreams that led up to them. Once in a while, when watching a sexually explicit movie or in response to blatantly seductive behavior by a pretty young woman, Bobby will feel sexually excited, but he reports that "it really isn't all that enjoyable. I've felt better after a long run or watching the Chicago Bears win a close football match."

The fact that everyone around him constantly talks about sex makes Bobby anxious and uncomfortable. "I play along because I don't want them to find out I'm a virgin or think I'm gay or something. But I'm almost always thinking, 'What's the fascination? Can't we talk about something else for a change?' "

At the same time, Bobby finds himself worrying about his own mental and physical health. "There's got to be *something* wrong with me," he sighs. "I'm probably the only twenty-year-old male virgin in America and it's not like I have to be. I know lots of women. I like women. There are half a dozen I can name right now who would sleep with me in a minute, but I'm just not interested."

Bobby has always had an extremely low sex drive and throughout his life has experienced only the slightest sexual desire. Wendy, once easily aroused and highly interested in sex, lost her desire during a crisis and can't seem to get it back. Other people we will describe in this book have experienced sexual desire problems in other ways. These individual differences are just some of the many factors that make ISD such a complex sexual difficulty.

What's more, with or without desire difficulties, no two people experience sexual desire in precisely the same way. You might feel sensations in your genitals, for instance, while someone else might feel vaguely sexy, open to sex, or just generally restless. Similarly, on one occasion, you might experience desire as a powerful rush that sets your heart racing, skin tingling, and so on. Yet, on other occasions, your desire may be much more subtle, perhaps consisting of brief thoughts about sex that slip in and out of your awareness during the course of the day.

In addition, each person has unique ideas about what constitutes a sexual turn-on. You may respond to many different external clues or only a few specific ones—sights, sounds, touches, smells, suggestions, or settings that you consider sexually exciting. Or you may seek out or become receptive to sexual activity in order to fulfill one, or a great many psychological wants and needs, including wanting to have an orgasm, to feel closer to your partner, to relieve boredom, or to confirm your attractiveness and adequacy. For some, the muscle tension, racing heart, and heavy breathing following a physical workout, the longing you feel in the pit of your stomach when you're sad, the hunger for human contact you feel when you're lonely, and even the pulsing energy you feel after you've narrowly escaped some sort of disaster may automatically trigger sexual desire. For others, these feelings would be a complete turn-off.

What activates your sexual desire, how often or urgently you experience it, and what you do in response to your sexual urges are influenced by:

- your preconceived notions about sex
- the expectations you bring to sexual encounters
- your sexual education and past sexual experiences
- your comfort or anxiety in sexual situations
- any performance anxiety or sexual problems—other than ISD—that you may be experiencing

Because these factors can and often do contribute to sexual desire difficulties, we will briefly explore each one in the remainder of this chapter.

PRECONCEIVED NOTIONS

When Barbara and Dan walked into our office for the first time, we thought we had found living proof that opposites attract. A petite, blond, blue-eyed bundle of energy, Barbara, at forty, is proud of looking ten years younger and dresses in colors and fashions more commonly seen on college students than suburban housewives. In contrast, Dan, with his graying hair, conservative gray suit, and serious demeanor, seems older than forty-three. Tall, thin, and always looking somewhat fatigued, Dan speaks softly and slowly, while Barbara is a veritable whirlwind of words and movement. Both used to believe that approaching life so differently had kept their marriage interesting. Recently, however, they've seemed to be moving in completely opposite directions. The problem, according to Barbara, always came down to sex, specifically Dan's lack of interest in it.

Married for fifteen years and the parents of two sons aged ten and twelve, Dan and Barbara met and began dating several weeks before Dan left the area to work on his master's degree at a university two hundred miles from the town where Barbara lived.

Dan was immediately attracted to Barbara. "There was just something exciting about her," he remarks and recalls being flattered by her attentiveness and how she made him "feel alive and important."

Barbara openly admits that she flirted with him only because flirting with men was something she did well and often. "I thought he was very intense, very serious," she adds. "It was a challenge to see if I could get him to smile, you know, to lighten up a little bit."

She liked his serious side too. "He seemed solid and dependable," she says, explaining that she had begun to tire of the kinds of relationships she had been having, relationships that had plenty of sexual chemistry but little substance. And soon Barbara also sensed the sexual chemistry between herself and Dan, deciding that Dan had "a sort of passion smoldering underneath that cool exterior." She wanted to be the one to unleash it.

They slept together the first time she visited him at graduate school and at every opportunity thereafter. Both were sexually experienced, although Dan acknowledges that none of his previous lovers had been as enthusiastic about sex as Barbara.

Because they lived so far apart, Barbara and Dan were able to see each other only one weekend a month. "I wanted him like crazy by the time I saw him," Barbara recalls. "It was great. The minute we were alone together, we had sex."

Dan felt that was expected. "Sometimes I didn't really feel like it. But we didn't see each other that often and Barbara was impossible to resist. Don't get me wrong, the sex itself was good. It's just that even back then it was usually Barbara's idea." After they married, sex continued to be initiated mostly by Barbara.

"My sex drive was never as strong as hers," Dan sighs. "She could have sex every night—no problem. I was satisfied with once or twice a week, and if I had other things, like work, on my mind, I would just lose interest for as long as a month at a time. Barbara always pushed for more."

In the early years of their marriage, Dan rarely refused Barbara's sexual invitations. They might have discovered their desire differences earlier if he had, or if Barbara hadn't held her seductions down to once or twice a week. "I'd wait for him to make a move," she says, "and after a couple of days had passed, I stopped waiting and came to him. I thought he liked it that way because he never said otherwise." And she never asked. You were supposed to *have* sex—not *talk* about it—she believed.

Barbara says that the first time Dan turned down a sexual advance, "It was like a slap in the face. But I tried to understand. I told myself he was working hard and worrying a lot."

Five years ago Dan left his secure position with a large engineering firm and began his own business. He considered this the most exciting—and frightening—thing he had ever attempted. Exhausted and preoccupied, Dan spurned more and more of Barbara's invitations to make love. She began to worry. Since men were supposed to be highly interested in sex, easily aroused, and always willing, the only "logical" explanation for Dan's lack of interest had to be that he was no longer attracted to *her*, that she had lost her touch, failed somehow.

So Barbara took stock and went to work on herself—dieting, exercising, changing her hairstyle, and trying other new approaches to interest Dan in sex. Nothing helped for long.

"No one tried harder than I did," Barbara explains. "But Dan was in his own world. I might as well have been invisible. His life was work, work, and more work."

Dan does not deny this, but adds, "She doesn't understand the pressure I'm under—she just piles on more. It's irritating when she expects me to drop everything, turn off my brain, and perform for her benefit."

"Obviously something is very wrong," Barbara declares during the couple's first therapy session. "Men don't lose interest in sex. They're the ones who are supposed to want it more. I've never heard of a man who didn't. So I don't see how he expects me to believe that he doesn't feel like having sex, period. *That just doesn't happen.*"

Dan's lack of interest in sex makes no sense to Barbara. It doesn't fit into her picture of what sex is or should be. Barbara's high level of interest in sex is equally baffling to Dan. Indeed, as his own sexual appetite has decreased, he has come to the conclusion that Barbara is obsessed with sex.

When Barbara and Dan came to us for therapy, their marriage was deteriorating, Dan's sexual desire was virtually nonexistent, and the vast differences in their feelings, beliefs, and attitudes about sex were obvious. *Yet, those differences had always been there.* Since early childhood, Barbara and Dan had been accumulating ideas about sex and relationships. Long before they met, they had begun to piece together a picture of what sex was supposed to be like and what they should expect from themselves and their partners in sexual situations, as well as what they could expect to gain or lose from engaging in sexual activity. This vision helped them understand, organize, and know what to do during one of the most complex and emotionally charged of all human interactions—having sex.

SEXUAL SCRIPTS

We, as well as many other psychologists and sociologists, use a metaphor from theater to describe this organized set of ideas, attitudes, and expectations that direct people as they participate in any kind of complex activity. We call it a *script*.

Giving direction without actually specifying everything that must be done, social scripts are not written down on paper. And although everyone uses them to guide thoughts and behavior, their existence is rarely recognized. Scripts for sexual behavior help influence how you act now based on what you have learned in the past. These scripts also help you to plan what you are going to do in the future. They do this by helping you define what you do with whom, when, where, under what circumstances, and for what reasons.

Your sexual script contains all the thoughts and feelings that move you to seek out, become receptive to, and engage in sexual activity. You have organized these ideas consciously or subconsciously, and they either motivate you to have sex or convince you not to.

If we asked why people have sex, you could immediately think of several motives, including to experience pleasure, to express love or affection, to feel close to their partners, to have fun or relax. But there are many, many more reasons for engaging in sexual activity and not all of these motives are sexual in nature. They include:

- to gain more control in a relationship
- to capture or retain someone's interest
- to prove your love, loyalty, or commitment
- to prove your masculinity or femininity
- to demonstrate your maturity and sophistication
- to feel good about yourself; to affirm that you are attractive, worthy, lovable, and competent both as a sexual partner and as a human being
- to relieve loneliness
- to reduce tension and anxiety or relieve depression
- to relieve boredom
- to obtain bodily contact; to be cuddled and physically comforted
- to soften up your partner in order to obtain a favor—or to repay your partner for one
- to avoid arguments or uncomfortable conversations, or even emotional intimacy, by switching the focus to sex
- to make up for some transgression or assuage guilty feelings about not spending enough time or paying enough attention to your partner

And finally, you may engage in sexual activity because you believe that is what you are *expected* to do at that time with that person in that situation. In essence, the other elements of your script sometimes convince you that you should have sex even when other motives are not present.

Acting Out Your Script

No two sexual scripts are identical, but then, they do not need to be. As long as there is some common ground and as long as motives are not in direct conflict with each other, two people can come into a sexual encounter with different preconceived notions and still have sex that both find acceptable and satisfying.

Every sexual interaction is a negotiation between two "actors" who may be pursuing the same thing for very different, and perhaps conflicting, reasons. Many of us are able to negotiate those differences most of the time by subtly altering our own expectations. However, if you are unwilling or unable to compromise about the differences you do have, problems are more likely to appear in your sex life. If getting your needs met means preventing your partner from getting his or her needs met—as happened in Barbara and Dan's case—those problems are probably going to be dramatic and distressing. In fact, sex may become a source of tension, anxiety, and conflict—so much so that interest in it may decrease markedly and at least one partner may experience ISD.

By the time Barbara and Dan came to us for help, they resembled two actors appearing on the same stage but performing two different plays. Barbara's script, like those of many high-desire individuals, involved wanting to engage in sexual activity frequently and for many different reasons, including to experience physical pleasure and excitement, to express and obtain love and affection, to unwind, and most significantly to bolster her sense of self-worth, affirm her attractiveness, and prove her competence as a sexual partner and a person.

Although Barbara did not recognize the connection between having sex and her self-esteem, when Dan began to rebuff her sexual advances, she reacted vehemently and felt extremely threatened. According to her internal sexual script, Dan was not only keeping her from engaging in an activity she enjoyed, but also withholding a major source of positive feelings about herself.

On the other hand, Dan not only assigned sex a low priority in his life, but also viewed it as frivolous, an activity that consumed valuable time he believed should be devoted to meeting his many "responsibilities." In addition, he interpreted Barbara's sexual overtures as demands to "perform for her benefit." This made him feel pressured, and as far as he was concerned, he already had more pressure in his life than he could handle. Her script said "more sex" at the very same time his was suggesting "less."

As you can see, ISD is often the result of *incompatible* scripts. Equally disastrous, however, are compatible scripts that contain unrealistic expectations and unattainable standards.

EXPECTATIONS AND SEXUAL DESIRE

- A normal couple *should* have sex at least two or three times each week.
- If two people still care for each other and are still attracted to each other, they will want to have sex and *should*, regardless of problems or demands in other areas of their lives.
- If a couple's sex life originally included frequent, spontaneous, and exciting sex, it *should* continue to be that way unless something is wrong with one partner or the relationship.
- If a couple's sex life is less than thrilling and they want it to improve, they *should* just devote more time and effort to it.
- Sexual desire *should* be perfectly synchronized; that is, when one partner is interested in sex, the other *should* be equally interested.

- Normal men and women *should* always enjoy sex, be good at it, and look forward to having it on a regular basis.

These are just a few of the expectations that have probably found their way into your sexual script. Unfortunately, each of these standards, as well as many others, may not be realistic. In fact, trying to live up to them—and being unable to—is often a major source of frustration, anxiety, and feelings of inadequacy.

Andrea and Paul

"We don't make love nearly as much as we should. We never seem to have the time—or the energy," Andrea explains succinctly, as one might expect from a woman who writes ten-second radio spots and one-page news releases for a living. At just thirty years old, she heads the public relations department of a national corporation. He husband, Paul, also thirty, is an associate in a prestigious, high-powered law firm that handles corporate clients all over the United States.

Andrea and Paul are both intense, goal-oriented high achievers who expect their lives to be organized, efficient, focused, under control, and moving ever upward to new peaks of personal and professional success. They have the same mannerisms, the same laugh, the same habits of glancing quickly at the wall clock and tapping the arms of their chairs when they feel uncomfortable during a therapy session. They both wear short, stylish haircuts and sport similar tortoiseshell glasses. Even though Andrea is short and slightly overweight and Paul is slender and long-legged, if you saw these two on the street you could easily mistake them for sister and brother.

Andrea and Paul met at a party five years ago, moved in together six months later, and got married two years after that. From their first encounter—which Paul describes as "lust on first sight"—sex for this couple was frequent, spontaneous, and pleasurable, which makes their present lack of interest and dissatisfaction all the more baffling and distressing to them. From our vantage point, however, it was relatively easy to understand. No real, live, flesh-and-blood human being could expect to lead a life like Andrea's or Paul's and still have time and energy left over for sex. But of course, they did expect just that.

Like many young, upwardly mobile, dual-career couples, Andrea and Paul constantly seek out new challenges, including Paul's recent decision to start training to run a marathon and their joint decision to buy an old house and renovate it themselves. They attack each new project with gusto, logic, and determination, but as you might expect, their quest for fulfillment often exhausts them.

In fact, just listening to Paul and Andrea describe their hectic, jam-packed schedules exhausted us! On a typical day, they awaken at roughly the same time. He runs while she showers, showers while she dresses, dresses while she drinks coffee. Then both skim through two morning papers. They wave goodbye to each other from cars heading in opposite directions. Then they both work until seven or eight P.M., and before coming home, Andrea stops at a health club to exercise. Several nights each week she has publicity functions to attend or Paul has dinner meetings. Weekends are filled with all the things they could not get to during the week: housekeeping, running errands, shopping, entertaining friends, or visiting relatives—and, of course, working on the remodeling of their house. Sunday morning offers the only uncommitted time during their week and "nine times out of ten, sleep is far more appealing than having sex," Paul explains. "We don't get enough of either, but sleep is harder to live without."

At first, Andrea and Paul did not pay much attention to the fact that they were having sex less often than they had in the past. However, once they realized that they were having it once a month at most, they were shocked, and, like many other couples in the same situation, began counting the days when they did not have sex and critiquing their performance when they did. Alarmed by the infrequency and mediocrity of their lovemaking, they approached the problem as they would any other. They applied time management principles, synchronized their schedules around predetermined lovemaking sessions, read books, and attempted new techniques they hoped would stir up more passion.

But no matter what they did, Andrea and Paul could not alter the fact that they had sex less often than they thought they should. They observed that they were not as "good" at it as they believed they were supposed to be, and neither partner enjoyed or looked forward to sex as much as they had earlier in their relationship.

When they first came to us for help, they were frantic about a sex life that was not what it used to be. The thrill was gone—and both were secretly terrified that their entire relationship would soon go with it. Andrea and Paul experienced unrealistic expectations about what sex should be like and felt like failures because they could not live up to their own standards.

You may be caught in this double bind too, especially when it comes to the issue of how often you *should* be having sex.

Frequency

A recent survey of sex therapists revealed that most of their patients believed a normal person wanted to have sex at least two to three times a week. Where did they get this impression? Probably from the widely publicized Kinsey studies, and more recent surveys, which established this as the *average* frequency of sexual intercourse.

But what does that statistic mean? Is it telling you that you are abnormal because you have sex less than two or three times a week? Is it a reason to be concerned or to take action to bring your sex life up to par? We definitely do not recommend trying to have intercourse more often because of some statistical average. A mathematical figure simply should not be allowed to dictate how often anyone engages in sexual activity. Besides, if matching the national average really indicates that you are normal and not matching it irrefutably proves that you have a sexual problem, why aren't people who have sex *more* than two to three times a week upset and worried that they might be oversexed?

When all is said and done, an average is only a statistic. It may not even reflect what most people do most of the time. A recent study of married couples, for example, did show that the largest percentage (31 percent) had sex two to three times a week. However, 24 percent of those surveyed had sex just once a week and 23 percent had it just two or three times a month—which means that at least 47 percent of married couples have sex *less often* than the national average.

That statistic may help you feel better if the only reason you felt you were not having sex often enough was because you weren't measuring up to national average. However, it won't be much help to you if—based on your own past level of sexual desire and your sexual expectations—you would like to have sex more often or less often than you do now. You will have to take a closer look at what may be influencing the frequency of your sexual activity, asking yourself if, under those circumstances, it is reasonable for you and your partner to have sex more often than you do.

As Your Sex Life Evolves

Nothing about sexuality or sexual behavior stays the same forever. In fact, sex often *improves* as you gain experience and become more comfortable with your partner. But none of us is likely to complain about that sort of change. On the other hand, having sex less often than you used to, especially if the sexual activity you do engage in doesn't seem to be as exciting as it once was, can leave you and your partner feeling baffled and frustrated. Indeed, such changes in your sex life may make you quite frantic. However, they are much more common occurrences than you might think. They are usually not permanent, nor necessarily signs of serious problems, although you can quite literally turn them into disasters by letting your fear overcome you and deciding that you, your partner, and your sex life are failing.

For instance, experiencing decreased sexual frequency and a few less "sparks" was particularly painful for Andrea and Paul because their sex life had once been the most exciting and valued part of their relationship.

"One of the first things I thought when I met Paul was that I wanted to sleep with him," Andrea admits. "The sexual chemistry between us was that strong."

Paul nods in agreement and they both chuckle as they recall their initial meeting at a cocktail party. There to conduct business, Paul was distracted by Andrea's presence. "Every time I talked to someone, I kept one eye on him and one eye on her." Similarly, Andrea constantly glanced in Paul's direction while trying not to let him or anyone else know she was looking. When their eyes did meet, the effect "was like being hit by a truck," according to Paul. Andrea managed to get someone to introduce them. "But I thought I had blown it," she laughs. "I was tongue-tied and blushing the whole time we talked." Actually, this anxiety and vulnerability reassured Paul that Andrea was indeed attracted to him and increased his interest in her.

Paul then invited Andrea to have a cup of coffee at a nearby all-night diner. "And we did stay there literally all night," Andrea reports. "We talked and talked for hours." But sex was never far out of either of their minds. "We got to know each other by accident," Paul claims. "We found out we had a lot in common only because we were involved in this sort of extended intellectual foreplay. We both knew we were going to end up in bed sooner or later."

They ended up in her bed, having sex as the sun was rising, and Paul spent the remainder of the weekend there, going home only long enough to pick up his toothbrush and a change of clothes. "We didn't waste any time," he chuckles. "It was probably the world's longest first date—the date never ended. . . ."

For a while, being together took priority over everything else in their lives. Whenever they were together they invariably had sex, even when meeting for a weekday lunch at his place. In the process, they grew to know each other even better and fell in love.

After they moved in together, their sexual desire became less urgent, but they still managed to have sex four or five times a week. "We were very innovative about it." Paul proudly describes how they used to juggle their schedules to accommodate their sex life. They didn't notice that they were soon down to having sex two or three times a week. They felt as close as they ever had and enjoyed sex every bit as much.

Like most couples, as they grew closer, Andrea and Paul found that they enjoyed other forms of intimacy in addition to sex. The frequency of their sexual activity decreased. They were not alarmed and did not need to be. Actually, some studies show that during the second year of marriage the majority of married couples have sex half as often as they did the first year.

However, Paul and Andrea's sex life took a turn for the worse soon after Andrea became head of the publicity department. "She would bring home a briefcase full of work," Paul says, "and fall asleep over it in the den. She could barely manage to *get* to the bedroom, so we could pretty much forget about having sex in it."

Paul began initiating sex less often at that time, and Andrea appreciated his consideration. But then Andrea started hinting about having a baby and Paul's interest in sex seemed to disappear completely. "He stopped coming on to me at all," she recalls. "And he always seemed to be busy with something else when I let him know that I was in the mood." Now Andrea and Paul were faced with a new dilemma—in addition to not having sex as often as they thought they should, they were far less interested in it than they believed they were *supposed* to be. As you can see, this couple's ISD was sparked and maintained by their unrealistic expectations. Yours may be too.

SEXUAL EDUCATION AND EXPERIENCES

Sexual scripts, sexual expectations, and sexual desire itself are all influenced by what you know about sex in general and the specific sexual experiences you've had in the past.

When we met them for the first time, Janet, twenty-four, and Tim, twenty-five, had been married for a little over a year. Despite the fact that they were very much in love and interested in starting a family, they had managed to have intercourse only a few times since their wedding night and had stopped trying altogether six months before they came to us for help. During their initial therapy sessions with us, they both found it extremely difficult to talk about sex in general. And when we tried to discuss their specific problems, Janet became tearful and Tim grew tongue-tied.

"If you put together everything Janet and I know about sex, it would fit on the head of a pin," Tim sighed. Indeed, as we got to know this couple better, we discovered that their sexual scripts consisted of a great many blank pages. What's more, the ones that were filled primarily contained restrictions and negative past experiences.

A dark-haired, delicate woman who wears no makeup, Janet dresses in floral prints and lacy clothing, which add to her air of youthful vulnerability and innocence. She is the only child of protective Italian Catholic parents. Born fifteen years into their marriage and after several miscarriages, Janet was her parents' "little miracle" and they doted on her. Wanting to make life easy and comfortable for her, they devoted themselves to her care, often anticipating or actually telling her what she needed before she knew herself. To Janet, it seemed natural to return their love by faithfully adhering to their rules and meeting their expectations. She was to be a "good Catholic girl who minds her manners, respects authority, and never shames her family."

Janet's mother was especially protective and always seemed to be warning her of the potential dangers that lurked around every corner. If Janet wanted to run or climb or use the slide at the playground, her mother told her not to, because she would fall and hurt herself. And she was not to talk to strangers, especially male strangers, because they might be "bad." Janet was not even allowed to go the her friends' homes. "They had to come to my house," she recalls, "so my mother could keep an eye on us and make sure nothing happened to me."

While these messages were similar to those most children receive, Janet heard them more often and urgently from a mother whose anxiety was literally contagious. Seeing the world through her mother's eyes, Janet came to believe it was a dangerous place indeed. The shy, compliant child became a timid, fearful adult. "I still worry a lot that bad things are going to happen to me," she admits.

In addition, Janet's mother did not hold boys in high esteem. "Even when I was little, I wasn't supposed to be alone with them," she reports. "She never really said why, except that they got girls 'in trouble.' " It would be years before Janet figured out what sort of "trouble" her mother was talking about, and by then, the notion of keeping a safe distance from the opposite sex had been reinforced by her religious training and her teachers in Catholic schools. Throughout her adolescence Janet always felt most at ease in groups of young women who shared her views and values.

Dating, on the other hand, was a nightmare for Janet, a source of stress she did not experience until she began college. Attending a Catholic university did not prevent Janet from meeting "the kinds of boys the nuns and my mother warned me about.

"You couldn't just go out and have fun," she explains. "You had to kiss at least, and if you kissed they tried for more, and if you said no they gave you a hard time." Janet hated to say no but knew she had to, despite her desire to please. The alternative was doing something she strongly believed she should not do. Anticipating the moment when she would have to ward off her date's advances, Janet could think of nothing else the entire evening—and sometimes for days before the actual date. Often Janet worked herself up into such an anxious state that she suffered migraine headaches or broke out in a rash. Prior to meeting Tim, she had given up dating and had not been alone with a man for more than a year.

An illustrator of children's books, Tim is boyishly handsome, with blond hair that needs trimming and kind slate-gray eyes. The oldest of six children, Tim, like Janet, was raised as a Catholic, although his parents were not active in their church.

They sent their children to a Catholic school simply because it offered a better education and a more disciplined environment than an inner-city public school.

Tim's parents had a laissez faire approach to child rearing. "They didn't have much to say about what we should or shouldn't do," he recalls. "If one of us did something we weren't supposed to, we heard about it after the fact. And unless it was something really major, like breaking someone's window or spray-painting curse words on the sidewalk or something, they didn't make that big a deal about it." And when it came to sex, according to Tim, his parents "really never talked about it at all."

As a teenager, Tim was a loner and a self-proclaimed book-worm who did not get involved in sports or other school activities. He favored books on theology, philosophy, and Greek mythology. He rarely read popular fiction and preferred to sketch or paint rather than watch TV or "hang out on the street." At about age fifteen he became fascinated with the notion of "a truly spiritual, all-consuming love."

That wasn't what he found with the girls he dated. "They thought I moved too slow," he sighs. He then tells us about a particularly bitter confrontation with one girlfriend who insisted that he was "really a homosexual and using her to keep people from finding out." He began to doubt his masculinity and, when his worry reached a fever pitch, intentionally set out to lose his virginity to a girl in his neighborhood who he knew was sexually experienced.

"It was a disaster," he declares. "It was over in a flash. This girl made sure I knew this was definitely *not* okay and I felt horrible afterwards." He would have half a dozen equally un-satisfying encounters before retreating to his original position of waiting for the woman with whom he could have a deep emotional and spiritual connection.

Janet, fearful of men and anxious about sex, and Tim, with only negative sexual experiences, managed to find each other and fall in love. They dated for several years, doing no more sexually than some passionate kissing and occasional tentative touching—and Tim always discontinued this touching as soon as he sensed that Janet was getting tense. If he became sexually aroused, Tim considered it his problem and would take care of it himself by masturbating after Janet had gone home. In an early therapy session Tim acknowledged that rather than feeling sexually frustrated, he was relieved that Janet placed no pressure on him to become sexual.

They did eventually decide to get married and, Tim recalls, "We had to talk to the priest before he would agree to marry us. There were a couple of meetings, and during one when it was just me and him, he asked about sex. I admitted I didn't feel all that sure of myself. He told me everything would be okay. That it would work out all by itself." Tim couldn't forget, however, that it had never worked out before.

Janet too remembers a prenuptial conversation about sex—with her mother. It was the first and only time they ever discussed sex directly, and Janet recalls that "she pretty much told me that sex was a woman's duty to her husband. She said it would hurt and I wouldn't like it, but I'd get used to it and learn to enjoy it because I was giving to my husband."

On the day that they were married, Janet and Tim were very much in love, trusted each other completely, and were looking forward to their life together. But in their hotel room on their wedding night, did they feel romantic or passionate? Were they intoxicated with desire? Not quite.

"I was petrified," Janet admits.

Tim whispers, "So was I."

Considering their past experiences and what little they had learned about sex, themselves, and relating to other people, their fear, anxiety, and even dread are hardly surprising. The sexual scripts Janet and Tim had pieced together thus far did not portray sex as an easy, enjoyable experience, to say the least.

Contrary to the popular notion that having sex is simply a matter of "doing what comes naturally," none of us automatically emerges as a complete, confident, and competent sexual being. We did not inherit a prepackaged sexual program that can be activated at the precise moment we need it to tell us what to think, feel, and do during sexual situations.

Although most of the time *we did not realize that we were learning or recognize what we were being taught,* we did indeed *learn* to be sexual. Beginning in early childhood and continuing throughout our lives, we learned our current sexual attitudes, beliefs, expectations, and behavior patterns from our families, fiction and films, our peers, and teachers and religious leaders.

From these sources we heard different, sometimes contradictory versions of what sex was supposed to be like, and we were left on our own to figure out which version was right. We picked up ideas indirectly and at random, grasping bits and pieces of information about sex, ourselves, and how to relate to and communicate with other people. Some ideas came our way long before we could put them into practice, and others, which would have come in handy when we began having sex, didn't come our way at all. Sometimes receiving no messages about sex created the most confusion. But in some haphazard manner, we managed to gather some information that was accurate and useful, as well as a great deal that was either incomplete or extremely unrealistic. We often ended up with "facts" composed of grains of truth that had been exaggerated or distorted and plenty of ideas that were completely untrue. *But we could not tell the difference,* and wove it all into the fabric of our sexual scripts, creating a crazy quilt of what we believed sex was supposed to be like and where it fit into our lives.

Unfortunately, the ideas we incorporated into our scripts during childhood and adolescence are not so easily removed or revised later on in our lives. In fact, whether we realize it or not, those ideas still influence what we think, feel, and do about sex.

For example, because Janet and Tim had sexual scripts that offered them almost no useful information about sex—and a great many anxieties—they did not consummate their marriage on their wedding night. In fact, they did not have intercourse at all during their honeymoon. They did try at first—because they knew they were supposed to—but Janet was tense and recoiled from Tim's touch, which understandably increased Tim's anxiety as well. By the third day of their honeymoon, the mere thought of trying to have sex caused so much distress that they agreed to wait until they returned home.

Once they were settled in their apartment, however, neither one was in a hurry to make love. They were content to kiss and hold each other, although, as it turned out, Janet was a bit more content than Tim. When Janet realized this, she felt terrible. She loved Tim and wanted to make him happy. With her guilt outweighing her anxiety, Janet gathered enough courage to let Tim make love to her. Since she was still too anxious to get aroused or lubricate adequately, intercourse was painful for her and distressing for Tim, who knew Janet was deriving no pleasure from it.

"She cried herself to sleep," Tim says. "I felt both completely inadequate about how I'd made love and selfish for wanting her to do something she obviously didn't want to do." He vowed not to have sex with Janet again until she told him she was ready.

Hoping that their lovemaking would improve with practice, Janet did periodically let Tim know she was willing to try again. "But half of those times Tim couldn't, you know, do anything," Janet stutters.

"I was so worried about her that I couldn't get an erection," Tim explains. "I'd start to get excited and then I'd think about the time before and her crying and apologizing. Any desire I felt just vanished."

For the next few months, too embarrassed to ask for advice from outsiders and reluctant to discuss the problem themselves, they alternated between avoiding sex and renewing their attempts to "get it right." Even those efforts ground to a halt five months after their wedding when Janet had an anxiety attack in the middle of one of their more successful attempts at intercourse. Shaking uncontrollably, gasping for breath, and crying hysterically, Janet felt "like I was going to die. I was terrified and it took hours for Tim to calm me down." They did not try to have sex again.

While couples like Janet and Tim, who rarely make love or have stopped having sex at all, are extreme examples of conflicts about sex and problematic sexual scripts, they are not as unusual as you might think. If sex is seen as dangerous or distasteful, as humiliating, or as a situation that reflects their own inadequacy once again, men and women simply are not going to experience much desire for it. What's more, their behavior will not change and their interest in sex will continue to be low or nonexistent until they revise some of the feelings, ideas, and attitudes contained in their sexual scripts.

Janet and Tim could have continued indefinitely in a loving but sexless marriage. However, they wanted to have children. And, as Janet put it, they wanted to have them "the normal way," which meant she and Tim would have to "get over whatever was getting in the way."

Although Janet and Tim are an extreme example of how anxiety can rob you of sexual desire and satisfaction, almost anyone can experience similar effects to a lesser degree.

ANXIETY AND SEXUAL DESIRE

"Sex is a real source of stress," says Rachel, the single thirty-three-year-old computer-software sales and service manger whom we introduced earlier. "First you get yourself all worked up trying to attract the guy, worrying about how you look, what you'll say, if he'll come on to you, and if you actually want him to. Then there's all the usual awkwardness about having sex with someone for the first time. It was never a picnic, but now with the whole AIDS issue to deal with, it's a nightmare. Do you talk about it? If you do, what do you say? Can you trust what he tells you? And then you have to insist that the guy wears a condom—it's just a nerve-racking experience from start to finish."

As a result, although Rachel experiences sexual desire on a fairly regular basis, she frequently stifles it. Rachel's comments reflect the anxiety and insecurity many single people feel when faced with the prospect of having sex with a new, as yet unfamiliar partner.

If you are a single man or woman who tends to feel anxious about having sex for the first time with a new partner, that feeling probably arises long before you reach the bedroom. In fact, you may begin feeling anxious as soon as you find yourself in a situation where you think you might be expected to have sex—on a first date or after connecting with someone at a party, for example. You may even experience anxiety while you are getting dressed to go out on a date. And if you are prone to feeling sexual anxieties, you most certainly will feel them when you have been seeing someone for a period of time and believe he or she is thinking that it is about time that the two of you became more sexual.

First-time sexual encounters are so anxiety provoking because they are accompanied by a long list of questions that you can't answer by yourself. Questions like: Does this person find me sexually attractive? Will this person think I'm fast and easy if I say yes or that there's something wrong with me if I say no? Will this person lose interest in me if I don't have sex or abandon me once I do? What will this person expect of me sexually? Will he or she want me to do things I don't feel comfortable doing? What if this person has had lots of attractive, terrific lovers and I don't measure up? How will our relationship change if sex is added? How will I deal with contraception? Is it physically safe to be sexual with this person?

Just reading these questions is mind-boggling, so it's easy to understand how anxious you are going to feel when you try to answer them while at the same time trying to figure out if you want to or are, in fact, expected to have sex, and whether you actually will. Of course, ISD can answer all of those questions for you, especially if you become so anxious that you go on red alert and shut down your sexual desire.

In addition, you may feel anxiety and self-doubt about your sexual attractiveness or adequacy. In fact, when you are faced with the prospect of being sexual with someone for the first time, it may seem as if every demon that has ever whispered self-doubts in your ear starts screaming at the top of its lungs. That was certainly what happened to Rachel, who, like many women, believed that in order to attract a suitable partner, she had to be physically beautiful and not too successful, assertive, or opinionated. And even women who fit the media and fantasy standard of attractiveness can feel insecure in new sexual situations, wondering if their partners like them for themselves or just their external appearance.

Single men seem to worry less about their sexual attractiveness, but they are often just as anxious as women about first-time sexual encounters. Their self-doubts tend to revolve around their own expectations and what they believe to be their new partners' expectations of an excellent sexual performance. As one of our single male ISD patients put it, "The more I like someone, the more worried I get that we won't click in bed." And, as is almost always the case, the more worried he gets, the less sexual desire he feels, and the more he avoids acting on it when he does feel it. "But by then I've passed the point of no return," he continued. "I have to go through with it."

As you have no doubt discovered, "going through with it" when you are already feeling anxious is not conducive to having a positive sexual experience. What's more, when you have sex with someone for the first time, you do not know what kind of sexual activity or touching that person likes and you rarely feel comfortable asking—or offering information about your own preferences. As a result, you are quite likely to spend this initial sexual encounter watching, worrying about, and inhibiting your own sexual responses, ending up with a sexual experience that is clumsy, uncomfortable, frustrating, or unsatisfying and that neither you nor your new partner will be particularly anxious to repeat anytime in the near future.

In fact, many of our single ISD patients, having had more than their fair share of nerve-racking and disappointing sexual first times, fall into a pattern of seeking out sexual encounters, having an unsatisfying experience, and then avoiding sex for a while before starting the cycle all over again.

Once you develop this pattern, you may notice that your periods of sexual avoidance, which often involve withdrawing from social situations as well, get longer and longer, as you consciously squelch your sexual urges rather than face the hassle of another unpleasant sexual experience.

Sexual anxieties are not restricted to single people or first-time sexual encounters. Indeed, they are quite common. To relax, enjoy, and obtain emotional and physical satisfaction from sex, you must first *feel comfortable*—with yourself and your body, your partner and your relationship, and sex itself, including the setting in which it takes place. When these conditions go unmet, sexual anxiety skyrockets and sexual desire is likely to plummet and maybe even disappear entirely. In fact, anxiety is one of the reasons people suffer from sexual problems other than ISD, as Al did.

SEXUAL DYSFUNCTIONS AND DESIRE

On his first visit to our office, Al, a forty-seven-year-old divorced insurance agent, sadly sums up his feelings about sex. "If I can't do it right, why do it at all?" he sighs and waits for our response to a story we have heard many times before.

Broad-shouldered and of average height, Al has a receding hairline, although he tries to disguise it by combing some of his remaining hair over his bald spot. Once a promising middle-distance runner, he now works out at a local gym and lifts weights. "I didn't want to go to seed completely," he chuckles and pats a beer belly that is only partially concealed by his V-neck sweater with the alligator appliqué. Calling himself a "man's man, a very traditional guy," Al admits he has very traditional ideas and attitudes on sexuality.

Faithful to his wife during their twenty-two-year marriage, Al describes his sex life while married as "sometimes good, sometimes not so good—never what you'd call fantastic." He wonders if his wife would give it a less favorable evaluation, since she left him for another man, a family friend with whom Al had a very competitive relationship and who Al always thought outshined him.

Depressed following the divorce, feeling displaced, and already questioning his sexual prowess, Al found himself thrust into a world of dating where all the rules had changed. "I'm no Robert Redford," he says, "but you'd think I was, the way women started coming on to me when they found out I was available. I was a hot commodity."

Al was unprepared for what he encountered and confused by it. "I had a hard enough time figuring women out when they did what everybody said they were supposed to," he sighs. "But now, nothing that was happening made sense. It was a whole new ballgame." What he perceived to be aggressiveness on the part of women—including many women he had never dreamed would be attracted to him—simultaneously excited and frightened him. "One part of me didn't like it and another part did," he explains. "I was free to do anything I wanted and God knows I had plenty of opportunities. But these women, they seemed to expect so much."

And sometimes Al couldn't deliver. The first few times he had difficulty maintaining an erection, he made light of the situation, blaming it on drinking too much earlier in the evening, being tired after a long work day, or not "really" feeling attracted to his partner. But even with these plausible explanations, Al began to feel anxious and fearful, always anticipating the next "test" of his manhood and worrying that he would fail to perform up to par.

This set off a vicious cycle of expecting sexual encounters to end in humiliation and failure while at the same time *hoping* the next sexual encounter would be different. But it was never different. And Al's anxiety increased to the point where he not only had difficulty maintaining an erection, but had trouble even getting one. Increasingly he became a worried spectator, waiting for something to go wrong. Eventually, his anxiety doused his sexual desire as effectively as an ice-cold shower.

Soon he began to avoid sex because he felt he could not risk the humiliation of another disappointing sexual performance. "I missed it for a while," he says. "But I really don't anymore. A really sexy young girl could walk in here right now, sit down on my lap, and start undressing, and I wouldn't react. I wouldn't feel a thing or I'd just turn it off if I felt it."

Fearing future failures, Al has stopped dating, and in fact avoids social situations that might lead to sexual ones. "The way I figure it," he says with a shrug, "why enter a race that you know you can't win?"

A full discussion of sexual dysfunctions and difficulties other than ISD is beyond the scope of this book. However, because some ISD sufferers also experience these other problems—before or after the onset of ISD—and because we will refer to these difficulties by name throughout the remainder of this book, you need to know what they are. The following tables briefly describe the most commonly experienced dysfunctions.

EXCITEMENT PHASE DYSFUNCTIONS

FUNCTIONAL RESPONSE	DYSFUNCTIONAL RESPONSE	MOST COMMON CAUSES
Abandonment of one's self to direct (e.g., touching) and indirect (e.g., thoughts) sexual stimulation leads to erection for men or lubrication for women	Impotence (erectile problems) or lack of lubrication. Problem can be failure to attain or maintain erection or lubrication.	*Psychological/Sexual:* *performance anxiety *pressure from partner to respond *anxiety about pleasing partner *Individual:* *conflict about sex leads to guilt and/ or anxiety *inability to let go of control *Relationship:* *mixed feelings about partner *fear of rejection or abandonment *unresolved conflicts *Physical:* *diabetes *problem with genital blood flow *hormones (e.g., low testosterone high prolactin, or estrogen inbalance) *drugs (e.g., anti-hypertensives or alcohol)

ORGASM PHASE DYSFUNCTIONS

FUNCTIONAL RESPONSE	DYSFUNCTIONAL RESPONSE	MOST COMMON CAUSES

Build-up of muscle tension, vasocongestion, and pleasure leads to ejaculation and orgasm for men and orgasm for women	Premature ejaculation (inability to control ejaculation)	*Psychological/Sexual*
		  *lack of awareness of physical sensations prior to ejaculation
		  *anxiety about ejaculatory control
		Individual:
		  *fear of intimacy
		  *generalized feelings of anxiety
		Interpersonal:
		  *unresolved conflicts
		  *mixed feelings about partner

	Retarded ejaculation (inability to ejaculate)	*Psychological/Sexual:*
		  *inability to let go during sex
		Individual:
		  *fear of loss of control
		Interpersonal:
		  *mixed feelings about partner
		Physical:
		  *trauma to or diseases of the lower spinal cord
		  *drugs

	Preorgasmia (inability to reach orgasm)	*Psychological/Sexual:*
		  *insufficient stimulation
		  *pressure to perform

FUNCTIONAL RESPONSE	DYSFUNCTIONAL RESPONSE	MOST COMMON CAUSES

		*lack of knowledge of one's own sexual response
		Individual:
		  *fear of intimacy
		  *inability to let go of control
		Relationship:
		  *mixed feelings about partner
		Physical:
		  *drugs
		  *advanced diabetes

SEXUAL DISORDERS ASSOCIATED WITH GENITAL MUSCLE SPASMS

MEN: Painful ejaculation, which can be caused by urogenital infection or mixed feelings about ejaculating, as a result of unresolved sexual or relationship conflicts

WOMEN: Vaginismus (involuntary contractions of the muscles surrounding the vagina), which can be caused by gynecological problems, prior sexual traumas, conflicts about sex, fears of intimacy, or relationship problems

DYSPAREUNIA

MEN AND WOMEN: Painful intercourse, often caused by a physical problem. It can also be caused by a hypochondriacal reaction to sexual stimulation, hysterical pain, pain-depression syndrome, or brutal sex.

If you want to know more about sexual dysfunctions, we suggest you consult any of the excellent resources we list on page 291.

Experienced by both heterosexual and homosexual individuals and couples, sexual dysfunctions sometimes lead to ISD or occur as a result of desire difficulties. For example, intense anxiety about failure to attain or maintain an erection, as well as repeated disappointment about not reaching orgasm, may cause individuals to avoid sexual situations and inhibit their sexual desire. Conversely, absent or infrequent sexual desire creates situations in which individuals—hoping to please or appease their partners—engage in sexual activity even though they are not particularly interested in sex. They tend to experience less excitement or arousal, which may in turn lead to problems of impotence or inhibited orgasm. To further complicate matters, men in particular may complain of impotence when their real problem is ISD. They find it easier to tell their partners that they cannot get an erection than to say, "I don't feel desire for you," or "I am not interested in having sex with you."

THE WHOLE PICTURE

As you can see, a great many ingredients go into the recipe for sexual desire, and the ingredient considered to be most important varies from person to person. Even with room for personal preferences, however, one thing remains constant. If even one of the ingredients—especially the one that is most important to you personally—is missing, the whole recipe can fail. Or to put it a different way, when your conditions are not met, you do not get the sexual experience you want. Sex may be less satisfying than you want it to be, less satisfying than it used to be, or not satisfying at all. And quite frequently, dissatisfaction breeds lack of interest.

CHAPTER TWO
ISD

THIS CHAPTER EXPLAINS the most common signs and types of ISD as well as desire differences. We'd like to offer a warning here. Our intention is to paint a clear, accurate picture of sexual desire problems and *not* necessarily to convince you that you have those problems. We ask you not to jump to conclusions and we warn you that hasty self-diagnosis or diagnosing your partner can do more harm than good. Do not turn the following pages into ammunition to be used against yourself or your partner. Do not punish yourself or blame your partner for your sexual dissatisfaction. We urge you to consider instead the following comments as a guide to the *possible* reasons that your sex life isn't what you want it to be. Once you have that information, you can use the exercises in Chapters Six, Seven, and Eight to solve your mutual problem.

SIGNS AND SYMPTOMS OF ISD

Although it is one of the first things our patients mention, having sex less often than you used to or think you should does not necessarily mean you or your partner have a sexual desire disorder. Desire is an internal psychological state, and so it cannot be accurately measured by external standards. Frequency of sex is, in fact, an especially unreliable indicator of sexual desire. For one thing, many people have sex when they do not actually desire it. Believing that marital sex in particular is a duty or obligation, many men and women merely comply with their partners' wishes. Others want to please their partners or prove they've still got what it takes, and consciously decide ahead of time to have sex without feeling turned on.

Conversely and perhaps more commonly, many people feel desire *more often* than they make love. They may truly be interested in having sex, but choose not to because of fatigue, stress, or lack of time, opportunity, or a suitable partner.

While it often affects how often you make love, ISD *always* affects the *internal* process that creates interest in sex, an appetite that in turn prompts you to seek out sexual opportunities, become receptive to sexual overtures, or actually engage in sexual activity. When sexual desire is inhibited, the circuits in the brain's sexual pleasure center shut down. Like Al, who insists he would not be turned on by "a really sexy young girl" sitting on his lap and starting to undress, people with sexual desire problems do not respond, barely respond, or switch off their responses to external sexual cues. Few, if any, psychological wants or needs—from interest in physical pleasure or a desire to increase intimacy to relief from loneliness—activate their sexual desire. In fact, consciously or unconsciously, a wide range of *negative* thoughts and feelings are used to squelch sexual feelings, inhibiting desire before it is strong enough to move these individuals toward actual sexual activity. Just when they begin to enjoy their sexual feelings and look forward to the prospect of making love, some ISD sufferers suddenly and inexplicably feel uncomfortable, tense, angry, anxious, or repelled by their partners. Others don't even get that far; they simply feel nothing at all.

In addition to these general features, the following feelings and behaviors are common among individuals who are experiencing ISD:

- feeling irritated, tense, pressured, angry, or disgusted in arousing situations, as Bobby does during explicit conversations about sex, for instance, or as Dan does when Barbara puts on a sexy negligee and attempts to seduce him

- finding that the first stirrings of sexual desire are immediately followed by negative or distracting thoughts or images—memories of something your partner did that was insensitive or irritating, images of your mother as she looked the day she caught you playing doctor with a neighbor, flashbacks of an unpleasant sexual experience, distracting thoughts about work or your children, and so on
- never or rarely fantasizing about sex or thinking about anything related to sex
- rarely recognizing or responding to sexual cues and barely reacting to people, places, things, or situations that are erotic or sexually provocative
- needing intense stimulution to create sexual excitement or finding that only one or a few very specific sexual cues turn you on
- feeling no desire for an attractive and appropriate partner—like your spouse or lover—and perhaps even feeling disgust or repulsion in your partner's presence
- feeling desire for unattainable or unavailable partners—like *Playboy* centerfold models or rock stars—but feeling no desire or shutting it down in the presence of a real partner or whenever the possibility of actually having sex exists
- fearing and/or mistrusting a partner who is actually loving and giving
- rarely engaging in sexual activity despite ample opportunities and/or repeatedly and routinely refusing your spouse's or lover's sexual invitations
- going out of your way to avoid sexual situations or situations that might lead to sexual situations
- engaging in sexual activity primarily for reasons other than sexual desire, such as obliging a partner
- find that when you do make love, sexual pleasure is limited or fleeting—like eating a meal when you are not hungry

Most of us have responded to sexual situations in at least one of these ways at one time or another. However, one or more of these signs do point to sexual desire problems if they are your usual or most frequent responses to situations and potential partners that in reality are safe, acceptable, and perhaps even optimal for sexual activity, or if they concern you or your partner or create conflicts between you.

TYPES OF ISD

Primary ISD, which is sometimes called hypoactive sexual desire, is less common than other types and is defined as a lifelong absence of sexual desire similar to what Bobby described in Chapter One. It may be caused by conflicts about sex, hormone deficiencies, or other physical conditions that interfere with the brain's ability to receive and transmit sexual messages. Primary ISD may not be considered a problem by those who have it. However, it is frequently a cause of concern to their partners. Fortunately, many of the exercises in Chapters Six, Seven, and Eight can help the sexual responsiveness of the primary ISD sufferer—if he or she *desires* such an improvement.

Low sexual desire is also considered to be primary when someone appears to have a naturally, constitutionally low (although not entirely absent) sex drive. For instance, although not as asexual as Bobby, Tim—who, as described in Chapter One, took several months to consummate his marriage to Janet and completely stopped making love two years ago—has always had a limited response to sexual stimuli and only sporadic interest in sex.

Unlike Bobby, Tim has masturbated perhaps two or three times a month since he was thirteen and he does have sexual fantasies, although they tend to be more romantic than erotic. "There will be a lot of kissing and touching," he explains. "But nothing really explicit. In fact, sometimes I'll skip over the really sexual stuff and go right to images of cuddling and feeling close afterward."

While other boys were ogling centerfolds and bragging

about their sexual exploits, Tim, a self-proclaimed bookworm, was immersed in Bible stories and Greek mythology, sometimes spending days at a time alone in his room drawing the pictures he visualized in his mind. None of them had sexual themes. His early sexual experiences were prompted by his interest in proving he could "do it" and were, for the most part, disastrous—reinforcing his doubts and proving that sex "really wasn't all it was cracked up to be."

With his naturally low sex drive, Tim made the perfect partner for Janet—whose lifelong anxiety about sex had blossomed into a full-fledged phobia. Their sexual desire difficulties ended up being less of a problem than they might have been for another couple.

Secondary ISD is defined as *lost* interest rather than lifelong low or absent interest, and it is more common than primary ISD. People with secondary ISD used to experience sexual desire but no longer do, or feel less desire than they once did. The onset to secondary ISD is often associated with psychological crises, depression, stress, anger, anxiety, and relationship conflicts, as well as physical problems.

Wendy is an excellent example of secondary ISD. Recognizing that her sexual feelings could not be accommodated by her terminally ill husband, Wendy consciously suppressed her sexual desire. Under the circumstances, this was completely appropriate. Two years later Wendy realized during therapy that "deep down inside, I still saw making love and feeling sexy as betraying Mark. That made me feel guilty and guilt kept me from being interested in sex."

Simplistic as Wendy's explanation might be, it is fairly accurate. In many cases of secondary ISD, an underlying psychological conflict—which the ISD sufferer is rarely consciously aware of—stirs up guilt, anger, anxiety, or other feelings that interfere with sexual desire. Most secondary ISD sufferers assume, as Wendy did, that they just are no longer interested in sex, when actually the interest is there but they are unconsciously stifling it.

Some secondary ISD sufferers *can* identify the source of their desire difficulties, most notably when that source of anxiety involves sexual performance. If other sexual problems preceded the onset of ISD, these individuals may even be well aware of what they do to turn themselves off. For example, Al, who prefers not to risk having another session of sex ruined by his erection problems, easily lists the "tricks" he uses to take his mind off sex. "I think about work," he says. "Or I try to remember people's phone numbers. Or I think about somebody who really ticked me off and dream up ways to get back at them. But mostly I just think about the last time I tried to get it up and couldn't. Nothing stops the juices from flowing like knowing you aren't going to be able to perform."

Global ISD, whether long-standing or recent, is a lack of interest or loss of desire in *all* sexual situations. Those with global ISD do not feel turned on regardless of the circumstances, the partner, or any other variable. They lose their appetite for all flavors, forms, and features of sex. Global ISD is most often brought on by depression, severe stress, physical illnesses, sexual traumas like incest or rape, or serious relationship conflicts. In addition, it is often seen in adults who were "perfect" children and received strong negative messages about sex or about experiencing pleasure in general.

Such is the case for Maggie. The daughter of an alcoholic father and a mother who periodically escaped from the household by having "nervous breakdowns" and checking herself into psychiatric hospitals, Maggie is a thirty-six-year-old magazine editor who is three years into her second marriage. The first ended in disaster when her husband left her for another woman. She came to see us for the first time without her new husband, claiming that "it's my problem, not his. I'm the one who can't relax in bed."

However, as we worked with the problem she presented to us, we soon discovered that Maggie also had a problem feeling sexual desire—under any circumstances. Growing up as the always responsible daughter in a chaotic household, Maggie had learned that "looking forward to feeling good meant setting yourself up to be disappointed." Her early sexual experiences, which were clumsy and unfulfilling, seemed to confirm her theory. So Maggie learned not to look forward to sex either.

If she did feel desire she tended to tell herself, "This is pretty pointless, don't you think?" and turn her attention to more "productive" endeavors like work or household chores. Like many adult children of alcoholics, Maggie had a highly developed sense of responsibility and put pleasure of any kind last on her list of personal priorities. What's more, Maggie, whose response to any sort of conflict was to shut down all emotions, often experienced additional drops in sexual interest whenever her work, her home life, or especially her marriage was not running smoothly. And like Wendy, Maggie was not consciously aware of turning herself off or of how she used obligations and more pressing matters to shut down sexual desire.

Situational ISD, as you might guess from the label itself, is losing your appetite for sex or feeling no sexual desire at all *in certain situations* but not others. Relationship troubles or life adjustment problems such as work-related stress, concerns about aging, fear of intimacy, or attempting to be a "superwoman" or "superman" can lead to situational ISD. When these or other underlying problems are solved, sexual desire usually returns.

More often than not, the situation in which desire is inhibited involves making love with a spouse or another safe, seemingly suitable and receptive partner. For instance, Ed, a fifty-three-year-old vice-president of marketing for a major pharmaceutical company, feels little or no desire to make love to his wife. "She just doesn't turn me on anymore," he says. "I know it's not her fault that she got old, but the truth is that when I look at her I actually *lose* whatever interest I was able to drum up in the first place."

However, Ed feels a great deal of sexual desire for younger women. Over the past five years, he has had several affairs. And even while seeing us for couples therapy, he was giving serious thought to beginning an affair with his new twenty-four-year-old secretary, who was, in Ed's words, "a luscious redhead with legs that won't quit and a great body in general. When I take her out to lunch, every guy in the restaurant turns to look at her and I know they're looking at me and thinking, 'There goes one lucky son of bitch.' "

This is precisely the reaction Ed used to get when he went places with his wife, Pat. "You should have seen her when she was younger," he says. "My wife was a real beauty. She knew how to dress and anywhere we went she turned heads. My male friends and business associates always made a point of saying how gorgeous she was." This made Ed feel good about himself; it boosted his sense of self-worth, because, whether in business or on the racquetball court or when it came to his marriage, Ed has always found that impressing other people made him feel good about himself. Soon after we began to work with this couple we started wondering if the real reason behind Ed's situational ISD might not be that his wife had become physically unattractive as she aged, but rather that the admiration of other people, and thus positive feelings about himself, were harder to come by the older *he* became.

At fifty-three, Ed had gone as far as he could with the pharmaceutical company. Although vice-president was good, it was not as good as president or CEO, which were realistically beyond his reach. In business, there were no new mountains to climb, no new achievements or promotions to celebrate, and therefore few opportunities to bask in the glow of other people's praise. In addition, although he had always worked out in order to stay trim, no amount of exercise could disguise the fact that his body was aging. His hair was thinning on top and turning gray, his face bore wrinkles around the eyes and mouth, and he simply did not have the strength or stamina he'd once had. Sometimes, after playing racquetball, he even thought he felt pains in his chest.

It was true that Pat, although still quite attractive and well-dressed, was showing the effects of age even more than her husband. She had never lost all the weight she'd gained after the birth of their children, her breasts had begun to sag a bit, and her thighs had lost some of their muscle tone. No matter how much makeup she wore, there was no hiding the fact that her face belonged to a fifty-two-year-old. People called her "handsome" now instead of gorgeous. When he looked at Pat, Ed thought about how much she had changed. These thoughts stirred up his own anxieties about what he had not done well enough in the past and might never get the chance to do in the future. When he looked at his wife, Ed felt old, and he did not like that feeling.

On the other hand, he felt no self-doubt whatsoever in the presence of younger women. "They still have stars in their eyes," he explains. "They don't see my flaws or know about my failures. They see a guy who is important and successful and still in darn good shape. They laugh at my jokes and trust my judgment and when I'm with them I feel young again."

Whom we find attractive is a matter of personal taste and Ed is far from alone in his preference for young women who resemble the models of physical beauty presented to us by the media. Yet not every man who admires and even gets turned on by "a luscious redhead with legs that won't quit" feels no sexual desire for his wife or is repulsed by the idea of making love to her. In Ed's case, and in the vast majority of situational ISD cases, lack of desire has more to do with personal insecurities and relationship problems than with the actual attractiveness of a potential sexual partner or the appropriateness of the situation in which sexual activity will occur.

Some situational ISD sufferers fear intimacy or commitments, and feel desire only when a potential partner is clearly not interested in a relationship of any depth or duration. As one client told us, "I'm dating a really nice guy now, considerate, sensitive, ambitious—and rich to boot. But I don't tingle when I'm with him; my heart doesn't race; my palms don't sweat. The spark isn't there and I won't sleep with him." Her lack of desire for this man is part of a pattern she developed after a lengthy and intense love affair ended abruptly and painfully. Love is dangerous, she concluded, and now she says, "Put me in a room with a married man or a traveling salesman who's leaving town in the morning, and I'm interested. Heck, I have enough sexual desire for the both of us. But, if they're going to want more than a good time from me, forget it."

Situational ISD also refers to losing sexual desire temporarily, such as during times of stress or while grieving a loss. Or you could develop situational ISD under certain circumstances; for example, you may be turned off by sex with a partner but not by masturbation.

Situational ISD is also experienced by people whose marriage or relationship is in trouble. Conflicts over money, child rearing, or household chores, unresolved anger and pain about one partner's extramarital affair, general disillusionment, and lack of communication can get carried into the bedroom, making a partner seem unappealing—although sexual desire may still be activated by external cues or fantasies about other partners, and acted on through masturbation.

Sometimes the guilt and other bad feelings created by not wanting to make love to your spouse will turn situational ISD into global ISD. For instance, when Sally married Jack, he was a handsome college football hero who seemed to have a bright future ahead of him. He had already been signed by a professional football team and the young couple dreamed together about wealth, fame, and success. But those dreams died when Jack sustained a career-ending knee injury during his very first pro-football season.

Sally nursed Jack through physical pain and emotional devastation, putting up with his drinking binges, listening to his endless tales of what could have been, and working two jobs until Jack finally pulled himself together.

Even after he had been back on his feet for several years, Sally was constantly reminded that Jack wasn't the man he used to be. He walked with a limp and his muscle had turned to fat. His sense of humor ran toward biting sarcasm and he was still likely to descend into deep depression, sulking and withdrawing for days and sometimes weeks at a time. To make matters worse, Sally was often overwhelmed by her own bitter disappointment about *her* dreams that had not and apparently never would come true. While helping Jack get through the crisis, she had put her own anger and frustration on a back burner, and now they welled up inside her whenever Jack tried to show affection or initiate sex.

She felt terribly guilty about no longer feeling sexually attracted to Jack and also about her frequent fantasies of hav-

ing sex with other men. Soon enough, the lie she used to tell
Jack when she didn't want to have sex—that she just wasn't
interested in sex at all anymore—turned into the truth. Lack of
physical attraction and resentment led to situational ISD; then
the guilt and anxiety about it caused Sally to lose her sexual
appetite altogether.

The exercises in Chapters Six, Seven, and Eight address
many of the underlying issues that cause situational ISD, although individual or couples counseling may be necessary, as
well.

"TURNING OFF": HOW SEXUAL DESIRE IS INHIBITED

Some people consciously choose to switch off sexual desire—
because their partners may want more closeness than they do
or because having sex will take them away from other priorities or because they are angry and want to get back at their
partners.

However, it is more common for desire to be suppressed
unconsciously. Instantly and automatically, an ISD sufferer can
go from turned on to anxious, irritable, and turned off—
without ever knowing what happened or why. In fact, many
people with ISD suppress sexual interest so rapidly and invol-
untarily that desire disappears before they even realize that it
appeared in the first place.

How Do We Do It?

Sexual desire is governed by sexual pleasure centers in the
brain and these centers are "wired" to many other brain centers. When activated by sexual thoughts and fantasies, emotions, or various psychological wants and needs, the sexual
pleasure center creates physical sexual excitement. The process
cannot occur, however, if sexual desire messages are overrid-
den by other emotions or if the circuits are shut down by other
brain centers, most notably the ones that protect us from pain.

Avoidance of anticipated pain *always* takes priority over seeking pleasure.

It is normal and customary to inhibit sexual desire in dangerous or inappropriate situations—when a partner is unattractive, unavailable, abusive, or a family member; when there is too little time or too great a risk of being interrupted; when we are tired, worried, or ill; or when the situation poses a real threat to our physical or emotional health. However, people with sexual desire problems often perceive danger where there is none and shut down sexual feelings in situations that are, in reality, safe and appropriate.

How Do People Shut Down Sexual Feelings When They Perceive Danger?

ISD sufferers reflexively experience feelings that resemble those they might have in a truly threatening situation, most notably fear, dread, and anxiety. Without consciously trying, they:

- evoke negative thoughts or associations or allow random negative thoughts to distract them
- focus their attention on their partner's most unattractive features or their own flaws
- think about work, children, money, or any other stressful topic

Recently a friend who does *not* suffer from ISD offered us an excellent example of how sexual desire can be switched off by anyone at any time. A writer with a deadline to meet, she found herself distracted by sexual fantasies about a man whom she had just begun to date. She did not know where their relationship would lead them; all she knew was that thoughts about when, where, and how they would make love were taking up far too much of her time.

"From out of nowhere, this thought popped into my head," she told us: " 'You know, he's just like my brother-in-law.' I *really* don't like my brother-in-law, and even though they don't really have much in common, the thought that he *might* be like my brother-in-law was a complete turn-off. I stopped tingling. I stopped hearing him whisper terribly romantic things in my ear. The thrill was gone—completely."

Our friend was subsequently able to get back to work. Also, when she was with the man she was dating, she made sure *not* to think about her brother-in-law, for if she had, she would have turned off her sexual desire in what was actually a safe and appropriate situation.

Chances are that you are not aware of the thoughts, memories, or emotions you use to suppress sexual desire. However, if you suspect that negative thoughts and images are suppressing your sexual desire, you can begin to help yourself by looking for the switches you flip to shut off the desire—in situations that are truly dangerous as well as those that are actually safe.

You might ask yourself what thoughts come to mind as soon as your spouse or another potential sexual partner sends out signals that he or she would like to have sex. Do you instantly remember something hurtful that the person once said? Do you immediately look at your watch, think of the unpaid bills on your desk or the sales meeting you have to lead in the morning? Do you conjure up images of the last time you had sex or any time your sexual activity was less than satisfying or a dismal failure? Do you find that some physical characteristic or idiosyncrasy of your partner's that didn't bother you in the past now bothers you all the time? If you do, there is a good possibility that you use these thoughts to inhibit desire even though you are not aware of doing so.

Why Do People Inhibit Sexual Desire?

To answer that question, think about the people you've already read about in this book. Why weren't they interested in sex? Al had failed on several occasions to attain or maintain an erection. Sexual desire created anxiety because it would most likely lead to another humiliating performance failure. Andrea and

Paul's sex life wasn't living up to their high expectations. Their single-minded pursuit of sexual excellence turned sex into a chore. Wendy associated sexual feelings with guilt and betrayal. Janet knew almost nothing about sex, had learned it was bad, and guessed that it would be painful. Looking at his wife reminded Ed that he had limitations, that he was aging, that his ability to achieve had plateaued, that time was running out for him. These thoughts and feelings shut down his desire for sex. Dan was drained by work-related pressures and angry at Barbara for failing to be sensitive to his needs. Sally resented the way her life had turned out and could feel no desire for Jack, whose needs she'd met by sacrificing her own. What's more, she was scared to death that she would succumb to sexual desire and have sex with other men. Maggie protected herself from disappointment by never looking forward to pleasure—sexual or otherwise. Bobby was essentially asexual, while Tim had never paid much attention to his own sexual urges.

Other ISD sufferers perceive certain sexual situations as dangerous because of painful past experiences. Still others fear intimacy. They believe making love might bring more closeness than they can tolerate, or that a partner will become dependent on them, hurt them, or leave them. And many think that giving in to sexual feelings will distract them from more important matters, while a few simply want out of their present relationships but feel guilty or afraid to say so.

Obviously, the physical, psychological, and interpersonal causes of ISD are varied and complex. We will explore them in detail in the next three chapters. For now, however, it will suffice to say that:

- ISD occurs because, for one reason or another, sexual feelings themselves are considered dangerous, create anxiety, conflict with other feelings, or are objectionable, and therefore they are shut down or not acted upon.
- Most ISD sufferers do not consciously know that they inhibit their sexual desire, but instead believe that they rarely feel desire or never experience it at all.

This last belief may be a matter of perception or faulty learning. Tim and Maggie—as well as a number of other patients we have treated—rarely recognize their own states of sexual arousal, never learned *how* to turn themselves on, experience very few sexual cues as sexually stimulating, and have a limited amount of experience in feeling sexual pleasure. As a result, they label *themselves* as "not very sexual" and behave accordingly.

More common, however, are the ISD sufferers who know what desire and arousal feel like—because they experienced it in the past or still experience it in certain situations—but who rapidly, and for the most part unconsciously, shut it down.

But the *greatest* number of people with sexual desire problems may not be suppressing desire at all. They are the men and women in relationships with partners whose level of sexual desire is noticeably different than their own.

DESIRE DIFFERENCES

Since sexual activity between partners takes two, one partner's lack of interest in sex—whether it is the result of ISD or not—invariably affects the other partner. Of course, if both partners have relatively low sex drives, neither one may mind the other's lack of interest. And if one partner never really enjoyed sex, that person may actually be relieved when the other's sexual desire decreases or disappears. Others feel disappointed, but not threatened by the situation.

However, many men and women do indeed feel threatened by their partners' lack of interest in sex. They interpret it as a personal rejection and feel deprived, frustrated, hurt, or furious. Some become depressed or obsessed, devoting enormous amounts of time and emotional energy to finding ways to ignite their partners' sexual desire and suffering additional anguish each time they fail to do so—as Barbara and Dan dramatically demonstrated. In fact, Barbara and Dan originally suffered from a desire dependency disorder. But because of the additional stress Dan experienced after he started his own business and his passively angry reaction to Barbara's escalating demands for more sex, he went from having low desire to feeling no desire and suffering from ISD.

Couples with Desire Differences

When we talk about sex drive, we are referring to your *natural capacity* to respond to sexual stimuli, including how often and the specific ways you react to sexual cues or situations. And just as all of us have different natural capacities in other areas, we also have different sex drives. Your level of sexual desire, like Tim's or Dan's or Maggie's, may be relatively low. You may be perfectly happy making love two or three times a month or even less often, and there may only be a few types of sexual cues or settings that really turn you on. Or, like Barbara, your sex drive may be quite high. If you could, you would have sex every day, or you normally think about sex many times a day and can turn everything from a suggestive television commercial to boredom with a tedious task into a sexual cue. Whether very low, very high, or somewhere in between, this innate capacity is rarely viewed as a problem when both partners have nearly equal sexual appetites.

When a couple that comes to us for sex therapy consists of one partner who says, "He (or she) never wants to make love," and another who complains, "He (or she) is constantly pressuring me to make love," it is relatively easy for us to identify them as a couple with desire differences. And like many other sex therapists, we find that the lower-desire partner overestimates the frequency of lovemaking while the higher-desire partner underestimates it.

However, frequency is not the only issue these couples disagree about. They may also have differing opinions about *when* to make love. As one man put it, "My wife thinks having sex first thing in the morning is the best of all possible ways to start the day. Personally, I need a good hour of peace and quiet and a couple of cups of coffee before I can even talk to someone, no less make love." Another patient, a young divorced mother of two, says, "My boyfriend is into spontaneity. He wants to be able to surprise me in the shower or walk through the door at five o'clock and have sex on the kitchen floor. The other day he showed up during his lunch hour with sex on his mind and he got really angry because I wouldn't drop everything and go to bed with him. I'm sorry, but I just can't get turned on knowing that the baby is about to wake up from her nap and my son is due home from kindergarten in ten minutes."

In addition, these couples often disagree about *how* to have sex. It is not uncommon to hear one partner call the other "abnormal" for showing interest in oral sex or new sexual positions. Or the higher-desire partner may label the low-desire partner "frigid" or "uptight" or "too mechanical" for always insisting that sex be performed in the "same, exact, incredibly boring way." Couples with desire differences also may not see eye to eye on the subject of who should initiate lovemaking.

Kevin, a thirty-seven-year-old concert promoter, and his lover, Carl, a thirty-three-year-old graphic artist, sought treatment for desire differences approximately six months after Kevin suddenly seemed to lose interest in sex. Previously, Kevin's level of sexual desire had been somewhat higher than his lover's. After six years together, both partners were baffled by the change.

During an early therapy session, Kevin complained about feeling "disgusted and put down" whenever Carl made sexual overtures. "I don't like him being so aggressive—and impatient. Too impatient to wait for me to start things rolling, so he just takes over the controls. And he does it without considering that I might be stressed out or tired or whatever. It's really insensitive behavior."

As Kevin spoke, Carl's brown eyes widened and his mouth dropped open. When we asked the reserved, soft-spoken young man how he felt, he said, "Amazed. If you don't count the first few months we were together, Kevin has never made the first move. We've even discussed this before. I *told* him I felt weird about always being the one to suggest sex. With other lovers, I had always been more passive, and coming on to him made me feel awkward and needy. *He* said he liked me to put the moves on him. It made him feel great to know I wanted him. He *said* it turned him on."

"Sometimes it does," Kevin conceded and we soon learned that Kevin did indeed enjoy his lover's sexual overtures when he was already feeling sexual desire—an emotional state Kevin believed he nonverbally communicated to Carl. He claimed that when he was interested in making love, he "sent out little signals." However, we soon discovered that those signals were confusing at best. For instance, when feeling sexy, Kevin might ask Carl to rub his back, but he also requested backrubs when he was feeling tense—and not the least bit interested in making love. Since the signal was the same in both situations, Carl could only guess at its meaning. When he guessed wrong, Kevin became irritated and repulsed. And Carl—already uncomfortable with the initiator's role—felt hurt and confused. Even though the actual differences in their sex drives were minor, Kevin and Carl wound up in a steadily escalating conflict over when and how often to have sex, and who should initiate it.

In the not too distant past, gay men with desire differences were unlikely to end up in a sex therapist's office. Sex was often the highest priority in their relationship and many times it was the only way they could demonstrate their commitment or express intimate feelings and other emotions (gay men were, after all, raised to be men, hearing the same negative messages about displaying feelings as their heterosexual counterparts). As a result, when one partner lost interest or could not keep up with his lover's sex drive, either the relationship would come to an end or the higher-desire partner would simply get his sexual needs met elsewhere. Neither option is as appealing now that AIDS is decimating the gay community. So gay men are undertaking what is for many of them a new and unfamiliar challenge—working to maintain the relationships they are in already. This is difficult enough to do without the added problem of desire descrepancies.

A Destructive Cycle

In nonsexual situations as well as sexual ones, people who have strong, clearly defined ideas about how other people *should* behave tend to become outraged when those people behave in some other way. For instance, the higher-desire husband in one couple we treated bitterly complained that "I only get no for an answer. 'No, I'm tired.' 'No, it's a bad time of the month.' 'No, because the kids might wake up.' Even when she says yes, I feel like she's thinking, 'Well, I've turned him down twelve times in a row, so I guess I'll throw him a crumb tonight and let him make love to me.' Do you know that in all the years we've been married, she never once made the first move!"

"*You* never give me the chance," his wife retorted angrily. "If I didn't say no once in a while, we'd be having sex every day, morning, noon, and night. If I say I'm tired, I really am. And if I'm not in the mood, I'm not. But does he care how I feel? Of course, not. Sex is for him. It's all about *his* needs and *his* urges. I don't matter. I'm just a means to an end. It makes me so mad. Even when I might actually want to have sex, I don't do it because I don't want to give *him* the satisfaction."

These angry words and bitter, resentful feelings are typical of the emotional fallout from the constant tug-of-war between partners with desire differences. In addition to the persist-resist battle that Barbara and Dan's story so clearly illustrates, both partners inflict and sustain various war wounds. Lower-desire partners are often left feeling sexually inadequate and guilty, while at the same time resenting their partners' demands and insensitivity. Higher-desire partners may feel deprived of sexual pleasure and guilty about having sexual needs and urges at all. Often, higher-desire partners feel personally rejected. Even when lower-desire partners insist that they simply aren't interested in sex, their spouses or lovers believe what they want, sometimes even badgering the lower-desire partner into confessing that "yes, it is about you. I don't want to have sex with you."

As the conflict continues, both partners may begin to withdraw emotionally as well as physically. To avoid giving the impression that they are making sexual overtures, lower-desire partners may not want to show warmth or affection of any kind. Hurt and angry, higher-desire partners get back by withdrawing emotional support. These couples communicate less and less, and expressions of intimate or loving feelings become fewer and farther between. Not only their sex lives, but ultimately their relationships deteriorate.

Whose Problem Is It?

Thanks to the media, most of us tend to believe that wanting more sex—within limits, of course—is normal and healthy, while wanting less is downright pathological. As a result, the lower-desire partner in a couple with desire differences is usually identified as the partner with the problem.

However, the higher-desire partner may experience as many—and sometimes more—problems. Higher-desire partners are frequently plagued by feelings of inadequacy and failure. They may even consider themselves "sick" or "indecent" for wanting more sex than they are getting. They certainly devote more time and energy to worrying about and desperately trying to fix the problem—often to the point of obsession. And of course, there's always the question of *why* these men and women go right on pushing and pressuring partners who have clearly signaled their lack of interest, as well as why individuals who react so strongly to rejection continue to set themselves up to be rejected.

The truth of the matter is that neither one is the villain on whom all the blame can be heaped. Neither one is an innocent bystander either. Two people participate in conflicts over sexual desire, and sexual desire problems themselves leave two victims in their wake.

Turning Differences into Disasters

The escalating conflict between partners with desire differences is even more pronounced when one partner does indeed suffer from ISD, especially if this person's sexual interest suddenly takes a nose dive.

For instance, during the six years that Kevin and Carl had been together, they had weathered many hard times, admitting that more than once the only thing that had kept them together was dread of having to start over with someone else. Both had had many sexual relationships prior to "settling down" and felt extremely lucky that they had not been infected with AIDS. Like other couples, both heterosexual and homosexual, they had experienced a slow but steady decline in the frequency of sex, but both agreed it had not been anything to be alarmed about. What did alarm them was Kevin's dramatic loss of interest in sex, a change that had occurred six months ago when he was chosen to head the national concert promotion company whose local operation he had run for the past five years.

To oversee a multimillion-dollar business with branch offices in twelve states was both an honor and a challenge. It also brought with it tremendous responsibility, longer hours, and constant headaches. It was not uncommon for Kevin to receive crisis calls at home and be on the phone late into the night, trying to resolve problems with artists and venues and managers. Fatigue, stress, and anxiety about his ability to handle the job all took their toll on Kevin's sexual desire.

Never one to discuss the things that bothered him, when Kevin did talk about work, he always focused on the positive aspects. He gave Carl no verbal clues about the strain he was feeling. Instead, as in signaling sexual desire, Kevin just expected Carl to know what he was going through. Carl couldn't help but notice that Kevin was more irritable and tired than he used to be and even rightly attributed his mood to work-related stress. But he did not make the connection between stress and the change in their sex life, because in the past, when Kevin had been "wired" about work, sex was exactly what he'd looked for to help him relax and feel better. With this in mind, Carl more frequently made sexual overtures, which Kevin rebuffed. Because the change was sudden and drastic, and because sex was highly valued as their main emotional outlet, Kevin and Carl's battle, unlike Barbara and Dan's, escalated rapidly. Nightly "screaming matches" were commonplace by the time they called our office for an appointment.

A sudden, noticeable change in one partner's sex drive is almost always greeted by a noticeable reaction from the other partner. Quite often, the initial response to a drop in a partner's sexual desire is to suspect infidelity, which is sometimes the case. Guilty feelings about extramarital affairs and anxiety about getting caught, along with general relationship tension, do inhibit interest in having sex with your spouse or long-term lover.

Another common reaction is for higher-desire partners—male or female—to assume that they have done something wrong, that they are no longer attractive to their partners, or that there is a problem in their relationship that their partners are refusing to discuss. Again, the higher-desire partner may at times be right, although the lower-drive partner—who is usually unaware of the underlying problem—may adamantly deny that anything is wrong.

Without an acceptable explanation, partners of ISD sufferers rarely tolerate the situation for long. ISD and desire differences may cause more distress and marital discord than other sexual problems—probably because problems like being nonorgasmic, impotence, and premature ejaculation do not completely stop sex or are often perceived as being out of anyone's control. Desire is not seen in this light, however. Men and women see sexual interest as something their partners can switch on and off at will, and become preoccupied or even obsessed with the idea that their partners are turning it off to hurt them or because they have somehow failed. In nearly every case, the higher-desire partner's relentless effort to fix the problem actually aggravates the ISD partner's condition.

SEXUAL AVOIDANCE

From earliest childhood all of us have been conditioned to avoid anything that makes us feel anxious. Parents and teachers always seemed to be one step ahead of us, anticipating negative consequences and steering us away from them. Intending only to protect us from pain or failure, they unwittingly taught us to fear and avoid situations that *might* lead to pain or failure.

Our own experiences—both as children and as adults—reinforced this lesson. Lovers reject us. A promotion we expected is not given to us. Friends we trusted betray us. Spouses are unfaithful. Regardless of the circumstances, we learn to anticipate and fear situations that have the potential to hurt or disappoint us again. This is simply human nature.

Whether we were warned about its negative consequences as children or had negative experiences with it as adults, sex is a source of considerable anxiety for any of us. And for some of us, that anxiety is so great that we actively avoid sexual activity or situations that might lead to it.

The Many Forms of Sexual Avoidance

Sexual avoidance ranges from relatively mild avoidance of real situations that provoke anxiety to extreme panic states that cannot be logically explained.

Performance anxiety prompts some people—whether they have ISD or not—to avoid sex. In addition to experiencing other sexual problems, many men and women temporarily avoid sexual situations after they get divorced, are widowed, or end a relationship. Sex could lead to intimacy and they are still recovering from the emotional fallout from their last intimate relationship. As a result, they "take themselves out of the game" for a while.

Many of us have aversions to specific aspects of sex. Because of the negative messages we received as children, we may feel disturbed or disgusted by certain sexual acts or various body parts. Women's genitals, for instance, are sometimes assumed to be unclean or even repulsive. Some of us abandon this notion completely. Others compensate for it, using feminine hygiene products—and contributing to a multimillion-dollar industry, which exists precisely because of our discomfort with female genitals. At the extreme are people who interpret the original message to mean that sex itself is dirty and disgusting and avoid any contact with female sex organs under any circumstances.

In addition, people who avoid certain aspects of sex may have aversions to:

- male genitals
- female genitals
- their own genitals
- homosexual activity
- heterosexual activity
- secretions and odors
- breast touching
- kissing
- being seen nude or seeing a partner nude
- giving or receiving oral sex
- anal sex

For the most part, people with specific sexual aversions may generally enjoy sex and engage in it regularly—as long as they can avoid the aspect that creates feelings of repulsion and anxiety.

However, sexual aversions can extend to aspects of sex that are quite difficult to avoid. To varying degrees, anxiety or disgust may compel people to avoid penetration, sexual arousal, orgasm, pleasure, or sex itself. Obviously, such aversions, and the extremes to which some people are willing to go to avoid them, can create problems. Sometimes fears about certain aspects of sexuality or anxiety about sex or intimacy in general become so extreme that actual phobias develop.

Sexual Phobias

A **sexual phobia** is an intense, *irrational* fear of sex and a *compelling* desire to avoid specific or all sexual situations. Sexual phobias may be experienced by women who were sexually abused as children or raped as adults, or by men and women with a history of other panic disorders like fear of heights, flying, enclosed places, and so on.

Unlike avoiding sex to protect yourself from the humiliation of impotence, to make sure you do not contract a venereal disease, or to keep from performing an act you have learned to view as repulsive—all examples that are based on reality—*phobic* avoidance of sex is rarely connected to anything that is happening in the present or, for that matter, to anything you can pinpoint at all.

Eleanor, for example, is a forty-eight-year-old woman from an extremely wealthy family who was widowed seven years ago and remarried during the past year. The mere thought of making love with her husband panics her, just as it did with her first husband. Yet, prior to her first marriage and during the years between her first husband's death and her remarriage, Eleanor was involved in a number of torrid love affairs. With these men, whom Eleanor described as "not the marrying kind," Eleanor enjoyed lovemaking and looked forward to it.

Throughout her life, Eleanor had experienced other kinds of phobias. As a young child she was so frightened by enclosed places that she would not retrieve clothes from her closets and insisted that car windows be kept wide open even in the most frigid weather. When she was in her early twenties, she developed a fear of heights so severe that she immediately moved out of her penthouse apartment, would visit no one who lived in an apartment any higher than the third floor, and became obsessed with plotting trips through the city that would not involve crossing a bridge.

Eleanor admits that she chose both of her husbands because they could offer "precisely the lifestyle I had as a child." However, in both instances, upon first meeting these handsome, intelligent, exceedingly kind men, she had instantly felt repulsed. "Sometimes I think that's why I married them," she says, agreeing that such a statement makes little sense. But then her phobic aversion to sex makes just as little sense. It is, according to Eleanor, "something with a mind of its own. These horrible doom feelings, these waves of fear and disgust literally possess me and make me do things I cannot justify or explain."

Most people with sexual phobias find that their aversions do indeed seem to take control of their emotional state and their actual behavior. When they do engage in sex—out of a sense of duty or a sincere desire to please their partners—men and women with such phobias may be able to calm themselves, push past their anxiety, and even enjoy sex. As one of our patients, an incest survivor, explains it, "I squeeze my eyes shut and say over and over, 'I am not a child. This is not my father. I love my husband. He won't hurt me.' And after a minute or two, the panic goes away. I settle down and get into making love."

Other sexual phobics never actually enjoy a sexual experience, but instead detach themselves from it, counting the cracks in the ceiling, thinking about what to cook for dinner. "I let my body do its thing," said another of our patients, a young man who suffered from severe claustrophobia as well as sexual panic. "But in my mind, I'm reciting the starting lineups of all the major-league baseball teams."

Still other people with phobic aversions to sex cannot detach and merely endure the experience. As Janet did, many people with sexual phobias experience full-fledged panic attacks when they attempt to make love. They are overcome by feelings of terror and impending doom. They experience heart palpitations, difficulty in breathing, and dizziness, sometimes fainting. Always there is an urgent wish to escape.

Avoiding More than Sex Itself

Whether phobic or not, people who are prone to avoid sex develop **anticipatory anxiety.** Simply thinking about the situation they wish to avoid stirs up the same fears and even creates the same physical symptoms as the situation itself. As a result, these individuals begin to avoid any activity that *might lead up to* the anxiety-provoking sexual situation.

Although he is not phobic and actually enjoys making love with Barbara when he is in the mood, Dan hates the arguments and recriminations that he knows are sure to follow his refusal to make love. Dan says he goes through every evening "waiting for the ax to fall." Anticipating Barbara's next attempt to seduce him, his anxiety increases with each minute that passes. "I keep an eye on her," Dan says, and as soon as he can tell that Barbara is about to make a move, "I pick up the telephone and call my business partner or go into my den and shut the door or suddenly remember something I left at the office or need to pick up at the store."

Like claustrophobics who will climb twenty flights of stairs to avoid riding in an elevator, or people with agoraphobia who restructure their entire lives to avoid the panic attacks they fear will occur if they leave their "safety zone," people with sexual aversions can become obsessed with avoiding sex and/or situations that might lead to sex. For instance, another one of our patients who suffered from ISD and sexual avoidance kept track of the days she and her husband did not have sex so that she could anticipate the next time he would want to. "When that day rolled around, I immediately panicked," she said. " I spent hours trying to figure out how I would get out of it this time. I'd work myself up to the point that I made myself physically ill."

Avoidance Rituals

Even people with mild sexual aversions and relatively low levels of anxiety worry in advance about the possibility of being in an unwanted sexual situation. They adopt a variety of avoidance rituals, including:

- bringing work home from the office
- beginning tasks like washing clothes or cleaning out kitchen cupboards just before bedtime
- insisting they "don't feel well"
- making phone calls
- watching TV
- leaving the bedroom door open "in case the children need us"
- making sure to go to bed before or after their partners
- filling every available evening and weekend with social engagements

- starting an argument just before bedtime
- making themselves physically unattractive by gaining weight, wearing curlers and cold cream to bed, or paying the bare minimum of attention to personal hygiene

Some people sabotage sex, seeing to it that sexual activity is boring or stressful so that their partners will lose interest; others cloud their consciousness with alcohol or tranquilizers. Single individuals may date, but refuse to have sex on moral or religious grounds. They may develop any number of ingenious methods to discourage romantic advances altogether, whether by making sure they don't look attractive or by behaving in a cold or rude manner. Many singles avoid sex and intimacy unconsciously by deeming every potential partner unsuitable and breaking off each relationship before it really begins.

Avoidance and ISD

While some individuals who avoid sex do experience sexual desire on a regular basis, ISD frequently leads to sexual avoidance—as it did for Dan. A lack of sexual desire put him in the uncomfortable position of repeatedly rebuffing Barbara's sexual advances. Hating the confrontations that always followed his refusals, feeling guilty about hurting Barbara, and also angry about her lack of understanding, he adopted avoidance rituals to protect him from the consequences of ISD. Other men who suffer from ISD avoid sex because they fear their lack of desire will prevent them from getting an erection. Even though they may never have actually experienced a performance failure, their anxiety about the possibility persuades them not to risk it. Both men and women who engage in sex even though they feel no desire may experience little pleasure or even feel angry, resentful, and used throughout the experience. These negative feelings may lead to sexual avoidance as well.

In addition, sexual aversions and phobic avoidance can lead to ISD. We often see patients who have made conscious decisions not to feel desire precisely because they want to avoid sex or certain aspects of it. Quite often they will use food, alcohol, or tranquilizers or develop physical ailments to help them anesthetize or ignore their sexual feelings.

A LITTLE BIT OF KNOWLEDGE . . .

We hope you took the advice we offered at the beginning of this chapter and haven't jumped to any conclusions about yourself or your partner. You should not play amateur detective or sex therapist and start thinking "Oh, no! I do that. I must really be sick," or "Aha! My partner does that. I knew he (or she) needed help and now I can force him (or her) to get it!"

If you have been worried about your sex life or been having lots of arguments with your partner about sex before you began reading this book, you now have a better idea of what your problem *might* be. But there is a good deal more you need to know—even if you have already decided to consult a sex therapist or marriage counselor. For instance, you will be better able to help yourself and your partner once you understand *why* ISD occurs.

The many possible causes of sexual desire problems are the subject of the next three chapters, beginning with a chapter on "ISD and the Body," which details various physical factors that can inhibit sexual appetite.

CHAPTER THREE
ISD and the Body

A SEX THERAPIST'S OFFICE was probably the last place on earth Larry, a fifty-five-year-old line supervisor at an auto parts factory, ever expected to be. Yet, there he was, his discomfort and embarrassment obvious as he squirmed in a chair that seemed too confining for his burly, bearlike body. He kept his deep blue eyes trained on the scuffed toes of his work boots.

Natalie, twelve years younger than Larry and his second wife, appeared nervous as well. Coming to our office directly from her job as a waitress, Natalie kept her coat buttoned over her uniform. Proving the more talkative of the two, Natalie informed us that she and Larry had been married for five years but had known each other much longer—since she had first begun waitressing at the restaurant near the factory where he worked. He was one of her regulars, she explained, adding that she had been attracted to him immediately. "He came off like this big tough grizzly bear"—she smiled affectionately and glanced in his direction—"but I could tell he was just a pussycat on the inside." She discovered that this hunch was accurate once she got to know Larry better—during the months immediately after he and his wife separated. "He was really broken up about it," she said, and having recently ended a six-year relationship herself, she was well able to commiserate with him.

Calling his divorce "a real blow to the old ego," Larry had "no use for women" for over a year afterward. But when he did

become interested in a new relationship, Natalie was the woman
who caught his eye. Their six-month affair led to a spur-of-
the-moment trip to Las Vegas to get married, which neither
Larry nor Natalie has ever regretted. Our first impression—
that they had a solid relationship and loved and enjoyed each
other—did not change during the time we worked with them.

Both agreed that their sex life had been satisfying at first.
"We had a good time," Natalie reported, blushing and looking
over at her husband, who nodded in agreement.

"Our sex life would probably be good now too," Larry
commented, "if we had one." But they did not. For the past two
years, Larry and Natalie had not had any type of sex at all.
When they came to us for help, Larry claimed to feel no sexual
desire in any situation. "I don't even think about sex anymore,"
he sighed and then chuckled nervously as he told us that he
"actually reads the articles in *Playboy* nowadays." He explained,
"I just can't get turned on. I want to. I should. Sometimes I
even start to, but then the urge disappears."

Natalie's sexual desire had not diminished, however. She
tried to compensate for Larry's lack of interest by pushing sexual thoughts out of her mind, but this strategy didn't always
work. Acknowledging that she masturbated occasionally and
that the thought of having an affair had crossed her mind
recently, she said defensively, "Two years really is a long time to
go without sex."

Wincing at the thought of Natalie with another man, Larry
told us, "I don't know where my sex drive went, but I sure
would like to get it back."

Before we could help Larry reignite his sexual desire, we
too needed to know where it had gone, and we began our
search by doing a comprehensive evaluation, including **a complete medical history.** Even though ISD is most often the result
of psychological or relationship conflicts, it can be caused or
influenced by a wide range or physical conditions that:

- directly or indirectly affect the brain centers that trigger
  or inhibit sexual desire
- cause hormonal fluctuations that decrease sexual desire

- cause pain or fatigue that can block or diminish sexual desire
- lead to depression, anxiety, or other psychological side effects that alter your mood and/or feelings about yourself

The connections between ISD and the body are exceedingly complex. For instance, the fact that Larry had suffered a heart attack two years earlier did not in itself explain his global loss of desire. His ISD could have been a side effect of his medication, the result of the lingering depression he had suffered since his heart attack, linked to his fears about having another heart attack, or caused by any number of other factors connected to his cardiac problems. We could not solve the puzzle until we had collected all the pieces and understood how they fit together.

In some instances, medical treatment for illnesses or debilitating physical conditions will be enough to restore sexual desire. However, treatment can also have a negative effect, particularly if medication decreases the body's ability to respond to sexual stimulation. In addition, the body may be cured, but the negative emotional reaction to the illness remains.

In other cases, discussing and redefining how and when to have sex—taking your physical condition into account—can renew your interest in it. But most important, physical conditions are part of a larger picture, and the way they influence your emotional state, affect your body image, or alter the way you and your partner relate to each other must be taken into consideration.

If you, like Larry, suffer from global ISD or experience a sudden, noticeable loss of desire, the first thing you should do is identify or eliminate the possible physical causes for your condition—beginning with hormonal problems.

HORMONES AND ISD

Hormones play a role in numerous bodily functions, including sex. They also have an effect on mood and, more generally, how we feel about ourselves and life. When certain hormones arrive on the scene, they can really get things rolling. But other hormones can keep anything from happening at all. Although not the most common cause of ISD, lower-than-normal levels of the hormones thought to stimulate sexual desire, as well as unusually high levels of inhibiting hormones, can have a dramatic impact on sexual desire.

Testosterone

Certain hormones, testosterone in particular, apparently excite cell membranes in the brain, activating the circuits that trigger sexual desire. Thus, even though it is commonly thought of as the "male sex hormone," testosterone plays a role in the stimulation of sexual desire in both men and women.

Men with abnormally low testosterone levels suffer from ISD, including those who test at the low end of the normal range. Testosterone production gradually decreases in men during middle age and men over the age of forty who suffer from global ISD should have their testosterone levels checked by a physician. Giving testosterone to men with abnormally low levels of the hormone often increases sexual desire. However, the hormone will not increase desire in men whose testosterone levels are well within the normal range—so don't rush off to your doctor and ask for a prescription.

Although sexual desire in women is also affected by testosterone, unless they have been deprived of all sources of the hormone because their ovaries *and* adrenal glands have been removed, their ISD is unlikely to be caused by a testosterone deficiency. Testosterone injections or creams can increase a woman's sexual desire if she is deficient in this hormone, but because they can also produce increased facial hair and other "male" characteristics in women—as well as other, more dangerous side effects—such treatment should not be used casually.

Prolactin

Abnormally high levels of the pituitary hormone prolactin have also been linked to ISD. Men and women with global ISD, as

well as those who experience diminished desire and then epi-
sodes of impotence, should have their prolactin levels checked.

Thyroid Hormones

Abnormally low levels of thyroid hormones in men and women
cause diminished sexual desire. Other symptoms include weight
gain, decreased energy, a consistently bloated feeling, and eye-
brow loss. See your doctor if you experience any of these symptoms.

Estrogen

Commonly thought of as the "female sex hormone," estrogen's
role in sexual desire is less clearly understood than that of
testosterone or prolactin. Elevated estrogen levels in men—
most often associated with liver damage caused by alcoholism—
do tend to suppress desire.

For most women, sexual desire fluctuates during the menstrual cycle. Some women are most interested in sex when their
estrogen levels are the highest—prior to and during ovulation.
Others feel the most sexual desire before, during, and immediately after their periods—when estrogen levels are the lowest.
These fluctuations are normal, however, and should not be
considered a form of ISD.

On the other hand, when a woman complaining of ISD
also has a *history* of menstrual problems, we recommend a complete gynecological evaluation. Heavy bleeding, irregular cy-
cles, severe cramps, and other symptoms may point to serious
hormonal imbalances or various gynecological problems that
may also cause pain during intercourse, turning sex into an
activity that is dreaded rather than desired.

When they begin taking birth control pills, some women
find that their interest in sex drops off sharply. It is not clear
whether the estrogen in the pill itself causes diminished desire
or if its side effects—like spotting, nausea, and dizziness—are
the culprits. Regardless, after a woman has taken the pill for

several months, desire generally returns to previous levels. If it does not, you should consult your gynecologist in order to change the type of oral contraceptive you are taking or to explore other methods of birth control.

Menopause

Menopause, the permanent end to menstruation, brings with it a number of physical and psychological changes that can affect sexual desire. For one thing, estrogen levels decrease dramatically, making the vagina less pliable and slower to lubricate. As a result, it may take longer to get sexually aroused. If penetration occurs before you have lubricated adequately, intercourse may be uncomfortable or even painful—which obviously does little to nurture sexual desire. And some women become so preoccupied with hot flashes or vaginal irritations that they find it difficult to develop interest in or even think about sex. However, loss of desire and less sexual satisfaction after menopause are far from a biological certainty. In fact, after menopause many women find sex to be more satisfying.

By using lubricants during intercourse or simply adapting what you do, you can continue having comfortable and satisfying sex. And estrogen replacement therapy, which improves lubrication, controls hot flashes, and often enhances a woman's general sense of well-being, can have a positive effect on sexual desire.

Unfortunately, these physical remedies may have little or no impact on ISD if menopause triggered it. Low self-esteem, anxieties about aging or the end of the child-bearing years, negative feelings about sex or a strained relationship with your partner—all of which contribute to ISD—cannot be cured by taking a pill or trying a new approach to sex. And these problems plague many postmenopausal women and their partners.

DRUGS AND ISD

Because chemical as well as hormonal imbalances can adversely affect sexual desire, we always ask our ISD patients about the prescription medications they are taking and their alcohol or recreational drug use.

Prescription medications that can reduce sexual desire and/or performance (see the table below) include sleeping pills and painkillers, which depress the activity of the central nervous system; allergy and anti-inflammatory drugs, which can block the action of testosterone; and blood pressure (antihypertensive) medications. In addition, drugs used to treat psychoses

---

DRUGS THAT MAY DECREASE SEXUAL DESIRE

ANTIADRENERGIC DRUGS
> beta blockers

ANTIANXIETY DRUGS (*in high doses*)
> Valium, Librium, Tranxene, etc.

ANTIDEPRESSANTS
> lithium carbonate

ANTIHYPERTENSIVES
> centrally acting (*e.g., responsive alpha-methyl dopa*)
> diuretics (*spironolactone*)

ANTIPSYCHOTICS
> Stelazine, Mellaril, Thorazine (*in high doses*)
> Haldol

HALLUCINOGENS
> LSD, mescaline, marijuana (*in high doses*)

NARCOTICS
> morphine, codeine paregoric

SEDATIVES/HYPNOTICS (*in high doses*)
> alcohol
> barbiturates

STIMULANTS
> cocaine
> amphetamines

If you are currently using any of these drugs and are experiencing a loss of sexual desire, consult your physician. He or she may be able to prescribe a similarly acting drug that has fewer sexual side effects. Do *not* stop taking medication that has been prescribed by your physician without seeking medical advice.

and certain types of depression may lower interest. Large doses of tranquilizers may decrease sex drive, but some people have found small doses sexually *uninhibiting*. Although there are no conclusive results yet, researchers are now exploring the possible benefits of some antidepressants in stimulating sexual desire.

As a rule, if you have started taking any prescription medications and have notice a *subsequent* drop in sexual desire or a change in how you function sexually, you should consult the physician who prescribed those drugs. Your doctor can tell you if this is a side effect and may be able to prescribe something that is less likely to produce it.

Keep in mind, however, that research on the effects of prescription drugs on sexuality is still fairly new and, at times, unreliable. That's why it's important to determine if your desire for sex decreased at the same time you began taking the medication, or if the decrease came first. Only then will your doctor be able to evaluate the effect of that medication on your sexuality.

ISD, Alcoholism, and Other Drug Addiction

In addition to inhibiting sexual desire and functioning directly, use of alcohol and other drugs (even without addiction) almost always contributes to ISD indirectly, by altering your emotional state and straining your relationships.

Like prescription medications, alcohol and other drugs produce chemical changes in your brain and body. Even in small doses, alcohol, barbiturates, Quaaludes, and other central-nervous-system depressants go straight to the brain centers that govern fear, reducing your anxiety and inhibitions. This is why you often loosen up or even feel turned on after one or two drinks. However, as you drink more or when the effects of certain drugs actually kick in, your ability to respond sexually is decreased in the same way as your speech capacity, coordination, reflexes, and other bodily functions.

Narcotics like heroin not only depress central nervous system activity but also reduce your sex drive in general, and hallucinogenic drugs like marijuana and LSD disrupt the way sexual thoughts and feelings are received and transmitted by your brain and nerve endings.

If you use alcohol or drugs, you may believe that they increase your sex drive and improve your sexual performance. However, this perception tends to be a distorted one, influenced by the general sense of relaxation and confidence that alcohol and other drugs can produce. In fact, you may find that your partner gives your sexual prowess a decidedly lower rating than you do.

Gwen and Arthur are a middle-aged couple who have been married for twenty years, most of them difficult as a result of Arthur's alcoholism. A construction foreman who managed to earn a living in spite of his nightly drinking binges and morning-after hangovers, Arthur has been sober for the past eighteen months and is an active member of Alcoholics Anonymous. Unfortunately, none of the support and advice he has received from other recovering alcoholics has yet been able to help him improve his marriage in general or his sex life in particular.

"I think that if I could start acting like a real husband, things might get better between us," he said, attempting to explain why he was seeking the advice of sex therapists. To Arthur, "acting like a real husband" meant having sex with his wife, which he was unable to do when he came to see us. "You see," he continued, "I hardly ever really, you know, feel the urge. I sort of lost interest while I was still drinking, but I didn't get interested again after I got sober. I really thought I would, and the thing is, I guess I'm one of those guys who can't force it. If I'm not in the mood, I can't do a darn thing in bed."

Actually, most men can't force themselves to perform sexually if they don't feel sexual desire, and prolonged alcohol or drug use will, in fact, lower your sex drive. Like other recreational drugs such as marijuana, alcohol has a direct and toxic effect on male testosterone production, which, along with similar effects created by alcohol-related liver damage and changes in the nervous system, is likely to inhibit sexual desire and functioning long after you stop drinking. What's more, as your addiction to alcohol or drugs progresses, your preoccupation with getting high will detract from your interest in having sex *and* your ability to perform or respond sexually.

"Oh, I suspect he thought he was a real stud," Arthur's wife, Gwen, said bitterly. "But he was one sorry excuse for a lover. Determined, though. I'll give him that. He'd come stumbling in after midnight hell-bent on having sex. Sometimes I could stall him. I'd go into the bathroom, saying I wanted to put in my diaphragm, and if I waited long enough he'd be passed out on the bed. But mostly, he didn't give me the chance to do that. He just used me, time and time again. To tell you the truth, I was glad when the drinking made him impotent, even if he did get nastier about that time too."

As the years went by, Arthur's behavior left its impact on Gwen. Her dread of her husband's insensitive demands for sex evolved into a complete lack of interest in it. "Sex is not on my list of fun things to do with my husband, or anyone else, for that matter," she said, adding that it would be fine with her if sex therapy failed.

"The man put me through eighteen years of hell," she asserted. "Now he stops drinking, says he's sorry, and expects me to forgive and forget. Well, it isn't that easy. If he thinks he's going to come home and find me waiting at the door all lovey-dovey in a sexy nightie, he's got another think coming. It's his turn now."

Clearly, discontinuing drug or alcohol use will not remedy all the problems that began before you got clean and sober. Physical factors, including medical conditions we will discuss in the next section, also negatively influence your emotional state and your relationship. It is often the *combined effect*—rather than the physical problem alone—that causes ISD.

MEDICAL CONDITIONS AND ISD

"I put off having the surgery for as long as I could," says Pat, who, along with her husband, Ed, was introduced in the last chapter. Because of recurring gynecological problems, Pat had a hysterectomy at age forty-six. Letting out a deep, heartfelt sigh, she explains, "I was afraid my marriage and my sex life would never be the same again, and I was right."

From a hormonal standpoint, a hysterectomy should have no more effect on sexual activity and desire than menopause does. Indeed, in some instances, relieved of worries about pregnancy and the discomfort of menstruation, women actually feel more uninhibited and interested in sex than ever before. Yet, sometimes the psychological impact of "surgical menopause" can be devastating.

"I was very depressed afterward and it took longer to physically recover than I thought it would," Pat recalls. "But the real problem was that I couldn't shake this feeling that the best part of my life was over, that when those doctors took out my uterus and an ovary, they took away something else too. My femininity, maybe. I don't know, but I felt like something was missing and I'd never get it back."

Pat's doctor, the nurses at the hospital, and even her friends who'd had hysterectomies themselves told her that the surgery couldn't change who she was as a woman or a person and that it didn't have to limit what she did and enjoyed sexually. But their reassurances fell on deaf ears. "Every time I looked in the mirror, all I could see was a shriveled-up old lady." She shudders at the recollection. "And most of the time I just turned around and crawled back into bed."

Although the postoperative blues eventually lifted, her interest in sex took longer to return. "By the time it did, it was too late," she concludes. "Ed just wasn't interested anymore."

As you may recall, Ed suffers from situational ISD, feeling no sexual desire for his wife but plenty of it for younger women. Seemingly unaware of Ed's affairs—or the reasons for them—Pat blames their lack of a sex life on her hysterectomy. "At first I didn't take care of myself the way I used to," she explains. "I put on weight, went without makeup unless I had to go out somewhere with Ed—and that was sheer torture. I just didn't feel attractive anymore. I didn't feel sexy, which didn't surprise me. It was exactly what I expected to happen."

Prior to a hysterectomy, many women fear that the operation will leave them less interested in sex, less sexually responsive, less attractive to their partners, and "less of a woman" in general. They may unwittingly turn these expectations into self-fulfilling prophecies. And when a woman's husband or lover also has a negative reaction to the surgery, the damage to self-esteem, the couple's relationship, and their sex life is bound to be even more extensive.

"Ed's attitude was less than comforting, to say the least," Pat recalls bitterly, recalling how her appearance-conscious husband would comment on the tightness of a dress that once fit her more comfortably or suggest that she change her hairstyle to make the wrinkles around her eyes less noticeable. "But I didn't expect much support," she adds. "Ed had never been particularly sympathetic to anything I was going through."

Indeed, he had not, and it was virtually impossible for him to relate to Pat's feelings about the hysterectomy. He was too consumed by his own. "When she was lying in her hospital bed," he says, "white as the sheets, no makeup, her hair a mess, too weak to even smile or talk, well, it just sent shivers up my spine." Although concerned about Pat's health, he could not shake the sense that he had seen his own future, his destiny to grow old with a fragile, sickly wife. "It wasn't a pleasant thought," he says flatly, and it came back to haunt him during the rare occasions over the next five years when he and Pat did attempt to make love. To make matters worse, Ed, who wasn't exactly well informed about female sex organs and had never felt entirely comfortable touching or looking at them, got a "queasy" feeling when he thought about "whatever it was that was missing."

Worried that intercourse might hurt Pat, Ed tried to "get through it as quickly as possible," which was the worst possible approach, now that it took Pat longer to lubricate. "I tried to explain it to him," Pat claims. "But he stayed as impatient as he ever was." At her wits' end, Pat consulted her doctor, who reluctantly began administering estrogen. It increased Pat's general sense of well-being and seemed to increase her sexual desire and responsiveness. Unfortunately, it had no effect whatsoever on her sex life with Ed.

As Pat and Ed's situation so vividly illustrates, even though the surgery itself and hormonal changes undoubtedly play a role in how women feel after a hysterectomy, the psychological side effects are more likely to be caused by:

- preoperative expectations—like Pat's assumption that the surgery would undoubtedly damage her sex life
- postoperative complications—pain, fatigue, and others
- failure to relieve the symptoms that led to surgery in the first place
- the husband or partner's adverse reaction to the illness and/or medical treatment
- the relationship conflicts that existed before the surgery

The Connection Between Medical Conditions and Sexual Desire

Although separating psychological causes of ISD from physical ones is often difficult to do, current research does indicate that certain diseases have a direct impact on sexual interest and functioning. These are summarized in the table on page 93.

Some of these diseases include renal (kidney) problems—especially those requiring dialysis—chronic alcoholism, cirrhosis and other liver diseases, and testicular cancers and prostate problems, which adversely affect testosterone production. Other illnesses and chronic medical conditions—such as some types of cancer, diabetes, epilepsy, hypertension, multiple sclerosis, and spinal cord injuries—influence sexual responsiveness and functioning. This can lead to ISD because, unfortunately, when sexual response suffers, anxiety or depression increases, and desire often diminishes.

For instance, men with long-term diabetes may experience difficulty in getting or maintaining erections. If they also work from a relatively traditional sexual script—one that tells them that sex equals intercourse, and includes few acceptable sexual behaviors that can be engaged in without an erect penis—they may avoid sex, consciously or unconsciously blocking thoughts or emotions that might trigger sexual desire, leading to ISD and/or sexual avoidance.

ILLNESSES THAT MAY DECREASE SEXUAL DESIRE

Testosterone deficiency caused by aging, diseases of the testicles, surgical or traumatic injury to the testicles, diseases of the pituitary, surgical removal of the adrenals or ovaries

Cardiac disease, including coronary artery disease, postcoronary syndrome, hypertension

Liver problems, including hepatitis, hepatic failure due to alcoholic cirrhosis, postmononucleosis hepatitis

Kidney problems, including nephritis, renal failure, dialysis

Pulmonary diseases

Degenerative diseases

Thyroid deficiency states due to a trauma to or surgery on the thyroid gland

Head trauma

Hypothalamic lesions

Psychomotor epilepsy

Pituitary gland tumors

Advanced malignancies

Virtually *any* medical condition that involves discomfort can indirectly diminish sexual desire. Just think about the last time you had a bad cold, the flu, or even a pulled muscle. Was a night of passionate sex on the top of your list of the things you most wanted to do? Of course not. What's more, recovering from surgery, recuperating from major illnesses, and coping with pain require enormous amounts of physical and emotional energy. With your body mobilizing all of its resources to combat infections or restore your strength, and your mind focused on how lousy you feel or what you have to do to get better, it is hardly surprising that your sexual desire is nowhere to be found.

Your interest in sex may return once you begin to feel better. Or it may not—especially if your medical condition is accompanied by pain or leaves you or your partner fearful and depressed. Your medical condition may change how you feel about your body, sexual activity, or yourself, and may influence the way you act with your partner. That's the reason *all* the changes that accompany various medical conditions need to be examined in order to understand truly the possible causes of decreased desire.

Pain

Pain is perhaps the most potent of all sex drive inhibitors. As soon as your brain recognizes that you are in pain, it goes on red alert status, switching off all circuits to nonessential functions, including sexual desire. Postoperative pain, pain caused by injuries, and pain that accompanies treatments like radiation therapy literally shut down sexual desire until sex is once again perceived as safe and acceptable. Unfortunately, your brain cannot give the "all clear" signal until your pain goes away, and sometimes it doesn't.

Ellen is a thirty-two-year-old special-education teacher who has been married for six years to David, a thirty-four-year-old architect. Two years into their marriage, after David was offered a job with a company in his native Chicago, the couple moved there from southern California. Several months later, Ellen, who was unaccustomed to driving in winter weather, got into an automobile accident. At first she appeared to have escaped injury, but by the morning after the accident her lower back was in extreme pain, a pain that has plagued her almost continuously ever since.

There are few things more stressful and draining than being in physical pain over prolonged periods of time. Your pain demands your full attention. You may even spend your pain-free moments anticipating the next onslaught. In fact, it frequently becomes the sole focus in the lives of people with back problems, severe arthritis, cancer, or other debilitating conditions, causing numerous life-adjustment and relationship problems that provide a natural breeding ground for sexual desire discrepancies and ISD.

Like many chronic pain sufferers, Ellen often talks at great length about her discomfort as well as everything she has done to try to relieve it. In fact, most of Ellen and David's first therapy session was devoted to the topic. As Ellen spoke, David's body language alternately conveyed extreme boredom or barely containable fury. He had, he told us, "heard it all a million times."

He loves Ellen, he added emphatically. He has tried to be patient and understanding; but he simply did not know how much longer he could endure a life that revolved around Ellen's back pain.

Ellen was frequently irritable or depressed and exhausted. Responsibility for most of the household chores fell upon David, who often got home from work to find Ellen stretched out on the floor with a heating pad on her back or in bed, where she would remain until she had to get up for work the next morning. Their medicine chest was clogged with miracle pills that had proved to be less than miraculous, and Ellen's trips to doctors and clinics all over the country were beginning to strain the couple's finances. They had not taken a vacation together since the accident and any social plans they made were likely to be canceled at the last minute by Ellen, who "just didn't feel up to them." When Ellen did got out socially, she subtly and sometimes not so subtly let David know about the physical and emotional price she was paying.

Four years after the accident, Ellen was a slave to her pain, David was drained dry of patience and understanding, their relationship was a mess, and, as you might expect, the impact on their sex life had been dramatic. Over the years, they had abstained from sex whenever Ellen was in pain, when her pain medication knocked her out, when one of the many "experts" she consulted advised her not to have sex, and even on numerous occasions when Ellen was *not* in pain but feared that sexual activity would make her back start hurting again.

Since Ellen rarely felt sexual desire anymore, when she did have sex with David it was out of a sense of guilt or obligation. "I know this situation isn't fair to David," she sighed. "So sometimes I have sex with him even though I don't really feel like it and know I'm going to suffer after it."

"Don't you think I know that?" David responded angrily and directly to his wife. "Don't you think I feel like an insensitive creep the whole time? You can stop playing the martyr, Ellen. I won't bother you anymore." He folded his arms across his chest, silently fuming as Ellen began to cry.

David may seem insensitive, but after four years of trying to accommodate every aspect of his life to Ellen's condition, his emotional turmoil was as real and debilitating as her physical pain. They came to us asking for advice on how to have sex in ways that would not cause Ellen more physical discomfort, but it was clear to us that even with a repertoire of new sexual techniques, their individual psychological states and the conflict and stress in their relationship was likely to prevent them from improving their sex life.

Fear, Depression, and Guilt: The Psychological Side Effects of Life-Threatening Illnesses

Larry, the line production supervisor we introduced earlier, was fifty-three years old when he suffered a heart attack that, in his own words, turned his whole life upside down. Once his condition stabilized, Larry underwent a procedure called angioplasty, which unclogged the blocked artery leading to his heart. His doctors told him to quit smoking, cut down on his drinking, lose weight, exercise more, and change his diet—which he did. They assured him that it would be safe to have sex at about the same time he resumed other normal daily activities. "They said it was fine as long as I didn't feel pain during it," Larry recalls. "Only I was afraid to take a chance."

As a result, Larry kept postponing the day when he would once again make love to his wife, assuring her—and himself—that once he had a few months of normal living under his belt, he'd want and be able to have sex again. "But the longer I went without it," he explains, "the less I wanted it, until I really didn't want it at all."

Any kind of heart ailment brings your sex life to a major turning point. However, the damage to your heart is *almost never* responsible for the decline. From a physical standpoint, *you are capable of safely having intercourse with your partner as soon as you can climb two flights of stairs without experiencing pain.*

When he was rushed to the hospital after collapsing during a company softball game, Larry was convinced that he was about to die. "I'm not going to be macho about this," he told us two years after the cardiac episode. "I was scared. Anyone who tells you they had a heart attack and wasn't scared is lying. It's scary as hell." The fear often remains long after you are out of physical danger. As Larry put it, "I can't help worrying about having another heart attack. Only the next time I might not be lucky enough to live through it."

In spite of his doctors' assurances that it was safe to have sex, Larry was terrorized by the thought of "dying in the saddle." At some level he mistakenly believed that the physical demands of sex could quite literally kill him—which is a fear shared by most heart patients (and their partners) as well as people who have had strokes and organ transplants or who suffer from hypertension.

Fear always inhibits sexual desire, and you may be plagued by fears other than the specter of dying during sex. You may be afraid that sex will trigger or worsen pain, that your physical condition will make intercourse painful or result in a humiliating episode of impotence, or that your partner will find you unattractive. Often unwarranted or exaggerated, these fears can linger indefinitely and intensify at a subconscious level. As a result, without even knowing that fear is what you are feeling, you may begin to feel turned on, but then "something clicks" and the urge to have sex disappears.

Larry's heart attack reminded him that he would not live forever—a fact that he, like the rest of us, preferred not to think about. Cardiac patients may feel depressed for several years after their heart attacks, and during the course of their illness most patients with cancer or other life-threatening diseases go through at least one episode of severe depression. Their psychological condition often prevents them from engaging in many activities that they are *physically* capable of performing and enjoying— including sex.

Depression is, in fact, one of the most common causes of ISD. Even mildly depressed men and women report that they have less interest in pursuing sexual activity than they once did and are difficult to seduce or arouse. Indeed, the two disorders are so closely linked that the vast majority of depressed individuals report that they lost interest in sex at the same time they began to feel depressed.

To further complicate matters, depression is often accompanied by guilt feelings, which can further dampen sexual desire. Guilt is the by-product of believing that your past behavior—sexual behavior in particular—somehow caused your present illness. You can experience this guilt when there is no direct connection between your illness and sex. But it may be difficult to avoid—and exceedingly difficult to overcome—if your illness is related to or contracted through sexual activity.

Not Feeling Sexy: The Side Effects of Disabilities and Disfigurement

Ours is a culture that shows little tolerance for physical flaws. And although in recent years we have made tremendous strides in sensitizing the public to the capabilities and humanness of physically disabled or disfigured individuals, we anxiously circumvent the matter of their sexuality. Indeed, people with certain diseases and disabilities are seen as asexual—and they may view themselves that way as well.

Unfortunately, health care professionals may offer little if any information or encouragement to change this impression. They may not discuss sex at all or focus entirely on the negatives, explaining what cannot be done without mentioning what can. As a result, if you are disabled or have had certain types of surgery, you may assume that sex is off-limits forever and find ways to shut down desire so you can comply with the "rules."

However, even when doctors or counselors do take the time to explain that you are able to have and enjoy sex after a mastectomy, colostomy, amputation, or paralyzing spinal cord injury, this information may do nothing at all to promote sexual interest.

"I'm deformed, a freak," Jean croaked in a voice hoarse from crying. "I can't imagine any man looking at me without being completely repulsed." A year after having a mastectomy, Jean still draped a towel over the bathroom mirror before disrobing to take a shower. "I repulse myself," she said. "I don't want to look at me and I don't want my husband to look at me."

Comfort with your body is a prerequisite for satisfying sex. Unfortunately, various medical conditions can prevent you from feeling comfortable with a body that no longer fits the standard for physical attractiveness or performance that you once set for it. The more closely your expectations of physical appearance and abilities are linked to your sense of self-worth and sexuality, the more difficult you will find it to adjust to disabilities or disfigurement.

For instance, Jean, a former beauty queen and model who works with gorgeous young women at the modeling agency she runs, once built her entire identity around her physical appearance. So it comes as no surprise that her reaction to disfiguring surgery was so extreme. Her self-consciousness and self-loathing escalate even further each time she "forces herself" to have sex with her husband—which is not very often, since she places so many restrictions on what her husband can do and where she allows him to touch her that he has begun to avoid sex as well.

Sexual desire may also be diminished in the aftermath of various medical conditions by:

Stress related to job loss, financial difficulties, medical bills, or possible setbacks in your recovery.

Feelings of inadequacy and decreased self-esteem associated with being dependent on other people, especially if you previously took pride in your self-sufficiency.

Self-monitoring during sex—anxiously focusing your attention on your heart rate, breathing, pulse, or twinges of pain—making you less aware of your sexual feelings.

Lack of information about when it is safe to resume sexual activity.

Difficulty adapting to physical limitations that prevent you from having sex in the same way that you once did.

When Your Partner Has a Life-Threatening Illness

When Larry had his heart attack, he was not the only one who felt frightened, sad, and helpless. Natalie experienced these emotions as well. "The thought of losing him made my blood run cold," she says, tears welling up in her eyes. When Larry came home from the hospital, Natalie nursed him back to health while also working extra shifts as a waitress to make ends meet.

"It got tough, though, when Larry's sick days ran out before he could go back to work and we had to live on my tips for a couple of weeks." The stress of those times made sex the "furthest thing" from Natalie's mind. "But once things settled down, I got interested again," she recalls, admitting that she had no idea when it would be safe for Larry to have sex again. "I waited for him to let me know. I guess you could say I'm still waiting."

As the months passed, Natalie found it more and more difficult to stop herself from thinking about sex and she often found herself trying to block out feelings of anger, fear, and resentment as well. "I'm not proud of it," she confesses. "But sometimes I felt real sorry for myself. I would wonder what the hell I had gotten myself into. Forty-three years old and married to a man who couldn't or wouldn't have sex. I'd be so ashamed of myself for thinking like that. I tried hard not to think about sex at all, but it didn't work."

When one partner in a marriage or relationship becomes seriously ill, the couple's usual pattern of give and take, dependence and independence, closeness and distance, is disrupted. Roles may change, most notably if a wife who once stayed at home must go out to work or a husband must assume responsibilities that were once his wife's domain. The "strong" partner may suddenly become weak and dependent. As a result, the partner who once needed more attention and emotional support must attend now become the "caretaker," as well as attend to his or her own needs. Further complications arise as schedules must be rearranged to accommodate hospital visiting hours, doctor's appointments, medical treatments, and many other changes in the couple's "normal" routine. Clearly, the partner who is not ill has as much adjusting to do as the partner who is.

Your Immediate Reaction

When you learned that your partner had a heart attack, was seriously injured, was terminally ill, needed surgery, or had developed a chronic, debilitating condition, you may have been flooded by a tidal wave of shock, sadness, fear, and confusion. But you had no time to dwell on these emotions. You "put them on the shelf" because you had to be strong. Your partner's survival seemed to depend on that. The stress you experienced was enormous and frequently you felt inadequate in the face of all the demands you had to meet. This, along with the fear that was your constant companion, pushed sexual desire far beyond your grasp—which was fine in the midst of a crisis. But what happened to your sex drive and your sex life once your partner was out of immediate danger or well on the way to recovery?

Although we have focused exclusively on the negative effects of serious illness, the truth is that sexual desire can bounce back for both partners. Indeed, serious, even terminal illness sometimes brings partners closer together. The crisis leaves them more committed than ever to fully enjoying each other and their lives—including sex. However, this return to sexual intimacy may be far from easy.

You Want Sex but Your Partner Doesn't

In some instances your interest in sex will return but your partner's will not. Like Natalie, you may consciously suppress your sexual desire while you wait for your partner to let you know that it's once again possible to have sex. Initially, this will not disturb you. In fact, you may be as anxious and confused about when to resume having sex as your partner is, and your physician may have offered few clues.

But sooner or later, you will begin to feel frustrated by the situation—especially if you are convinced that your partner is well enough to have sex, but he or she continues to show no interest in it. At the same time, like David, you may feel guilty or insensitive for wanting to have sex in the first place. You might share the sentiments Natalie expressed when she said, "It's selfish of me to want him to have sex. I should be more understanding. After all, look at everything he's been through."

But what about you? You've been through a lot too.

When Your Partner Is Interested, but You Are Not

If you put your emotional and sexual needs on a back burner for weeks or months or longer, you will probably find anger, resentment, and self-pity bubbling to the surface. You may discover that you are the one who has lost all desire for sex with your partner, sometimes feeling no interest in having sex at all.

Although Jack, the would-be football star whom we introduced in the last chapter, did not suffer a life-threatening illness, his career-ending injury had a similar psychological impact on him and his wife, Sally. As you may recall, Sally's interest in having sex with Jack disappeared at the same time that he got back on his feet. When we pointed out this "coincidence," Sally had no trouble explaining it. "Once he was okay, it was okay for me to be angry, and believe me, I was," she said. "He'd been acting like a big baby the whole time. I did everything for him and he acted like that was *expected*. He never once said thank you. He hadn't spent one second thinking about how I might be feeling. Then one day it was 'Okay. I'm fine now. Let's make love.' Well, I was too furious to be interested."

When your partner has recovered or stabilized, you too may find your relief giving way to fury or self-pity or other uncomfortable, desire-inhibiting emotions. Thoughts that you buried may rise up to haunt you, thoughts about your own mortality, about whether or not your partner would be as caring and supportive as you were if you became ill, about what the future will be like with a spouse who has a heart condition, diabetes, hypertension, or a kidney transplant. You may wonder when the crisis will occur. If the illness drew the two of you closer, you may fear that the closeness and safety you've been feeling will disappear now that your partner no longer needs your care. You may also worry that what originally attracted you to your partner—a spirit of independence, a fun-loving attitude, a sense of adventure, or an ability to give you support—is gone forever. Or you and your partner may simply fall right back into your old patterns, renewing the power struggles and conflicts that made sex dissatisfying in the past. All of these thoughts and feelings can lead to ISD.

When Nothing Is the Same as It Used to Be

After abstaining from sex during your partner's illness, you may find lovemaking strange at first, and you may have trouble "getting into it." The tension between the two of you may become unbearable, rising noticeably each time you feel compelled to ask, "Are you sure this is okay? Do you feel up to it? Am I hurting you? We don't have to do this if you don't want to. Are you sure you want to?"

Your sexual desire may also diminish because:

- Your partner now has sexual performance problems.
- You treat your ailing partner so delicately and have sex so cautiously that neither of you obtains much pleasure from it.
- You do not feel attracted to your partner now that hair loss from chemotherapy, weight loss or gain, disfigurement, or other physical effects of illness have caused alterations in appearance.
- The adjustments you must make so that sex can be comfortable and satisfying for your partner may disgust or bore you, or are too much trouble for you.

Such problems and feelings will not just go away. They must be addressed, discussed, and explored so that solutions can be found. Suggestions on how to go about that healing process will be discussed in Chapter Six.

ISD AND AGING

There was only one reason that Raymond, a seventy-year-old retired dentist, acquiesced to the demand by Cynthia, his sixty-four-year-old wife, that they see a sex therapist, and he explained it to us only moments after he entered our office. A dapper man with a full head of wavy silver hair and a coarse, slightly crooked moustache, Raymond sat with legs crossed and arms folded across his chest. The expression on his face was stern, almost belligerent, as he informed us, "This shouldn't take long. All you have to do is tell my wife that a man my age can't have sex. Then she'll stop pestering me and everything will be fine between us again."

"Don't be so sure," Cynthia retorted, giving us our first glimpse of a personality that was as fiery as her bright red hair. She expected to have a sex life. "And if you can't give me one . . ." she began, but did not get to finish because Raymond interrupted her.

"This is what I get night and day, day and night," he sighed. "Where she got the idea that a seventy-year-old man could do anything in bed, I'll never know." He shook his head and rolled his eyes, letting us know that he considered his wife to be woefully uninformed and perhaps a bit nuts.

We were more curious about where Raymond got *his* idea that men his age could no longer engage in sexual activity. He told us that he had "figured that out the hard way" seven or eight years ago. Cynthia was Raymond's second wife. Acknowledging that having sex with his first wife had never been particularly exciting, Raymond explained that his sex life had ended completely and abruptly five years before she died. Although up to that point he had sometimes experienced difficulty maintaining an erection, he discovered—on one memorable occasion—that he was unable to get sexually excited at all. "I got the message," Raymond said and acted as if we were idiots when we asked what that message was. "Sex was a thing of the past," he replied impatiently, adding that after this one episode of impotence, he had never again attempted to have sex. He simply accepted what he believed to be "a fact of life," that men who reach a certain age lose their ability to have sex and their interest in it as well.

Is Raymond's notion that sexual functioning stops and sexual desire disappears after a certain age similar to your own opinion? In our culture, passion, romance, and sexual activity are generally believed to be the exclusive domain of young, attractive individuals who are able-bodied and in perfect health. As a result, when the realization that you are getting older hits home—often after you are afflicted with one or more of the medical conditions described earlier—your sexual interest may indeed begin to wane. But neither it nor sexual activity *has* to be abandoned altogether.

Men, Sex, and Aging

We are not going to tell you that aging does not affect sexual performance and desire. It does. All things slow down for all men as they get older and this process begins long before you find your first gray hair or realize you are running out of steam on the racquetball court sooner than you did when you were younger. The urgent, ever-present sex drive you had during adolesence simply does not last forever. By your thirties you may be less preoccupied with sex, and, unless you are exceptionally performance conscious, by your mid-forties you are less focused on orgasms and ejaculation, instead deriving pleasure from the general sensuality of sexual activity. After age fifty, the physical changes—which have been happening all along—do become more noticeable. You can no longer ignore these facts:

- It takes longer to get an erection.
- Your erections are not as full or as hard.
- It takes longer to get a second erection after ejaculating.

- It takes longer to reach orgasm and ejaculate (which is one change you may actually welcome).
- Ejaculation is somewhat less powerful.
- You need more direct physical stimulation in order to get an erection and/or reach orgasm.
- You may engage in sex less frequently than you once did.

While sexual functioning may indeed diminish or change and you may occasionally experience various sexual performance problems, sexual pleasure and desire need not follow suit. If you aren't wedded to the idea that more sex is better, if you don't define satisfaction solely in terms of the firmness of your penis or the vigor of your orgasms, and if you are willing to engage in a variety of sexual activities rather than intercourse alone, your sex life will weather the effects of aging without causing you much distress or inhibiting your sexual desire.

Unfortunately, you may *not* be able to adapt to these inevitable changes easily or accept them gracefully. If your approach to sex has always been goal directed, performance oriented, and limited to a few minutes of routine foreplay leading up to intercourse, the physical effects of aging may deprive you of much and perhaps all sexual satisfaction. And if you are unable or unwilling to modify your sexual behavior, chances are you will lose your sex drive instead. If you agree with Raymond, who once insisted, "It's getting to finish line that matters," and if you cannot trust your body to get you there, you will consciously or unconsciously suppress your sexual desire to avoid the failure of not making it over that line.

Women, Sex, and Aging

Like men, women find that their sexual desire and responsiveness change during the course of their lifetimes, but they do not change in the same way. Just as your male partner's sex drive was starting to slow down, yours may have been revving up. In fact, your sexual responsiveness and interest may have been at its peak when you were in your late thirties or early forties.

Then menopause arrived. The average age for menopause is fifty-one, and it almost always represents a significant sexual turning point. While the psychological side effects of menopause vary, certain physical changes are fairly common. During sex:

- Your breasts may no longer swell and your nipples may not become erect.
- Your clitoris and labia are less engorged.
- Your skin may not flush as readily.
- It may take longer to lubricate.

These physical changes need not affect your sexual pleasure or desire. Yet, women often do experience dramatic drops in sexual desire as they get older. Unlike men, who worry about their ability to perform, women are more likely to experience ISD as a result of their anxieties about the effect aging has on their appearance and sense of self.

Gray hair, wrinkles, sagging bodies, and so on make old age seem "uglier" for you than for your male counterpart, and all too often the realization that you cannot look as sexy as before—in your own or your partner's eyes—prevents you from *feeling* sexy or maintaining your interest in sex.

A second factor that contributes to ISD in older women is the lack of suitable sexual partners. This sometimes affects women whose husbands are ill or not inclined or able to have sex, and it is a major problem for older women who are widowed or divorced. There are simply more women who fall into this category than available men in the same age range. If you are one of them and want to engage in sex with a partner, you may have to turn to a younger lover or a married man, and both alternatives may be unacceptable to you. In fact, the most acceptable alternative may seem to be suppressing your sexual desire altogether. After all, if you are not interested in sex, you certainly will not miss not having it.

Other "facts of life" that can diminish sexual desire in both men and women include:

- the increasing likelihood that you will suffer from one or more of the previously discussed medical conditions that affect sexual desire
- the reactions of your grown children and other people, which intimate that sexual urges and sexual activity in people your age are abnormal and may even be signs of senility
- the urge to fight the aging process in general—and your inability to win the battle—which may lead to desire inhibiting anxieties or depression
- boredom with a long-standing relationship, the stress of trying to make ends meet on a fixed income, the changes that accompany retirement from the work force, and other emotionally draining and relationship-straining issues

Yet, none of these factors or the physical effects of aging can dampen desire if the strongest foundation for continuing sexual activity is present. That foundation is a personal history that includes positive attitudes toward sex, positive experiences with it, and good feelings about yourself and your partner. Time and time again, experts on sex and aging have found that *sexual activity remains constant throughout life*. If you enjoyed sex and looked forward to it when you were thirty, chances are that you will still be pleased with it and interested in it when you are fifty or seventy, and right up until you draw your last breath. You may not have sex as often and you may not engage in the same way as you once did, but there is ample evidence that sexual interest and satisfaction can be part of your life no matter how old you are.

Unfortunately, this revelation is of little value to you if you share the sentiments expressed by Marjorie, a slender, impeccably dressed sixty-year-old woman whose husband was considering penile implant surgery to solve his problems in achieving and maintaining an erection. "I don't understand what all this fuss is about," she said, "In my opinion, sex is the most highly overrated activity in the world, and frankly, I'm relieved that

I've finally reached an age where it isn't expected of me any-more."

Regardless of your present age, your sexual desire may be long gone, if it ever existed at all. Like Marjorie, you may look forward to the day when sexual expectations have decreased and your partner has "slowed down." Some of you have already abandoned sex or avoid it whenever you can. Perhaps you have found an explanation for your indifference in the preceding discussion of ISD and the body, but if you have not, you may find one in the next chapter, which explores the various and vital connections between ISD and the mind.

CHAPTER FOUR
ISD and the Mind

"IT DOESN'T MAKE SENSE," Janet sighs, reaching for a tissue. Others, crumpled, scrunched, and shredded, are piled on the table beside her chair. This session, the first without her husband, has been the most difficult. "I love Tim," she continues. "I love to be with him. Even now, when I see him walk through the door after work, I feel like I'll burst from loving him so much. I want to rush over and throw my arms around him, but I can't. I do feel safe with him. I know that he loves me and would never hurt me. Never. So why am I afraid to show him any affection? Why do I panic when I even think about having sex with him?"

"I don't understand it, I really don't," Wendy groans. With too much nervous energy to sit still, Wendy is, as usual, on her feet, moving around the office, looking at pictures she has seen before, lifting objects and examining them, doing anything that will distract her from the turmoil churning inside her. "I used to think Bill was the sexiest guy I'd ever met. Now I don't even like kissing him. I used to be into sex. Now that interest is completely gone. You say it has to do with Mark's death, but I've accepted that, I'm over the worst of it, and I want to get on with my life. I really do. I want to get married, have more kids, be normal again. But this problem, this ISD thing, is still getting in the way. I just don't understand it."

*   *   *

"It's a mystery to me," Larry shrugs, folding his arms across his barrel chest. "After I had my heart attack, my sex drive hit the highway, and even though everyone keeps telling me it should be back by now, it isn't. I wish it was. I wish I knew where it went, because if I did, I'd be able to do something about it."

As you know, Janet, Wendy, and Larry suffer from ISD and they are baffled by their lack of interest in sex. If you or your partner are also plagued by ISD, it may not make sense to you either. Time and time again, you try to find a "logical" explanation for what is happening—or rather, not happening— only to come up empty-handed. And unfortunately, when you don't know what put out the fire in the first place, you can't figure out how to reignite it.

Sexual desire disorders are so difficult to explain because their cause is often confusing, if it can be understood at all. Frequently the cause is outside our conscious awareness and out of our control. Yet it's felt very directly as a lack of interest in sex.

IMMEDIATE CAUSES OF ISD

You do not necessarily have to delve deeply into your subconscious mind or analyze your entire life history in order to find some of the psychological forces that have an adverse effect on sexual desire. Sometimes you lose interest in sex because of events and conditions you are consciously aware of and currently experiencing. Al, for instance, knew right off the bat that his sexual avoidance was the direct result of his recent problems in attaining an erection and his concern that future sexual encounters would lead to more humiliating performance failures. And Paul, bemoaning the state of his sex life, could explain that "I'm trying to have my cake and eat it too. I want to get ahead at work, train for a marathon, fix up our house, have a social life, *and* have terrific sex with Andrea. I even know that it isn't humanly possible to do all those things. But that doesn't stop me from trying. It's like a treadmill I can't get off of. But it burns me out. I feel tired and anxious all the time—too tired for sex and too anxious to enjoy it when we do have it." Consciously recognized, troublesome, here-and-now issues represent some of the *immediate* connections between ISD and the mind, including:

- lack of information and/or communication, which keeps you from knowing what to do to create sexual desire and excitement
- making sex a goal-oriented performance focused on erection, lubrication, and orgasms rather than pleasure
- negative reactions to events immediately preceding sexual opportunities (like arguments, a disturbing phone call from your mother, or trouble at work)
- depression
- guilt
- feeling uncomfortable with your own or your partner's body or natural sexual responses
- stress
- "spectatoring"—either trying to keep tight control over your sexual responses or stepping outside yourself to observe what is happening to you critically, often judging yourself harshly
- unresolved relationship conflicts or anger
- physical problems that directly affect the brain or change the balance of hormones

Performance Anxiety

Whether you expect and try to avoid sexual failure or expect and strive to achieve sexual excellence, your determination to control and critique your sexual performance and sexual responses reduces pleasure, burying it under your fears that sex might turn out to be disappointing, unsatisfying, or—worse yet—humiliating. By spectatoring, you virtually ensure that what you fear is what will happen. What's more, you begin to think of sex as a chore, more trouble than it's worth, and a source of stress and anxiety.

Emotional Depletion

While performance-related anxieties cause you to focus too much emotional energy on critiquing your sexual interactions, ISD can also be the end result of having *too little* energy to expend on sex, as a result of stress and depression.

According to pioneering researcher Hans Selye, **stress** is "the non-specific response of the body to any demand made upon it." No matter what that demand is—a work deadline, car trouble, bills to pay, your upcoming wedding, a sick child, or a sexual overture—once you recognize that the situation requires you to *do* something, your body and your mind mobilize their resources to allow you to cope with the demand. From this perspective, stress itself is not good or bad, but simply a fact of life.

Problems occur, however, when your life circumstances present you with more demands than you can realistically cope with. Major life crises like the death of a loved one, illness, divorce, or job loss require enormous adjustments. Expectations about handling each new challenge perfectly or doubts about your ability to meet the challenges you do face only compound the stress.

This was certainly the case for Kevin, whose promotion, although welcome, brought him all sorts of new responsibilities that he was not always sure he could handle. He and other people we have mentioned in this book felt the effects of *excessive* stress. Their minds and bodies were constantly prepared to do battle with the next demand or perpetually feeling the aftereffects of the last. Just keeping up with the pressures of daily living left them with little or no physical or emotional energy for "nonessential" activities—like sex.

In addition, the cumulative effects of excess stress or acute distress are thought to alter body chemistry, probably affecting hormone levels and brain activity and thus physically inhibiting sexual desire. Excess stress also produces physical symptoms like headaches, fatigue, ulcers, lower back pain, or muscle stiffness, as well as making you more susceptible to colds and other illnesses. Being under constant stress isn't likely to make you a particularly loving or giving participant in a relationship. Indeed, having to adapt to your moods or sudden emotional outbursts, your partner may be tempted to stay out of your way as much as possible, ceasing to make sexual overtures or becoming unavailable when you do feel in the mood for sex. And finally, if you are preoccupied and distracted by other concerns during sex, perceive sex as an activity that consumes the time and energy you need to meet other demands, or view your partner's sexual overtures as just one more source of pressure, you are a prime candidate for ISD.

Depression, as we mentioned in the previous chapter, often leads to a loss of sexual desire. Unlike the emotional depletion of stress, the emotional depletion of depression is a reflection of the overall slowing-down of your bodily functions and your general loss of interest in almost all of your usual activities and pastimes. In fact, the loss of interest in sex is one of the symptoms psychologists use to diagnose depression, along with:

- sleep disturbances such as insomnia or awakening early in the morning and being unable to go back to sleep
- low energy or chronic fatigue
- feelings of inadequacy
- decreased attention, concentration, or ability to think clearly
- decreased effectiveness or productivity at school, work, or home
- social withdrawal
- limited involvement in previously pleasurable activities
- feeling slowed down
- being less talkative than usual
- a pessimistic attitude about the future or brooding about past events or a general feeling of hopelessness
- tearfulness or crying

- increases or decreases in appetite or weight
- thoughts about suicide or death

If you suffer from ISD and also have two or more of the symptoms above, some kind of depression is probably behind your diminished or absent sexual desire. In most instances, elevating a depressed mood also elevates sexual desire, so we recommend seeking treatment for depression, in the form of medication, psychotherapy, or a combination of the two. You should seek psychiatric treatment immediately if you are having suicidal thoughts.

Transitions and Turning Points

In addition to causing stress and perhaps depression, major **life changes** can create immediate problems and conflicts that can alter your sex life and dampen your desire. These include getting sober and coping with the illness or recent death of someone you love. **Turning points** in your relationship, like moving in together, having children, or seeing your children leave home, can also have the same effect. Anxiety, confusion, and frustration frequently accompany such transitions, especially when role changes are involved.

Both in their mid-forties, Phil and Anne have been married for twenty years and have two children in college. Up until several years ago their marriage was a very traditional one, with Phil serving as sole breadwinner and chief decision-maker while Anne remained at home raising their children and running their household. Then, when the children were in high school and able to fend for themselves, Anne decided to get a job. Phil was supportive initially, believing that Anne would "work part time at a department store or as an aide at a day care center or something harmless like that." He was surprised when she chose to get a real-estate license, but still did not expect it to amount to much. However, it did.

Anne proved to have impressive talent as a real-estate salesperson, and not only earned a substantial income but devoted larger and larger percentages of her time to her work, thriving on the challenge it provided as well as basking in the newfound knowledge that she was "good at something besides being a homemaker and taking care of people." Phil, however, had liked being taken care of. Indeed, one of the things that had originally attracted him to Anne was her ability to anticipate his needs and meet them, as well as the way she really listened to him, sympathized, and made him feel important.

As Anne became more wrapped up in her work—to the point of not always preparing meals or being available to go places and do things with Phil as she used to—and suddenly wanted equal time to talk about her work day in addition to listening to Phil talk about his, Phil found that many of the emotional needs he expected Anne to meet were not being met at all. Although he still *said* he supported her career and was proud of her, Phil began to withdraw sexually.

By the time they entered our offices, Phil and Anne rarely had sex. When they did, neither one felt satisfied and Phil was beginning to ejaculate prematurely—having his orgasm before or right after penetration—which Anne believed was just one more way to get back at her.

Phil and Anne came to us for help with sexual problems that were a direct result of the other problems in their relationship, which had changed drastically in recent years. Their case was far from unusual, for a satisfying emotional relationship is almost always a prerequisite for a satisfying sexual one.

Neither Phil nor Anne knew why they had lost interest in sex, which is not unusual since, most of the time, the individual and interpersonal dynamics that lead to ISD occur on a largely unconscious level. Through therapy, however, Phil and Anne were better able to understand what had happened to them.

Over time it became clear that because Anne was devoting time and energy to her career and paying a good deal less attention to him, Phil felt rejected. While he was thinking, "Anne's career is more important than I am," and sulking, Anne was feeling resentful and thinking, "Phil should be proud of me instead of trying to make me feel guilty." When Phil got angry and decided that "Anne is neglecting me," Anne got fed up and concluded, "If Phil is going to make me feel lousy, I'll have to put even more energy into work because it makes me feel good."

Baffled by the changes in his wife and his relationship, Phil began to lose interest in having sex with Anne, who he felt "wasn't the woman I married." Anne was furious, since she suspected that Phil was withholding sex to punish her for being more independent, and reported that she "would have to beg him to make love to me." Unwilling to "humiliate" herself on a regular basis, Anne stifled her sexual urges.

As you can see, the combined effect of Anne's newfound independence and Phil's old expectations was rather dramatic. Changes in life circumstances, like the other immediate influences we have discussed, drastically alter the way you think and feel about yourself, your roles, your partner, your relationship, and sex itself. When your relationship is under stress and takes a turn for the worse, as Anne and Phil's did, so will your sex life—since your feelings and expectations are always right there with you, consciously or unconsciously, when you have or consider having sex.

Negative Self-talk

A few dissatisfying sexual experiences, a single performance failure, or a handful of insecurities about your body, your self-worth, or your relationship can trigger a tidal wave of anxiety and negative thinking—a tape loop of negative self-talk that goes hand in hand with many of the immediate causes of ISD. For instance, Dan replayed a desire-inhibiting monologue in his mind each time Barbara tried to interest him in having sex. "I don't have time for this," he thought. "I need to concentrate on things that really matter, not something frivolous. Why is she pushing me to have sex, when she knows I have more important things to do? It makes me mad." When he's in such a state of mind, is it any wonder that Dan is not overflowing with sexual desire?

Andrea and Paul expect to be good at sex and get as much

as they possibly can out of it. They view sex not only as a command performance but also as the foundation upon which their relationship is built. Already alarmed by the infrequency and mediocrity of their lovemaking, each and every time they have sex both Andrea and Paul find their minds racing a mile a minute, churning up a whirlpool of doubt, self-criticism, and anxiety. Andrea thinks, "This isn't that great. It should be better. I'm not really into this. I wonder if Paul can tell. He seems to be enjoying it, but maybe it's an act to spare my feelings." Meanwhile, Paul is thinking, "Would it be better with someone else? Oh God, what if she's wondering about that too! If things don't improve soon, we'll both be looking for someone new. Oh no, now I'm losing my erection. No wonder this isn't as good as it used to be."

By worrying incessantly that sex would not be good, Andrea and Paul virtually ensured that it wasn't. If you listen to your own negative self-talk long enough, you are likely to turn it into a self-fulfilling prophecy too.

What's more, after each disappointing sexual encounter, Andrea and Paul would think, "Maybe we shouldn't try this again for a while." Unfortunately, a stockpile of unsatisfying experiences and negative expectations continued to grow. Furthermore, with their negative self-talk playing and replaying its prerecorded messages a little louder each time a sexual opportunity presented itself, "a while" became no time in the foreseeable future.

To make matters worse, negative self-talk about matters other than sex itself can also shut down sexual desire. Anxiety-provoking, judgmental, or disheartening thoughts about how you aren't competent, lovable, or physically attractive, along with a low opinion of your partner or your relationship, are particularly inhibiting. So are doubts about finding a suitable partner.

For instance, Rachel, the single computer-software sales manager, fell prey to negative self-talk whenever she found herself in a social situation that might lead to a sexual one. As soon as she spotted a man whom she found attractive or one who seemed to be attracted to her, her mind clicked into high gear. "Great-looking guy, intelligent, funny," she would think. "I bet he's married or gay or a jerk once you really get to know him. The ones I meet usually are. Why can't I attract guys who aren't losers? Why can't I let the guys who aren't losers know I'm attracted to them? Because they'll think I'm desperate or needy or sleep around for the hell of it. That's a laugh. The first time you have sex with someone, it isn't even any good. Who needs it?" By the time her self-doubts and negative self-talk reached their final deafening crescendo, Rachel's interest in sex would be long gone. She had literally—and consciously—talked herself out of sexual desire.

On the other hand, many of our patients are not aware of their desire-inhibiting thoughts until sex therapy techniques like those included in Chapter Six turn up the volume for them. This happened to Ed after he attempted a sex therapy "homework assignment" we had given him and his wife, Pat.

"Look, I tried what you said, but it didn't help," Ed declared, informing us that an exercise involving sensual but not sexual touching had been a total wash-out. "I tried to keep my mind on what I was feeling, but these thoughts just kept coming out of nowhere and they wouldn't go away, or at least not for long." The thoughts that Ed was referring to revolved around his perception that Pat was "no longer attractive and looked old." He even fantasized about how Pat would look when she was really old—with silver hair and sagging breasts and wrinkles all over her body.

"She was all dried up and brittle." He shuddered. "I felt nauseated, disgusted." Although Ed did indeed try to banish these thoughts from his mind, he could not. In fact, without telling Pat why, he became so uncomfortable that he refused to complete the exercise.

Intrusive thoughts, once you recognize what they are, provide valuable clues about what is going on in your subconscious mind before and during sexual encounters. Like Ed, you may not be aware of the thoughts and images that interfere with your sexual feelings. But chances are that they have long been doing a number on your subconscious mind, switching off sexual desire before you even realize it has been switched on. In

Chapter Six we will discuss exercises that may help you better understand and work through these less conscious, desire-inhibiting thoughts.

Emotions and ISD

Negative feelings—whether or not they are consciously connected to specific thoughts—also contribute to ISD. You are apt to feel less sexual desire when you are also feeling:

guilty	angry	frightened
anxious	ashamed	repulsed
depressed	resentful	unloved
mistrustful	insecure	frustrated
inadequate	pressured	apathetic
powerless	rejected	humiliated

More often than not, you may view these and similar emotions as danger signals that you are or soon could be in pain. And you may consciously or unconsciously put sexual desire on a back burner until you are feeling safer and better.

Since this happens to everyone at one time or another, the question that challenges us and our patients is *why* it happens so regularly—and so intensely—to people who have lost their interest in sex. *What* causes these feelings and *how* they block sexual desire are the questions that need to be answered. When given the opportunity to explore these questions in the safe, nonjudgmental atmosphere of therapy, many individuals and couples find answers that reopen the pathway for sexual desire.

REMOTE CAUSES OF ISD

Compared to immediate concerns, which you may be able to recognize and connect to your sexual problems, remote causes of ISD are even more difficult to identify. Indeed, they tend to operate subconsciously and may involve influences from the past. In other instances, you will recognize the issue but fail to understand the source of the problem, believing that you could not possibly be inhibiting your desire because of events or feelings you are sure you "got over" years ago. This was certainly the case for:

- Janet, who truly loved and fully trusted Tim but was terrified by the thought of having sex with him
- Wendy, who lost all sexual desire six months before her husband's death and has yet to get it back, even though she is now in love with a man whom she once considered extremely sexy and desirable
- Maggie, who wants to have sex so that she can please and hold on to her husband, but feels anxious, out of control, and turned off every time she thinks about sex
- Larry, who was given a clean bill of health two years after having a heart attack, but is still unable to feel any interest in sex

Like many of the other ISD sufferers and desire discrepancy couples who appear in this book, they are living proof that ISD is, more often than not, a case of mind over matter. While they want to enjoy sexual desire, they rarely or never do. Indeed, when they should be "all systems go," they unconsciously go on red alert status instead, shutting down the circuits that receive and transmit sexual messages. Because this process often takes place without their conscious awareness, they don't know what's happening, or why it's happening, or that anything is happening at all.

For instance, Larry, the heart attack victim, was initially convinced that his body had undergone a drastic chemical change that had robbed him of his sex drive. But there was no physical reason for Larry's global loss of desire. In fact, although he vehemently denied it at first, tucked in the back of Larry's mind was the idea that having sex would set off another heart attack, this time a fatal one. Strongly related to his current fear are his unresolved feelings about his father's death, which occurred when Larry was seven. Rather than admit to his fear of dying during sex or take the risk of disproving it, Larry, *without knowing he was doing it,* protected himself by not feeling sexual desire.

Of course, when ISD patients come to us for treatment, we attempt to identify the immediate and/or remote causes of their condition, and try to determine if there might be a physical cause. If there doesn't seem to be any immediate cause or if it doesn't respond to short-term sex therapy, we explore deeper, more complicated psychological issues, many of which we will discuss in the remainder of this chapter. In treating patients who mistrust a partner who is, in reality, loving and giving, or those who experience unprovoked anger, extreme anxiety, or total numbness in sexual situations, we look for and often find underlying fears—like Larry's—that are the cause of their ISD.

Underlying Fears

Denise, a thirty-year-old computer programmer, came to see us alone. Initially, she did not want her lover, Linda, a thirty-four-year-old college admissions counselor, to be involved in treatment, even though Linda was very aware of and deeply affected by Denise's recent lack of interest in sex. Denise was not ready to tell her that she had recently begun to feel repulsed and panicky during sex. She hoped that Linda had not noticed the severity of her sexual problems. "It would be the final blow," Denise told us. "It would end our relationship." And Denise most definitely did *not* want the relationship to end.

"Before I started having this problem," she explained, "when we had sex, I felt so close to Linda that it was almost like being part of her and her being part of me. I want to feel that way again."

We listened to Denise's pain and heard her wish, but based on the information she reported, we suspected that she was ambivalent about her desire for closeness with Linda. Experience had taught us that many people cannot tolerate such intense closeness, especially if they fear that they will get so dependent upon their partners that they will lose their own identity or independence. They may also worry that they will be suffocated or overwhelmed by a partner who needs more than they are willing or able to give. They may be concerned that the information they disclose to their partners will be used against them, or they think they will somehow end up hurting their partners and hate themselves afterward. And it is even more common to fear that the people they get close to will reject or abandon them. While these fears are usually unconscious, the effects are not. Because sharing yourself sexually can be such an intimate experience, people who fear intimacy often lose their desire for sex or the willingness to act on that desire. When you are involved in an intimate relationship, these fears often come with the territory. After all, caring or loving always involves risk taking, daring to be vulnerable, perhaps getting hurt. Yet, taking that risk also allows you to reap countless emotional rewards. Sadly, fearing the negative consequences of intimacy may prevent you from experiencing the positive ones. Fear may force you to keep your distance and never enter into intimate relationships at all. But more often, you carry your fears with you into your relationships and they may get in your way. They certainly did in Denise's case.

Denise's relationship with Linda began while Denise was still married to Roger, her high school sweetheart and the father of her three children. She had never acted upon her lesbian feelings before she met Linda. As often happens, openly acknowledging her sexual preference, although alleviating the stress of leading a "double life," brought numerous repercussions. "Everyone turned against me," Denise explained. "My parents, our friends, everyone. They all rejected me because I was gay." But the most devastating blow came when her husband was granted custody of their children after the divorce.

As painful as this period of Denise's life was, it did make her intimate bond with Linda even stronger. "No matter what happened, I had Linda," Denise sighed. "She was my lifeline." Indeed, their sense that it was "us against the world," which lasted throughout the first year they lived together, brought the two women closer together than they ever had been before—or would be again.

"I don't love Denise any less," Linda insisted when Denise finally agreed to include her in our sessions. In Linda's opinion their relationship hadn't changed drastically over the past three years, but had just settled down. "Oh, it's a struggle sometimes," she admitted. "But what relationship isn't? Except for Denise being a little more insecure than most people, our problems are just the normal day-to-day kinds of things all couples go through."

But Denise didn't see it that way. Having lost so much already and afraid of losing the only thing she had left—her relationship with Linda—Denise saw even the slightest conflict as a harbinger of doom. What Linda called a little spat, Denise labeled a horrible fight, invariably thinking, "Linda doesn't love me anymore. I don't know why she stays with me. I'm sure any day now she's going to tell me it's over and then I'll have nothing."

Convinced that Linda was eventually going to reject her, sure that the pain of rejection would devastate her, and believing—as most of us do—that "the closer we get, the more I'll be hurt," Denise unconsciously began to withdraw, taking a few steps back each time they argued. And since Denise felt closest to Linda when they made love, her withdrawal had an immediate impact on their sex life. "For some reason, having sex made anything I was feeling feel worse," she sighed. Fairly quickly, Denise became aware that she was likely to lose interest in sex after an argument—when she was feeling the most insecure. She did not realize that her fear of rejection and her sexual desire were fused in her mind. Soon, all of Linda's sexual overtures triggered Denise's unconscious fear of rejection, which, in turn, inhibited her sexual desire.

When we suggested that ISD helped Denise maintain a safe distance from Linda, she protested, "But being close to Linda is what I want!" We did not doubt that. However, we also believed that Denise's subconscious mind would have added, "But not *too* close!" Later Denise acknowledged, "If I let myself get closer, losing Linda would hurt even more. I guess in some ways I'm trying to protect myself."

The connection was difficult for Denise to recognize at

first, although she was at least willing to entertain the idea. Larry, however, was not. He did not take kindly to the idea that an underlying fear of triggering a fatal heart attack was at the root of his sexual problem. In fact, the first time we mentioned this possibility, he slammed his fist down on our desk and growled, "Stop making mountains out of molehills. You're making me sound like a mental patient just because I don't feel like having sex." Of course, we weren't labeling Larry as mentally ill and he eventually realized that. But the fact of the matter is that underlying fears are extremely difficult to identify, not only because they are lodged in the subconscious layers of your mind, but also because a part of you may not *want* to know what they are. They are confusing or threatening or simply hard to swallow—which is why they got buried in the first place.

To complicate matters further, the fears that inhibit sexual desire need not have anything to do with sex itself. For instance, a general fear of failure often leads to emotional depletion or gets channeled into performance anxiety. And anxieties about success—particularly when you are not able to appreciate the success you have attained or refuse to believe you were really responsible for it—can cause sexual dissatisfaction and tension. All the fears that you may experience in life can resurface in your sexual relationships and influence your behavior in a detrimental way.

What's more, because the part of your brain that controls sexual desire is connected to the brain centers that analyze complex experiences and are responsible for memory storage and retrieval, anything that even remotely *reminds you* of painful past experiences can set off the red alert signal and shut down your sexual desire circuits.

Unfinished Business

"I don't want to hear it!" Ellen furiously told her husband, David, who was caught completely off-guard by her angry outburst. To tell you the truth, we were also surprised by her response, since it occurred just after David had begun to convey how much he loved Ellen and worried about her, trying to decide what to do when she had woken up in excruciating pain on the morning after her car accident. We had no reason to doubt his sincerity, but Ellen obviously did.

"None of this would have happened if you hadn't made us move here," she shouted at him. "If you ever cared about me at all, you never would have forced me to move to the godforsaken Midwest!"

As you may recall from the previous chapter, Ellen and David's sex life and relationship had both gone downhill following an automobile accident that left Ellen in chronic pain. Up until this point, they had both blamed their problems on Ellen's physical condition and her preoccupation with it. But now it was apparent that anger and resentment had been brewing inside Ellen and inhibiting her desire long before her car careened out of control on an icy highway.

Looking back on the months following the move they had made more than four years ago, David recalled, "Ellen used to pick arguments right before we went to bed. She'd just go on about something trivial and then walk away, leaving me too ticked off to sleep and definitely in no mood to have sex. The fights never had anything directly to do with the move. She never said anything about that, although she did seem a little down."

"A little down!" Ellen gasped, finally able to let out the feelings she had suppressed for so long. "I was practically suicidal. I gave up my friends and my family and my home in the state where I had always lived so he could have the job he wanted. I hated the weather, our townhouse, the school where I was teaching. It was all I could do to get myself out of bed in the morning. I wasn't just a little down—I was depressed." And under the depression, she was seething with anger. David did not know any of this—not because he was exceptionally insensitive, but because Ellen had kept it all inside, never once objecting to a move she truly had not wanted to make.

Once pain became the primary focus and source of conflict in their lives, the anger and resentment Ellen had originally buried stayed buried. Yet, that bit of unfinished business did as much damage to their sex life as chronic pain did. It was the reason Ellen had resisted all the suggestions we had offered during the couple's sex therapy sessions. But more important, according to Ellen's medical records, the pain she experienced, although real and caused by the injuries from her accident, was intensified by stress, anger, and other strong emotions. In essence, the chronic pain that sustained Ellen's ISD was itself being amplified by her unresolved feelings and unfinished business about the couple's move to the Midwest.

Everything that has ever happened to you plays a part in defining who you are today, what you do in any situation, what you expect from your life and relationships, and how you interpret events and your interactions with other people. You are a product of your past experiences. Some people have *integrated* those experiences—no matter how traumatic. They learned from these events, then let go of the intense emotions surrounding them and moved on.

But these people are also a minority. Unfortunately, most of us do not completely resolve all the anger, pain, disappointment, humiliation, or confusion associated with our past experiences. Instead of learning to cope, communicate, and solve your problems, you may have learned to withdraw, overcompensate, or bury your feelings—including sexual ones. You may be thoroughly convinced that you have gotten over, forgiven, or forgotten certain troublesome past experiences, yet when you think about them, feelings of anger, pain, and sadness may be just below the surface of your consciousness. Indeed, yesterday's wounds are today's sore spots—the unfinished business that may be standing between you and your sexual feelings.

When your current partner is the one who caused you pain or disappointment—by having an affair, for instance, or taking you away from familiar surroundings and emotional support the way David did—it is not all that difficult to make the connection between unfinished business and ISD.

Yet while we are products of our past experiences, we need not be prisoners of them. The past cannot be rewritten or buried deep enough to render it impotent, but it can be integrated. You can begin this process by excavating these unresolved experiences and feelings. And if they involve your partner, you can deal directly with these obstacles that have so firmly blocked the growth of your relationship. Although it will not be easy or painless to do, you and your partner can clean up the unfinished business between you, and in the process restore your sexual desire.

However, the unfinished business that inhibits sexual desire may have very little to do with the partner you are with today or the situation you are in right now. Although your present circumstances or relationship can trigger painful memories, it is all too often the hurts others have perpetrated, the lessons others have taught you, and the losses you once suffered that haunt and sometimes poison your intimate relationships today.

Losses, Grieving, and ISD

"Mark was a miracle and a miracle worker in my life," says Wendy, her frown lines disappearing, her eyes brightening as they always do when she talks about her husband and their life together before cancer debilitated and ultimately killed him. Relaxed when he is being discussed in her therapy session, Wendy seems to find Mark's memory soothing and stabilizing.

Before she met Mark at her sister's wedding, Wendy was a nineteen-year-old college dropout, living with four other girls in a rough neighborhood, bartending until two in the morning, partying until dawn, and then sleeping all day. "Drinking, doing drugs, sleeping around"—Wendy lists the activities that consumed most of her time. "But everything fell into place after I met him," she continues. "He made me believe in myself. Didn't put up with my bullshit. Helped me see that my wild, crazy lifestyle was making me miserable."

Your first reaction to a great loss like Wendy's is likely to be *shock* or *denial*. You are literally blinded by the magnitude and repercussions of it. "This can't be happening" is apt to be the first thought that pops into your mind, quickly followed by "I can't deal with this. This pain is too much, too overwhelming."

Instantly and automatically, unconscious defense mechanisms take action to protect you, often doing such a "good" job that you feel completely numb. And until you are psychologically ready to face it, you continue blocking out, minimizing, intellectualizing, or denying outright reality and the pain that comes with it. The trouble is that while you shut out painful emotions, you anesthetize all of your other feelings as well—including sexual ones. As Wendy put it, "After Mark was diagnosed, I didn't feel anything for a while. Oh, I walked and talked, smiled, and even had sex if Mark was up to it. But I wasn't really there. My body worked, but I wasn't in it. I was like a zombie." And zombies are not known for their high sex drives.

With defense mechanisms keeping your emotions in check, you may go through a period of *outward adjustment* and, indeed, be determined to go on with your life as if nothing bad had happened. Sometimes this apparent return to normalcy takes the form of getting into a new relationship. Unfortunately, relationships that begin when you are "on the rebound" are rife with problems—including sexual ones. Because you are still numbing your feelings while unconsciously preoccupied with your loss, and because your conditions for satisfying sex are rarely met right away by a new partner, sexual failures are commonplace. And because your emotional state affects your judgment, you are more likely to make poor choices, ending up with an emotionally, as well as sexually, incompatible partner.

If you have chosen a partner quickly in order to replace your loss, what you feel for your new partner may be confusing. You may be attempting to have sex with someone whom you don't care about very much. Emotional attachment and satisfying sex are frequently linked and so you may find sex with your new partner distant and unsatisfying. As a result, your desire drops. Or you may care a great deal about your new partner, but you may be protecting yourself from new losses by maintaining a certain amount of distance, and suppressing desire, as Denise did, in order to do that.

When the reality of your loss sinks in, you may get *depressed*. Then you may get *angry*, sometimes directing that anger toward yourself, which creates guilt, shame, and decreased self-esteem. As you know by now, these psychological states inhibit sexual desire. Only after you successfully negotiate these stages of the grieving process can you truly accept your loss, put it in perspective, and get on with your life. Unfortunately, many of us get stuck in one of the early stages of grieving or, like Wendy, find one last obstacle blocking our path to *acceptance*.

We worked with Wendy for twelve weeks without seeing any change. Nothing we suggested enabled her to warm up to Bill and even the sexual fantasies she could conjure up were invariably interrupted by memories of Mark. There was a barrier that seemed inpenetrable, but on her thirteenth visit to our office, Wendy confronted it directly.

"Sometimes my memories are so clear," she was saying. "It's like my life with Mark was recorded on videotape and I can replay whatever I want to remember whenever I want to remember it. It's almost like he's still with me. It's . . ." She stopped in midthought, her eyes widening. We could practically see a light bulb go on in her head. "That's it, isn't it? That's why I don't want to have sex with Bill." She looked at us in amazement. "If I start a new life with Bill, I'm afraid I'll lose my old life with Mark, all those memories that have kept him alive for me since his . . . since his death."

As Wendy's breakthrough insight reflects, when you lose your spouse or lover through death, divorce, or the breakup of your relationship, you eventually reach a point where you truly have to let go, finally severing the ties that connected you to that person. Letting go *does not* mean forgetting that person or what the relationship meant to you. Moving on does not mean you didn't *really* love that person. Experiencing sexual desire and enjoying sex with a new partner is not an act of betrayal. However, if you consciously or unconsciously feel this way, you will not be able to accept and work through your loss—and ISD may be a way to make sure you don't have to.

Suffering ISD after losing a loved one or ending a relationship is also likely to occur if:

- Deep down inside, you harbor hopes and fantasies about rekindling your old relationship.

- You cannot bring yourself to take the risk involved in beginning or maintaining a new relationship (which could bring a new loss and new pain).
- You have been "out of circulation" for so long that social and sexual situations fill you with anxiety and self-doubt.

Family Issues

"When my father was on a binge he was completely unpredictable," says Maggie, the twice-married magazine editor and adult child of an alcoholic (ACOA) introduced in Chapter Two. "One minute he'd be Mr. Nice Guy and the next he would be yelling and cursing and turning over the furniture. He would be telling jokes—which he usually found a lot funnier than we did—laughing his head off, and then you'd blink and he was off in the corner crying his eyes out. He had no control over his emotions at all."

At thirty-six, Maggie is exactly the opposite, keeping a tight rein on her feelings at all times. She rarely cries or loses her temper or does anything that might look silly, irresponsible, or out of control. We have seen her smile only a few times. Even then she hesitated, thinking about whether she was expected to smile rather than doing so spontaneously. Indeed, the only emotions Maggie seems to feel on a regular basis are anxiety and depression. She shuts down even those feelings by withdrawing from the person or situation that seems to provoke them. Unfortunately, the people who cause her the most anxiety are the ones with whom she is most intimately involved, including her second husband.

As we explained previously, how you act in social and sexual situations, as well as your feelings about yourself, can be traced back to what you learned from your family. Indeed, the inner picture of the world and yourself that you formed during childhood provided you with the framework for perceiving reality as an adult.

"I know now that my family definitely was not normal," Maggie continues, sharing the insights she gained in a support group for ACOAs after accepting that her first husband, like her father, was also an alcoholic. "It was dysfunctional, chaotic, a very crazy situation to grow up in. My dad was all over the place emotionally. And my mom's feelings sort of stewed inside her until they boiled over and spilled out incoherently, often onto me and my sisters. She'd literally go crazy and have to be hospitalized."

Since her father, who let his feelings show, made family life frightening and unpredictable, and her mother, who was more passive, had nervous breakdowns, Maggie saw only one safe avenue available to her. "I guess I figured that my best bet was not to feel at all," she explains, citing a conclusion often reached by children living in alcoholic or otherwise dysfunctional homes. As adults, they may even realize they are doing this. They may even know why they began to do it. But, more often than not, they are as confused as Maggie is about why they are *still* doing it and how extensively it affects the quality and character of their lives and relationships.

"My mother died five years ago," she says. "My father's been sober almost that long. I haven't lived at home for more than a few months at a time in almost twenty years. I'm not even married to an alcoholic anymore. So why do I still feel like I did when I was eight years old?"

The simplest, most straightforward answer to Maggie's question is that old reflexes are hard to shake—for Maggie and everyone else. A dysfunctional family—whether one turned upside down by alcoholism and mental illness or one in which abuse, infidelities, divorce, or other traumatic events occurred—teaches children countless lessons that later have an adverse effect on adult relationships. And the lessons families *fail* to teach—about healthy communication, expressing affection, and resolving differences, to name a few—do plenty of damage too.

For instance, if your family life was unstable and especially if one of your parents was clearly identified as the "bad guy," you probably did not learn to tolerate ambivalence, to recognize and accept that there is good *and* bad in everyone—including you. As a result, everything is black or white to you. You simply cannot see the shades of gray. When people think or act in ways other than as you think they should, you instantly label them crazy, evil, completely unreliable, or thoroughly despicable. Rarely can you separate the person from the problem, and when the person is your partner, your all-or-nothing approach turns every disagreement into a full-fledged confrontation, a battle between good and bad, right and wrong, riddling your relationship with intense, often unresolved conflicts and setting up barriers to intimacy, sexual satisfaction, and desire.

We probably do not need to remind you that your family also left you with certain impressions about sex itself. But you might not be aware that your interpretation of the events that occurred may have convinced you that feeling sexual desire is a dangerous thing to do.

Dan, for instance, grew up under the influence of a father who gambled and had numerous extramarital affairs. "We all knew what was going on," he explains, "since my parents fought about both things constantly." Dan sympathized and identified with his mother, who somehow managed to be both mother and father to her sons, holding the family together while working to keep them from losing what little they had. "My mother was the responsible one," says Dan, who prides himself on being responsible as well. "My father was completely irresponsible. Gambling and screwing around was more important to him than paying the bills or taking care of us and we were the ones who suffered from it."

Dan grimaces, recalling the nights he went without supper because there was no money for groceries, the school days when he was ridiculed about his hand-me-down clothes, the countless times he lied to collection agents who showed up at the door. "My father's screwed-up priorities screwed up our lives," Dan concludes. "I mean, every guy gets turned on now and then, but that doesn't mean you drop everything and mess up your life because of it." Does this last statement sound familiar? It should, since it is almost identical to Dan's typical reaction to Barbara's sexual overtures.

Similarly, Paula, a single, thirty-eight-year-old financial planner, was raised by a passive, long-suffering mother and a hot-tempered, domineering father who not only "called all the shots" but also physically abused Paula's mother. "My mother loved the bastard," Paula claims. Clearly, her anger at her father has been buried alive. But unlike Dan, who put his mother on a pedestal, Paula's attitude toward her mother is decidedly unsympathetic. "She was a fool, a slave to him. She put up with everything he did because she didn't think she could live without him. If there was one thing I learned from my mother, it was not to let that happen to me." And Paula learned that lesson very well.

Today she is financially independent and plans to stay that way if she ever gets married. "No man's ever going to know how much I'm worth *or* be able to get his hands on my money," she says proudly. But then, it is unlikely any man will ever get a chance to try. Paula's relationships rarely last longer than a few weeks. They start out "hot and heavy," since Paula feels plenty of sexual desire right up until the moment when her latest lover indicates that he wants to see her more than once or twice a week. Then her sexual desire quickly begins to fade. "I don't think it through ahead of time," she claims, and we believe her.

"It's the weirdest thing." She shakes her head in bewilderment. "I wake up one morning thinking, 'What's this guy doing here?' Even if we had great sex the night before, I don't want him to touch me, because he not only doesn't turn me on any more, he actually repulses me."

Although she is aware of her determination not to get into the *kind* of relationship her parents had, when she came to us for treatment, she did not realize that, at some level, she saw intimacy and *any* relationship as threatening. For Paula, ISD was an unconscious defense that protected her from becoming "a slave," and prevented her from developing a stable intimate relationship.

If you grew up in a confusing or chaotic home, you desperately tried to understand what was happening around you. After all, that is the fundamental task of childhood, to create an inner picture of the world and how you fit into it. This background constructs a script that *makes sense* to you and will one day help you function independently. Unfortunately, sometimes your family may have handed you a script that made little sense in the world you lived in then or the world you live in today.

As a child, using the limited insight that is available to someone so young, you attempted to organize this script somehow; you created explanations for the unexplainable and managed the unmanageable by interpreting events in a way that made sense to you *at that time*. The conclusions you reached were stored away in some remote, largely unconscious corner of your mind, and will continue to influence you until you consciously confront and rewrite them.

Thus, Maggie figured out that withdrawing from conflicts and controlling her emotions kept her entire life from "falling apart" the way her family once had. And Janet learned to do everything possible to avoid the "horrible things" that could happen to her—which was the lesson drilled into her by her doting but overprotective mother. And based on what they had observed in their families, Dan and Paula concluded that feeling or giving in to sexual desire brings dire consequences. These and other interpretations of actual events—as distorted or inaccurate as they may have been—help people survive or at least make sense out of childhood. Unfortunately, they can and often do diminish sexual satisfaction during adulthood, leading to sexual avoidance and ISD.

Your Sexual History and ISD

If your life today is a product of your past experiences, then it stands to reason that your sex life today reflects your past sexual experiences. And if your early sexual experiences in particular were accompanied by feelings of failure, overwhelming guilt, shame, or humiliation, they may be contributing to ISD.

"I had sex for the first time when I was sixteen," Janet's husband, Tim, explains. As you may recall, he purposefully set out to lose his virginity to a neighborhood girl with a well-earned reputation for being easy and experienced. "I was so nervous you wouldn't believe it," he continues. "It took forever to get hard, and then after I did, I ejaculated right away, maybe fifteen seconds after I was inside her. Man, was she angry about that." Seven years later, her tirade and his humiliation are still alive in his unconscious memory, reopening old wounds and making him shudder each time he attempts to be sexual.

Tim remembers apologizing and explaining that he'd never "gone all the way" before. "And she laughed at me," he says, "and told me that she could tell I had no idea what I was doing." Her words still echo in Tim's mind. "She really hurt me. I guess that scar has never really healed."

Early sexual scars rarely do. "The problem was that I never got any better at it," Tim says. "It doesn't seem possible, but things actually got worse." The performance anxiety he felt during his early disappointing sexual liaisons and the sexual problems he and Janet have encountered since marriage seem to support his claim. "After a while I started to think, 'What's the point of trying?' "

Your past sexual experiences also helped you discover what excites you sexually. Unfortunately, some people learn to respond to only a limited number of cues and others never learn to identify feelings of sexual desire as such.

"I didn't even know what sexual desire *was* until I was almost forty," says Anne, the housewife-turned-real-estate-saleswoman whose marriage is floundering as a result of her transition from caretaker to career woman. "It took me that long to figure out that I could want sex—for myself, because I enjoyed it and it made me feel good."

Raised in a very traditional and unemotional family, Anne cannot recall either of her parents ever mentioning sex, never mind teaching her anything about it. Yet during her youth, Anne got the impression that when it came to sex, "men were in the driver's seat. They made all the moves, all the decisions. They felt the urges and we girls put on the brakes if the boy was going too fast for us."

As Anne recalls, what girls decided was too much or too fast had nothing to do with their own sexual feelings. Determining what was "allowed" was based on beliefs and values about what was right or wrong, good or bad, too soon to try or about time to permit. "It never dawned on me that I could feel interested in sex ahead of time," she claims.

Phil, whom Anne married when she was twenty-three, was the first and only man with whom she ever had intercourse. They had sex frequently during the early years of their marriage and, until recently, made love at least twice a week. "I've always kind of enjoyed sex," Anne says, and indeed, Anne was—and still is—easily aroused and usually orgasmic. Yet, until she was in her late thirties, Anne never recognized her own feelings of sexual desire. "I guess I never got a chance to"—she gropes for an explanation that turns out to be close to the truth. Because Phil's sex drive was a bit higher than her own and since Anne always accepted his sexual invitations, her sexual needs were met *before* she consciously experienced them. What's more, since the only cue to which Anne gave sexual meaning was Phil's interest in being sexual with her, she did feel sexual desire at times, but labeled it as something else. "When I would get all flushed and feel my pulse racing while watching a movie or reading a novel, I thought I was just upset or embarrassed," she explains.

Then, several years ago Phil became preoccupied with problems in his business and was sometimes too tired or tense to have sex. Gradually, they began having sex less and less often. Anne started feeling "keyed up" and restless, as well as distanced from Phil. "I found myself thinking about sex at odd moments early in the morning, in the middle of the day, while driving the car," she recalls. She mentioned it to a friend who chuckled and asked, "Do you mean to tell me you never felt horny before?" Anne had not. What's more, once she did, she had to learn what to do about it, including letting Phil know when *she* was interested in having sex. The fact that she was still uncomfortable doing that played a supporting role in escalating their sexual desire discrepancy.

As you can see, any element of your sexual history can have an impact on sexual satisfaction and desire. And as you might expect, the most damaging sexual experiences of all are traumatic ones—including incest, child molestation, rape, and other sexual assaults.

Sexual Trauma and ISD

"He would come into my room at night, late if my mother was home, earlier if she was working. I'd wake up and he would be there, standing over my bed, whispering my name." Sylvia, a schoolteacher who is in her third marriage, trembles as she recounts events that occurred almost forty years ago. "I wasn't scared the first time," she says. "I didn't know what was happening, and even when I did, I didn't understand it. I remember thinking it was just a bad dream. But it kept happening. There was nothing I could do to stop it. It wasn't a bad dream. I know that now. But it was a nightmare that I still live with every day."

At least once a month and sometimes as often as once a week, Sylvia's father, a dock worker whom she describes as "a giant, a huge, powerfully built man," sexually molested her. The incest, which involved fondling of her genitals and oral sex, began when she was six and lasted until her twelfth birthday. She never knew why it started or why it stopped. She always knew when it was about to happen, however. "I could tell by how he looked at me when I came downstairs to say good night," she explains. "I'd go back upstairs, get into bed, and lie there, waiting, so scared, my heart pounding so loudly that you could have heard it in the next room." Fear was only one of the painful emotions that washed over Sylvia during her father's unwelcome visits.

"I'd go back and forth like a yo-yo," she continues. "Sometimes it felt good. But then I would feel disgusted. I wanted to vomit, to scream, to scratch his eyes out. But I never did. It was out of control and I was completely powerless to stop it. I was terrorized." Eventually, young Sylvia discovered that she could "turn off my brain, just totally block out my feelings and remove myself from the situation."

That is precisely what she did each time her father molested her and what she continued to do forever afterward. In fact, Sylvia, who was forty-five when she came to us for sex therapy, completely blocked the incest from her mind, having absolutely no conscious memory of it. Then, after four months of therapy, the memories started coming back. After years of psychotherapy and participation in an incest survivors' support group that helped her face and work through many of her emotional conflicts, Sylvia has recently begun to experience sexual desire.

Up to one million cases of incest are reported each year. It is estimated that one out of every four adult women and one out of every eight men were sexually abused in some way during childhood, often by an adult whom they knew and trusted. As you might expect, and as you well know if it happened to you, when an adult has sex with or otherwise sexually abuses a child, the child does not welcome the activity, rarely understands what is happening, and almost always feels powerless to prevent or stop it. Incest, because it also destroys the child's trust and sense of safety, as well as the normal boundaries of parent-child relationships, inflicts deep psychological wounds that can last a lifetime.

Victims of incest and child molestation often go through life feeling helpless, dirty, damaged, or different from other people. They may blame themselves for what happened, think they have some inherently "evil" or "bad" part that draws unwanted attention to them, believe sex is dangerous or the only thing they are "good for," feel powerless to control anything about their lives, or attempt to control every aspect of daily living. More often than not, they find it exceedingly difficult to trust or share any details about themselves with other people, making relationships problematic and true intimacy out of the question. They have numbed any feelings, including sexual ones, that may be associated with the abuse. We have yet to meet a childhood sexual-abuse victim whose sexuality had not been negatively affected in some way.

If you had sexual contact with an adult during your childhood, chances are that you find sex confusing at best. As in Sylvia's case, the sexual abuse that frightened you and that you instinctively knew was "bad" involved physical stimulation that sometimes felt "good." Sex became hopelessly tangled up with fear, confusion, shame, powerlessness, guilt, and betrayal. You certainly are not alone if you concluded that it was bad to feel good. What's more, childhood sexual abuse probably convinced you that sexual *desire* is dangerous. Desire was a weapon used against you. After all, your abuser's lust was the out-of-control force that compelled this trusted adult to hurt you.

The end result of learning that sexual pleasure is "bad" and sexual desire is dangerous varies depending on the nature of the abuse; how old you were when it occurred; how many years it continued; the violence, threats of violence, or manipulation involved; whether anyone else knew about it; what happened if it was discovered or you exposed it; and the specific methods you used to cope with it. The survivors of incest and child molestation whom we have treated report a wide range of long-lasting reactions that affected them even while they were blocking all memories of the abuse from their minds. Having sex, or facing the possibility of having sex, can reactivate the *feelings* associated with traumatic sexual experiences even when you do not remember the experiences themselves. As a result, you may:

- "space out" during sex
- feel numb or panicky during sex and in sexual situations, sometimes to the point of having anxiety attacks
- avoid sex, using various tactics to keep yourself out of sexual situations and occasionally becoming extremely anxious when you *anticipate* sexual overtures
- use sex to meet *all* your needs, sometimes leading to promiscuous sexual behavior
- feel disgust with sex, certain aspects of sex, specific body parts, or being touched in any way
- try to control all aspects of a sexual situation in order to feel safe
- feel terrified by the mere possibility of engaging in sexual activity
- have sex even though you do not want to

In addition, if you are just beginning to remember or deal with traumatic sexual experiences, you may have flashbacks to the assault. During sex or in sexual situations, thoughts, feelings, and even visual images of the traumatic incident may appear in your mind, sometimes so forcefully that you actually confuse what is happening now with what happened then, or you look at your partner and see your abuser instead. This is a truly terrifying experience.

Indeed, Rebecca, a twenty-three-year-old sales clerk who could "go only so far" with her fiancé before feeling her sexual urges turn into panic and disgust, was disturbed by that type of flashback. She called our office one morning and insisted on seeing us as soon as possible. "It was awful," she declared. Her skin was pale, her eyes red-rimmed with dark circles around them. She did not have to tell us she had not slept since watching her fiancé turn into her stepbrother right before her eyes. "We were doing what we usually do," she continued, "making it as romantic as we could. We'd lit some candles and Joey turned around to switch off the lamp, only when he turned back he wasn't Joey anymore. He was Ronnie, my stepbrother. He looked like Ronnie, looked like he was wearing Ronnie's striped pajamas. When he took my hand I was sure he was going to put it on his penis and say, 'Make it feel good, Becky. Rub it like I taught you to. If you do it good, maybe I'll teach you something new.' That's what Ronnie used to say. I think I even heard Joey say it. I don't know. I'm so scared. Am I losing my mind?"

If you have a flashback, you too may think you are losing your mind. You are not. Many sexual assault victims have them and learn to overcome them by using specific techniques like those we have included in Chapter Six, or others you can find out about by reading any of the excellent resources listed in the Bibliography.

Of course, incest and child molestation are not the only types of traumatic sexual experiences linked to ISD. Rape or any other form of sexual assault—no matter how old you are when you experience it—leaves you terrified, emotionally devastated, sometimes physically injured, and almost always plagued by a pervasive sense of powerlessness and by fears about losing control. For months, years, or decades, you may find that you cannot become sexually aroused without feeling afraid and experiencing many of the same reactions to sex that incest victims do. A 1983 study of female survivors of sexual assault showed that more than half of them had long-standing sexual desire difficulties, including ISD.

Not Getting What Turns You On—and Not Wanting To

Do you remember Bobby, the pre-med student who came to see us because he could not explain why he had never experienced sexual desire or engaged in sexual activity despite ample opportunities to do so? We sent him to a physician for a complete medical checkup that revealed no physical cause for his non-existent sex drive. None of the sex therapy techniques we suggested activated his desire and no amount of exploration uncovered a clearer understanding of his condition. After three months of therapy and against our advice, Bobby, convinced that he was simply asexual, terminated treatment. But six months later he called us. "I started this, so I might as well finish it," he said enigmatically and scheduled an appointment. What we had started was a process of reflection and introspection that dug up fears and feelings Bobby had buried so deeply he had completely forgotten about them.

"I was wrong about having erections," he stammered, so obviously tormented that it was painful to witness. "When I was around thirteen, I had them all the time." And he was most likely to have them when he was with his best friend, Ray. Although Ray was several years older than Bobby, the two boys had been inseparable from the time Bobby was six.

When Bobby reached puberty, his feelings about Ray "got all mixed up," but from his description of them it was clear to us that what Bobby felt was sexual desire. Those feelings reached a fever pitch during two weeks spent at Ray's grandparents' farm. During that summer visit, when Ray was out of Bobby's sight, Bobby missed him. When he was nearby, Bobby trembled and perspired. And according to Bobby, "If he just brushed by me, I got hard." Ray found plenty of opportunities to "brush by" Bobby, for the attraction was mutual, and on their last night at the farm, Ray climbed down from the top bunk and got into the bottom one with Bobby. "We kissed and touched and masturbated each other," Bobby reports, taking an eternity to get those words to come out of his mouth. "It was the only time I ever had sex."

At this point, it is important to mention that Bobby had led a very sheltered life. His parents did not talk about sex and slept in separate bedrooms. Strict Christian fundamentalists, they did not own a television or permit their children to go to the movies. And although the restrictions had been lifted by the time Bobby reached high school, he was just thirteen when he had sex with Ray. All he knew about homosexuality was that it was a sin and that being called a queer or a fairy by your peers was devastating. While Bobby had been a willing participant in a sexual activity he had enjoyed, he had a vague sense that he had done something very wrong. He did not have enough sexual information or experience to attribute any particular meaning to it. That is, *until* Ray said, without malice, "So, Bobby, you're gay too." Bobby was shocked and confused. And Ray's explanation of the facts of life only left him feeling more mortified and baffled. Clearly, he had crossed the line between good and evil, become something he did not want to be, and behaved in a way that was completely unacceptable to him. Worst of all, he had enjoyed it.

Bobby immediately decided he would never, ever allow such a horrible thing to happen again. Indeed, he would not see or speak to Ray again. He did everything he could think of to bury all his feelings and stifle all his sexual urges while coping with the loss of his best friend. He blocked these feelings and urges so thoroughly that, until two weeks prior to his unexpected phone call to us, he had no conscious memory of the sexual encounter with Ray and had truly felt no sexual desire in any situation since.

Bobby's story is not as unique as you might think. Denying or suppressing a sexual preference because you or your partner cannot accept it is yet another remote cause of ISD. We see it in men who get sexually aroused by dressing in women's clothing or by wearing a specific piece of their clothing—such as pantyhose, dresses, or silky undergarments. Problems arise when these men cannot, or find it very difficult to, become aroused *without* cross-dressing, but their partners are repulsed by the practice and forbid it. This can also occur in people who practice so-called deviant sexual behaviors. These individuals are sexually apathetic unless the activity or partner is "different" or forbidden (and sometimes illegal), or the partner acts in very specific ways. And it plays a part in some cases of situational ISD where—like Ed, who feels no desire for his wife but plenty for women half his age—someone has mutually exclusive categories for "sex objects" and "love objects."

While homosexuality is *not* a sexual deviation, for some people it is a problem. Like Bobby, some men and women don't accept their own sexuality. Determined to change or deny their true sexual preference, they may "flee" to heterosexuality. They may enter a heterosexual relationship and even get married, doing their best to function sexually. Since one of the most fundamental elements of their sexual scripts—whom they find sexually attractive—is being ignored, they derive less satisfaction from sexual activity and often lose interest in it. In other cases, like Bobby's, the sexual preference is blocked completely from consciousness, and in the process all sexual urges may be blocked as well.

Regardless of your sexual preference or marital status, if you have ISD as a result of any of the immediate or remote psychological issues we have discussed in this chapter, your relationships will suffer because of it. It is time to explain what that means and to take a closer look at perhaps the most important connections of all—the connections among ISD, intimacy, and relationships.

CHAPTER FIVE
ISD and Relationships

"IT'S MY PROBLEM, not Michael's," Maggie said whenever we suggested including her husband in our therapy sessions. "This doesn't involve him," she would insist, reminding us that her ISD was connected to unfinished business from *her* past, not Michael's. True enough. Yet, our experience has taught us that people have an uncanny ability to choose or attract partners who inadvertently trigger their underlying fears or are perfectly cast to play a leading role in reenactments of unfinished business. This certainly was true in Michael and Maggie's case.

Dressed casually in faded jeans and a well-worn leather jacket, Michael, a freelance photographer, was a lean, almost skinny man with dark hair in need of combing, slate-gray eyes, and dimples that cut long, narrow creases on both sides of his face whenever he smiled, which he did easily and often, unlike his wife.

When we first met him, Michael seemed self-assured and easy-going, not the least bit nervous or apprehensive about coming to see us. When we commented on this, he shrugged and said, "Maggie told me I had nothing to worry about." Then with a grin on his face that made it clear he was joking, he turned to his wife and asked, "You didn't lie to me, did you, honey?" He even winked at her, but Maggie missed the humor in his statement. Indeed, she acted as if she had been slapped.

"Of course, I didn't," she replied, hugging herself tighter with arms already protectively folded across her chest.

"I was kidding," he gently assured her.

"Oh," she whispered, but did not relax at all.

How typical was this sort of exchange? we wondered. The answer was, very typical, according to Michael. "Maggie's really sensitive about certain things," he acknowledged, admitting that, two years into what was the second marriage for both of them, he still hadn't gotten used to her tendency to take things personally, especially things that seemed insignificant to him. "Sometimes she'll call in the middle of the day," he continued, "and I'll say, 'I can't talk now. I'm working.' Maybe she thinks I don't *want* to talk to her. I'm never really sure what goes on in her head. All I know is that once she gets home, she won't talk to me at all."

In the situation he just described, Michael usually tries to "loosen her up" with a little humor. But Maggie rarely recognizes or responds to humor other than jokes that are identified as such ahead of time. She usually misinterprets Michael's intentions, feeling more ill at ease than before. If he takes a direct approach, however, Maggie sees his attempts at communication as an interrogation. And if he resorts to sexual overtures to mend things, she feels pressured and intruded upon, thinking that Michael should know that having sex would be "the last thing" on her mind. Indeed, everything Michael has tried to bring her closer to him inevitably winds up pushing her further away.

Maggie, who grew up in a chaotic family, withdraws at the first sign of conflict, becoming emotionally distant when she feels the slightest twinge of discomfort. Yet she is married to a man who approaches life quite differently, preferring to "get things out in the open where you can deal with them." Not only does that make Maggie's behavior difficult for Michael to understand, but it also means that whenever Maggie retreats into her shell, Michael tries to draw her out of it. "I know he means well," Maggie says. "And he rarely yells at me or anything like that, but I just can't talk about what's bothering me while it's still bothering me. I need to be alone with my thoughts for a while and Michael just keeps pestering me."

Michael was raised in a tight-knit, working-class family where they all "yelled, screamed, and threw things" when they were angry. But they also hugged, touched, laughed a lot. As a result, Michael had few fears about expressing his feelings freely and frequently. "He's so excitable," Maggie sighed. "He screams at the TV when someone fumbles during a football game. He misplaces things and curses at himself while he looks for them. He laughs out loud in movie theaters and argues with repairmen when he thinks they overcharged us. And sometimes I'll get home from work and he'll be all excited about something. He'll just rush right up to me and try to sweep me off my feet and carry me into the bedroom."

While many people would not consider these displays of emotion to be inappropriate or excessive, Maggie often found them frightening. "I never know what he's going to do or say," she explained—which was precisely what had caused her so much distress while growing up with an alcoholic father and a mentally ill mother.

Maggie learned long ago that showing or even feeling emotions was a dangerous thing to do. So each time Michael displayed his emotions, Maggie reflexively shut down hers, including her sexual desire. Maggie's suppression of her feelings had been necessary, even adaptive, in dealing with her father. With Michael, however, the inhibition of her feelings was *un*necessary and *mal*adaptive. Yet she couldn't turn her reflex off just by "knowing" it was safe to do so. The groundwork for Maggie's ISD had been laid in childhood, but the way these partners interacted in their relationship contributed to her fears and sexual desire difficulties.

And that bring us to the main point of this chapter. While ISD is *sometimes* caused by physical problems and *often* relates to individual emotional problems, there is *always* a connection between ISD and your relationship. ISD *always* affects and is affected by your relationship. Even if, like Maggie, you are at first reluctant to believe it, as you read this chapter and take a closer look at your own relationship, you will find that a connection of some kind does indeed exist.

ISD is *never* just your problem or just your partner's. How can it be, when one partner's low or absent sexual desire inevitably shapes the sex life both partners share? However, the connections between ISD and relationships extend well beyond the damage done *after* one partner loses interest in sex. Not only do hurt feelings and conflicts over sexual desire problems spill over into the rest of your relationship, but they almost always reflect unresolved relationship problems that existed *prior* to the onset of ISD. In fact, if your relationship is already floundering, a sexual problem like ISD may be a symptom of the tension in your relationship, as well as the straw that breaks the camel's back.

The Last Straw

During their first visit to our office, Kevin and Carl, like many other couples we treat, immediately informed us that they had entered sex therapy as a last resort. "If this problem can't be fixed, our relationship will end," they agreed. After listening to them, we knew that ISD was not the only troublesome aspect of their relationship.

For one thing, when Kevin and Carl had begun their relationship, neither one had what Kevin called "much of a track record to fall back on." Doggedly pursuing a career in a high-pressure, highly competitive field, Kevin had avoided long-term involvements. "When a lover started making demands, I was out the door in a flash," he explained. While Carl was more inclined to work at a relationship, until he met Kevin he had never encountered anyone he thought was "worth the effort."

Not only did Carl think Kevin was worth the effort, but, as he put it, "I guess I saw this relationship as a do-or-die situation." The irony of this remark did not escape him. He openly acknowledged that the AIDS epidemic had changed his attitudes, as it has for countless other gay men.

Carl was willing to go to any lengths to make sure he didn't contract the virus, including "settling down in a nice, stable monogamous relationship." Before he even met Kevin, Carl had decided that he was going to make his next relationship work, no matter what. As a result, he had a heavy emotional investment in Kevin, a hidden agenda that said, "You have to go the distance on this one. Breaking up is not an option. Sex outside the relationship is not an option. If you get involved, you have to stay involved."

Sticking to his agenda would have been a challenge under the best of circumstances, because Carl did not have a particularly clear idea of how to make a relationship work. At the same time, Kevin had an agenda of his own—devoting time and energy to the relationship only if doing so did not interfere with his career.

From the start, the road was rocky. Kevin, preoccupied with work, expected Carl to take care of day-to-day details including those he could have handled himself. He earned considerably more money than Carl and reminded Carl of this whenever Carl asked him to invest more emotional energy in their relationship. Carl knew that he could not accompany Kevin to certain social functions because many of Kevin's business associates did not know he was gay, but still Carl felt left out. Kevin hated it when Carl sulked. Carl wished Kevin didn't have such a hot temper. Their list of complaints went on and on. Although no single problem threatened their relationship, the cumulative effect took its toll. Yet, even this degree of relationship tension would not have driven them apart if they hadn't used sex as a cure-all.

For Kevin and Carl, sex was the glue that held their relationship together. They had sex to express affection, to confirm their commitment to each other, to stay close during the good times and get closer when bad times had torn them apart. Whenever they decided that an argument had gone on long enough, they ended it by having sex. Of course, having sex never actually solved a problem, but, as Carl put it, "It made the problem seem less important. As long as things were okay between us in bed, we managed to get through the rough times."

Understandably, when work-related stress caused Kevin's

sex drive to take a nose dive, every other aspect of their relationship went downhill as well. They had never been able to resolve problems and now they could not escape from them either. Without sex to hold them together, Kevin and Carl did not just drift apart, they blew each other away during frequent, bitter, and at times brutal arguments.

ISD was indeed the straw that broke the camel's back, but it could not have had that effect if their relationship had not already been overburdened with inequities, communication breakdowns, hidden agendas, outside pressures, and other unresolved problems. Yes, a sexual problem can deal the final blow to a relationship that is already on the road to destruction. But other forces steered you onto that road. And they may be the very same forces that shut down your sexual desire in the first place.

If you can't agree on who takes out the garbage, you can't expect to negotiate effectively about who does what to whom, when, and how often when it comes to a sensitive, emotionally charged issue like sex. If a spat over who drives the kids to their piano lessons can turn into a full-scale battle, a dissatisfying sexual experience or a rebuffed sexual overture is apt to set off the equivalent of World War III. When there is *conflict* in your relationship outside the bedroom, ISD may become your first line of defense—or attack—in the bedroom.

RELATIONSHIP CONFLICTS AS A SOURCE OF ISD

Your relationship is the setting in which your needs and expectations are fulfilled or thwarted. A confusing, chaotic, or strained relationship that makes you feel like your needs or expectations have been pushed aside will not make you want to be physically close to your partner. No couple we have ever treated has illustrated this point more dramatically than the one we are about to describe.

Frank, a local TV news anchorman, and Liz, who owns and runs a successful art gallery, have been married for less than two years, and although he is forty-five and she is forty-one, this is the first marriage for both of them. Frank and Liz look like the perfect couple. Attractive, articulate, extremely successful in professions that keep them in the public eye, they are apt to be seen in all the right places rubbing elbows with all the right people and playing the parts of adoring husband and wife. However, what looks like the ultimate intimate relationship from the outside is a disaster behind closed doors—including the closed door of our office.

"Everything is me, me, me," Liz sneers, shooting a venomous look at Frank, who is, as usual, the source of her wrath. She begins to imitate him. "How do I look? Look what I did. I really impressed so and so, didn't I? Aren't you going to thank me for the flowers? Don't you think it was nice of me to take you to the opera?" She shudders with disgust and wraps up her latest tirade. "He's like a drooling puppy dog, always begging to be patted on the head."

"Really, Liz, you must be talking about yourself." Frank shoots back a poison dart of his own. "But then that's all you can talk about."

"Oh, please." Liz laughs derisively. "I can't get a word in edgewise. If you aren't tooting your own horn, you're sulking or whining about something. When I was considering having a child, I didn't mean marrying one!"

"A child of yours would die from lack of attention," Frank retorts. "There isn't a maternal bone in your body. You're about as loving as a Sherman tank. But then you don't *have* a heart. You got rid of it to make room for your ego." He turns to us, hoping to drag us onto the battlefield. "Tell me the truth, now. Have you ever met anyone more self-centered than my wife?"

"They've met you, haven't they?" Liz hisses and they are off and running again. Things really heat up when the topic of discussion is sex.

"Frank has this fantasy that every woman over the age of twelve wants to have sex with him." Liz pauses to light a cigarette, then continues her attack. "I say, 'Go ahead, because you aren't going to get sex from me.'"

"Fine. I'm tired of trying to turn you on. You're just a frigid bitch," Frank snaps. "You aren't exactly a sex goddess, you know. Ninety percent of the time you don't want to have sex, and when you do, you just lie there expecting me to do all the work."

"Wake me up the day you do *any* of the work," she snarls. "You're so into yourself during sex, you don't even know I'm there. I'm surprised you don't call out your *own* name."

Actually, both Frank and Liz are "takers" in bed. They both want to have a thoroughly satisfying sexual experience and become quite absorbed in *getting* pleasure for themselves. To make matters worse, when Liz "instructs" Frank on how she likes to be touched, even if she is not being critical, he becomes enraged. He perceives a neutral request like "Touch me more softly" as meaning "You don't know what you're doing, you clumsy jerk."

Unfortunately, Liz reacts in a similar manner when Frank attempts to provide her with sexual information. The principle of *getting*, not *giving*, applies to their relationship outside the bedroom as well. Even when they talk about more neutral subjects, one partner often ends up feeling injured by what is truly an innocuous comment.

Liz and Frank both want to be number one in each other's lives, but that position is already occupied—by themselves. Their life together is an endless—and futile—struggle to get what they need from someone who has too little to give. As a result, they have what psychologists call a hostile marriage—one in which both partners feel extreme anger toward each other. This anger may not always be expressed in words, but it invariably gets acted out in every area of the relationship. This constant conflict has left Liz and Frank too furious with each other to have sex. Indeed, they feel no sexual desire for each other, and ended up in our office with each demanding that we teach the other how to be a decent lover.

The Nature of Conflict

Conflicts occur whenever getting what you want means that someone else cannot get what he or she wants. And this sort of conflict is inevitable when one partner in a relationship suffers from ISD. Simply put, if ISD sufferers get what they want—infrequent sex or none at all—their higher-desire partners cannot get what they want—to have sex more often than they do.

Conflicts can also occur when getting what you want means someone else must give up something he or she already has. For example, when Anne took on a career in real estate, Phil had to give up her undivided attention and emotional support. Yet, if Anne had devoted as much time and energy to Phil as he wanted her to, she would have to give up the sense of accomplishment and enhanced self-esteem that her career offered her. But conflict *does not* have to lead to dire consequences—or ISD.

When you openly discuss your needs and feelings and then negotiate a compromise that allows both you and your partner to get at least some of what you both want, conflicts get resolved. This "win-win" approach leaves neither partner feeling used, neglected, resentful, or angry. In fact, successfully rising to the challenge that conflicts provide and working together to resolve them can actually strengthen your relationship.

Unfortunately, this constructive approach is not the one most of us take. We are much more likely to get caught in "win-lose" conflicts—where one partner gains at the other's expense—or "lose-lose" conflicts—where one partner who can't "win" tries to make sure the other person doesn't win either. These approaches are unproductive and destructive because they inevitably escalate, leaving a trail of hurt and angry feelings, creating distrust, and failing to generate positive change.

As you could see from Liz and Frank's exchange of barbed comments, an unproductive conflict may begin when one partner says or does something that threatens the other partner's self-esteem, which the "injured" partner then defends by launching a counterattack, and the battle is on. Win-lose and lose-lose arguments include many accusatory "you" statements—universal indictments like "You *never* do anything to help around the house," or "You've *always* been a lousy lover"; and statements beginning with phrases like "Why did you do such and such . . . ?" or "If you really loved me . . ." or "If this relationship meant anything to you . . ." These zingers are usually aimed directly at your partner's sore spots—and you know where they are because they have been revealed during intimate moments.

This sort of unfair fighting is most likely to occur when you or your partner feel powerless or cheated. The ante also goes up if you believe that all conflicts are bad, as Maggie does, or that people in love do not have arguments—which is why Denise, who was afraid of rejection to begin with, believed that each "spat" with Linda proved that their relationship was about to end. When conflicts occurred, both Maggie and Denise "shut down" and shut their partners out, ensuring that neither the conflict nor anyone's feelings about it would get resolved.

How does conflict affect your sex life and your sexual desire? For one thing, in the immediate aftermath, you are unlikely to be in the mood to make love. Of course, some couples, like Kevin and Carl, use sex to curtail a conflict and even find that the "heat of battle" sets off sexual desire. However, most of us find it difficult, if not impossible, to feel sexual desire for "the enemy." Consequently, most couples simply must make up before they can (or want to) have sex. Unfortunately, many couples don't truly make up. Instead, issues and problems get buried for the time being. So, while the conflict seems over, an underlying tension remains in the relationship.

Repeated and escalating conflicts occur because these problems have not really been resolved. They can express themselves in loud verbal exchanges or quiet subtle wars, but overall, they are painful and destructive to your self-esteem and your relationship. It takes longer to kiss and make up. You may even come to believe what you say during a conflict and begin to think less of your partner, who then seems less sexually desirable. You may begin to accept the criticisms your partner directs toward you and feel withdrawn and depressed. As trust declines, you may constantly be on the lookout for the next conflict, wanting to protect yourself. ISD provides an obvious—although not necessarily conscious—solution.

As a result, sex becomes yet another source of conflict in your relationship. Thus, conflict that leads to ISD leads in turn to more conflict, which further dampens sexual desire and traps you in a downward spiral that may not end until your relationship has been damaged beyond repair.

Sex as a Weapon—Power Struggles and ISD

Long before Pat had the hysterectomy that she believes ruined her sex life, and long before Ed lost all sexual desire for her because she no longer turned heads, their marriage had plenty of conflict in it. From the outset, Ed, whose narcissistic personality traits included needing to have his self-worth constantly confirmed by other people's respect, admiration, and praise, was capable only of taking from Pat, who periodically got tired of doing all the giving when she was getting very little in return. "Oh, we had a great house," she said, "nice cars. He would buy me clothes and jewelry and he did take me out a lot, to dinner, to social functions for his company, things like that. He treated me well in that way, but I always felt like a 'Stepford wife,' you know, a little robot replica of a wife who did everything her husband wanted but wasn't supposed to have needs or a mind of her own."

For instance, Ed was very "particular" and demanding about everything from Pat's housekeeping to her hairstyle. "I don't think he means to be cruel or unreasonable," she commented. "He's just very appearance-conscious. He has certain ideas about how his children and his wife are supposed to look and act, especially in public. He wants everything to appear perfect, including me. We all try to please him, but sometimes he just goes too far."

According to Pat, asking Ed to change his behavior or lower his expectations was pointless. Consequently, from the start, whenever Ed became overly demanding, cruel, or insensitive, Pat, who knew that having sex with her "boosted Ed's ego," started withholding sex. "I just said no," she recalled. "And I kept on saying no until he started showing me a little more respect and affection."

In this way, Pat not only punished Ed for behavior she

found unacceptable, but also made an attempt to balance the give/get tally sheet in a relationship where she did most of the giving. Since Ed was basically incapable of giving, the only way Pat could achieve a balance was to *not* give Ed something that he wanted—sex.

Withholding sex is one way less "powerful" partners, like Pat, can exercise some power in their relationships. Through actions rather than words, they say, "Well, maybe you do make decisions without consulting me. Maybe you do constantly put me down and pay more attention to your career than you do to me and expect me to drop everything to meet your needs, but you do *not* have *all* of the power in this relationship. When you want to have sex, it's my turn to call the shots. In the bedroom, I have something you want, but you can't have it until I'm ready to give it to you."

What's more, even if you do periodically give in to your higher-desire partner's pressure and have sex, if you have ISD, you still have an ace up your sleeve. As Pat put it, "Sometimes, Ed can get me to have sex, but he can't make me want it or like it."

Higher-drive partners can also use sex as a weapon or means of expressing anger, such as when they initiate sex even though they know their partners aren't interested. In doing so, they may be disappointed, but also feel somewhat self-righteous. Meanwhile, because the higher-drive partner is using sexual advances as a weapon of humiliation, the other partner may feel sexually inadequate.

Unfortunately, while sexual withdrawal and sexual humiliation are powerful weapons and a way of evening the score, using them does not resolve the underlying problem. In fact, it usually only makes the problem worse.

TROUBLE SPOTS: POTENTIAL SOURCES OF CONFLICT FOR ALL COUPLES

Conflicts inevitably arise in every relationship. However, *more* conflicts occur and are *less* likely to be resolved constructively if you and your partner are not aware of or are unable to navigate through the trouble spots that come with the territory of intimate relationships. Trouble spots are the potential sources of conflict encountered by any two people who want to share their lives and also need to maintain their own identities and senses of self-worth. And the first of these trouble spots is intimacy itself.

Intimacy

The word *intimacy* is most often used to describe close, familiar, usually loving relationships that provide a detailed and deep knowledge of one another. But how close, how familiar, how loving do you want to be? How much closeness is enough for you? What happens when you want more or less than your partner does? *How much* intimacy can you tolerate in your relationship?

Most of us have personal limits on how close we can get to another person before we feel suffocated or intruded upon, as well as how much distance we can tolerate before feeling isolated or unloved. Our **intimacy comfort zone** varies from time to time; whenever we get pushed or pulled beyond its boundaries, we do something to get back to where we want to be.

Early in your relationship, while you and your partner were learning about each other, developing trust, and establishing the give-and-take of your relationship, sex may have helped you feel close to each other. It is only logical, then, to assume that *not* having sex could have the opposite effect.

With this in mind, many men and women withdraw sexually when they want or need to put some distance between themselves and their partners. And it usually works. For instance, long before he began to suffer from ISD, when Kevin was feeling a lot of work-related pressure, he would temporarily lose interest in sex. "Kevin would take his briefcase to bed," Carl recalls. "Or he'd wait until I was ready to go to bed and suddenly remember that he had to call California. Or he'd do a lot of little things to irritate me, knowing I would be less likely to come on to him when I was on the verge of telling him to go to hell. And of course, he'd just say forget it when I did come on to him."

Carl wasn't about to "hang around waiting for more rejection." Instead, he began to create some distance of his own. He stayed out of Kevin's way, going to movies by himself, having dinner with his friends, managing to be out of the house when Kevin got home, and finding reasons to leave the room in the middle of Kevin's nightly recaps of his workday triumphs and tragedies. In this way Kevin got what he wanted—distance. However, when a week or so had passed and Carl still was not showing interest in Kevin's career and was still excluding Kevin from his social plans, Kevin began to feel shut out. When he reached that point, Kevin took steps to get closer to Carl— primarily by letting Carl know he was once again interested in having sex.

As Maggie Scarf put it in her book *Intimate Partners,* "Over time it becomes clear that inside every distancer is a pursuer and inside every pursuer a distancer. Depending on the circumstances, the distancer will pursue (in order not to be abandoned totally) and the pursuer will distance (in order not to be exposed to an intimacy which might feel engulfing or overwhelming)."

Defining an intimacy comfort zone and staying within its boundaries is a challenge for any two people who want to establish and maintain a lasting relationship. Using sex to do that is a very risky business, however. When someone who prefers a lot of personal space and emotional distance gets involved with someone who prefers intense involvement and lots of closeness, sex becomes yet another battleground. For example, intimacy tensions surfaced almost immediately in Dan and Barbara's relationship, and sex problems eventually followed.

Recalling their long-distance courtship, Dan said, "I always looked forward to Barbara's visits, but when they were over I was always glad to see her go. By Sunday morning, I was checking my watch every ten minutes and thinking, 'Enough already. I need to be alone.' " It was not just Barbara's presence that left him feeling like he could not breathe, but also her personality.

Barbara was energetic and talkative, curious and bubbly—or, to quote Dan, "She wanted to know everything about me and do everything with me every minute of every day." Barbara thrived on togetherness. The closer she could get to Dan, the happier she would be. And she wanted this closeness to occur immediately.

While he was in graduate school, the geographical distance between their homes provided Dan with an external boundary to maintain the emotional distance he needed. However, once they married, Barbara immediately realized that Dan preferred "a lot of space," and she tried to give it to him. "It was easy enough to tell when I was getting on his nerves," she recalled. "He'd just shut me out, wouldn't hear a word I said even though he was looking right at me. So I'd just back off for a while. Lots of times I would want to have sex, but I figured that if Dan was off in his own little world and didn't want to do other things with me, he certainly wouldn't want to have sex with me. So, I just didn't let him know I was interested. I held back until I couldn't stand it anymore."

In this way, Barbara and Dan developed a covert, unsteady compromise on the amount of closeness in their relationship, staying well within their intimacy comfort zones for many years. "Having children helped," Barbara acknowledged. "They needed so much love and attention that I didn't have a lot left over for Dan and that seemed to suit him just fine." Things went awry, however, when the children grew older. Then outside pressures—connected to Dan's starting his own business— left Dan needing even more distance than before. Barbara, who was pushed beyond the limits of her own comfort zone, felt anxious, abandoned, and unable to back off any further. So, she began to pursue Dan sexually, sometimes with obsessive determination, in attempts to regain reassurance that she was attractive, needed, and loved. She did not realize that her attempts to get closer to Dan essentially resulted in his pulling further away from her. Because Barbara and Dan, like many other couples, were mismatched in their intimacy needs, they experienced a constant tug of war. While sexual contact became the means for Barbara to gain intimacy, ISD and sexual avoidance became the means for Dan to gain the distance he required.

Negotiating a "Relationship Contract"

In the last chapter, we described what happened to Anne and Phil's relationship and sex life after Anne embarked upon a career in real estate. As Anne took on the "career woman" role, she relinquished some of the responsibilities that went along with her old role as care-giving wife and mother. As you may recall, Phil was less than thrilled with this transformation. "I'm not saying Anne should just stay home watching soap operas or anything like that," he said defensively. "She's always had outside interests, but they never interfered with her real responsibilities. The house and our kids and being my wife always came first. That was the way we agreed it would be when we got married. Maybe that's old fashioned, but it was what we both wanted and I want to know who gave her the right to change it. What made her think that she didn't have to play by the rules anymore, that it was okay to put her career first, our home second, and me all the way at the bottom of the pile?"

As you can see, in addition to feeling neglected by Anne, Phil felt deceived and betrayed. By pursuing a demanding career and deriving so much satisfaction from it, Anne was not living up to her end of a bargain Phil believed she had made by marrying him. He believed he had every right to be angry and that he was justified in trying to coerce her to "play by the rules" of their relationship.

Each partner in a long-term relationship typically has some expectations (realistic or not) concerning how both partners will act. Changes in these expectations can cause tension. An affair outside the marriage, a wife's sudden decision to leave her career to have children or vice versa, or even the more stable partner's suddenly experiencing emotional distress may contradict relationship expectations. Each of these situations and many others will lead to relationship conflicts, *if they violate your "relationship contract"*—the rules you and your partner expect each other to live by as participants in an intimate relationship.

When you and your partner began your relationship, both of you also began co-writing your relationship contract, which provided a set of guidelines for the many and varied interactions that any relationship involves. Based on your preconceived notions about how people in love should behave, how an intimate relationship should be, or what your basic needs are, the contract you developed included certain bottom-line values. Loyalty and monogamy are examples of these values. Extramarital affairs, which most couples consider to be a serious breach of contract, usually bring serious relationship repercussions.

As your relationship evolves, each of you tries to define your own role and develops expectations concerning your partner's role. The priority you give the relationship in your life is also defined. In other words, each of you works out what you expect to give and get from the relationship. Your role may be defined as primary breadwinner, household manager, or child care provider, or it may be more diffuse. For example, you may play the role of the "social" partner, the partner who is strong and takes care of everything, or the partner who is less strong and more needy.

While these various roles and expectations help define the specific terms of your contract, they do not make the difference between a relationship that works and one that doesn't. What is crucial is that you and your partner both *agree* on what they should be. Unfortunately, reaching that agreement is the hard part.

While some relationship expectations and rules are negotiated verbally, most are not, at least not before a problem forces you to talk about them. As a matter of fact, some relationship expectations and rules are actually only wishful thinking. You hope your partner will act a certain way, without realistically evaluating his or her ability or desire to do so.

Most relationship expectations and rules are established through a more realistic trial-and-error process, by observing how your partner reacts in certain situations and adapting accordingly—as Barbara did when she realized Dan could tolerate less closeness than she could. However, while this attempt to adapt is better than the "magical" thinking described above, which is based on hope rather than reality, it is a difficult and often disappointing process. And many of us do not even do that much to obtain a workable relationship contract.

For instance, when Michael married Maggie he assumed they would adhere to a rule he had learned from his family—never go to bed angry. This rule worked for Michael's parents because they got over their anger quickly and reached compromises with a minimum of difficulty. Michael, of course, thought everybody did things this way. But as you may recall, Michael's attempts to "play by the rules"—by trying to get Maggie to talk about and work through whatever was bothering her—contributed to their relationship problems and played a role in maintaining Maggie's lack of sexual desire.

You too may *assume* that you and your partner expect the same things from your relationship and would react to most situations in the same way. You may believe an agreement exists, but discover—usually in the heat of battle—that it does not. And that is what makes the relationship contract a trouble spot for most couples.

The second troublesome aspect of relationship contracts is the one Anne and Phil encountered. They did not renegotiate their contract to fit a relationship that changed once their children became independent and Anne's "full-time mother" role became obsolete. Anne believed the old rules no longer applied and behaved accordingly. But Phil saw things differently and reacted vehemently—breaking what Anne considered to be a cardinal rule of their relationship; that Phil was supposed to support her and be proud of her accomplishments whether they involved being a good wife and mother or being a successful career woman. Rather than renegotiate their contract, Anne and Phil each tried to get the other to play a part the way it was supposed to be played originally, creating conflict that devastated their sex life and deeply wounded their marriage.

To avoid similarly disastrous consequences, you and your partner must be sensitive and willing to adjust to changes that occur in your lives and your relationship. Outside pressures like work-related demands, financial setbacks, aging parents, and illness, as well as normal life-cycle transitions like having children, returning to the work force, children leaving the "nest," and retirement, all have an impact on you and your relationship. And, as we've stressed, change must be integrated; it cannot be ignored. You and your partner simply do not live and relate to each other in a vacuum. If you cannot bend, you will break.

Communication

"If you told me you felt that way, I wouldn't have done what I did," Michael said to Maggie when he learned that his efforts to ease tension only made her more anxious and more determined to withdraw from him.

"If you didn't want kids, why didn't you say so?" Andrea asked Paul, after he finally admitted that he was ambivalent about being a father as well as worried that a baby would put more strain on their already troubled relationship. "If you had just said something," Andrea continued, "maybe we could have worked it out and maybe I wouldn't have driven myself crazy thinking you didn't love me anymore and had found somebody else."

"You don't listen to me," Carl sighed. "You come home, spill your guts about what happened to you at work, and if I'm lucky I get five minutes to sum up everything that's happened to me in the past week. It's even worse if I have a problem. Then you cut me off after thirty seconds and launch into one of your standard lectures."

Effective communication is a skill. Sadly, it is one that most of us did not learn. In fact, few of us enter intimate relationships already knowing how to communicate effectively. This is unfortunate because any problem will get resolved more constructively and your day-to-day relationship will run more smoothly if you and your partner can:

- express your feelings and "own" them, using "I" messages like "I feel left out when you and your friends talk all through dinner about the places you've been that I haven't," instead of "you" messages like "You never include me in your conversations"

- listen to what is being expressed—without becoming defensive, forming a rebuttal before hearing the whole message, interrupting, walking away, or changing the subject
- respond by reflecting what you heard to make sure that you got the message
- give feedback that lets your partner know how you felt about what was said
- ask for clarification—again making sure that you understood what your partner meant to say
- express your viewpoint during *that* conversation—not three days or three weeks later—and do so without labeling your partner's point of view stupid, childish, or insensitive
- talk in specifics—tell your partner you'd like a goodbye kiss in the morning instead of simply saying, "I wish you would be more affectionate"
- feel comfortable with a free exchange of ideas, neither fearing "retribution" for expressing yourself nor handing out punishments (insults, sulking, sexual sabotage, or any other sort of payback) when your partner expresses thoughts and feelings

In addition to preventing problems from getting solved in a satisfactory manner, communication breakdowns leave a trail of hurt feelings, resentments, misunderstandings, and fuel for future conflicts. And certain types of communication—which we did learn while growing up—can actually create conflict and increase your chances of experiencing sexual problems, including ISD.

For instance, many of us seem to believe that being in an intimate relationship endows us with mental telepathy and **we expect to be mind readers.** But no matter how close you feel to your partner, you can still guess wrong—and often do. Likewise, if you expect your partner to know how you feel *and* to act on that knowledge, doing precisely what you wish, you *will* be disappointed, no ifs, ands, or buts about it.

Accusatory statements, which Frank and Liz specialized in, are outright attacks on your partner that escalate conflicts.

Kitchen sinking—bringing up past events, old injuries, and everything but the kitchen sink during arguments—ensures that conflicts will escalate, but never actually get resolved. Kitchen sinking is a habit many people with sexual problems display, either using other issues to keep the focus off the hot topic or using the sexual problem to hurt or humiliate the partner who has gained an advantage in the nonsexual conflict.

Linked to your own unrealistic expectations, **unreasonable demands**—like insisting that an emotionally depleted partner make time to make love, or repeatedly attempting to seduce a partner who has ISD—leave you feeling frustrated and your partner feeling inadequate, anxious, and angry.

Using sex as your only means of expressing affection is another mistake. Far too many of us, men especially, do not know how to convey tender or loving feelings in words or with nonsexual touches. Some of us can't even hug our partners—or be hugged by them—without turning the token of affection into a sexual overture or interpreting it as one. This contributes to ISD by:

- creating resentment and hostility in partners who come to believe they have to "put out" sexually in order to receive any affection at all
- limiting the amount of intimacy in your relationship by avoiding all physical contact, fearing that it will lead to sex when sex is not what you want
- leading you to assume that your relationship's low or absent sexual desire can mean only one thing—that your partner does not love you anymore

Finally, as we have pointed out in earlier chapters of this book and will explore as a part of the self-help strategies in Chapters Six, Seven, and Eight, **miscommunication or no com-**

munication about sex itself decreases sexual satisfaction, increases performance anxiety (as you guess about whether you are doing it right or pleasing your partner), and can make sex an activity you dread rather than look forward to.

Interdependence

Interdependence means that each partner in a relationship has achieved an individual identity and is also capable of intimacy. Within the relationship itself, both partners are aware that their actions, needs, and feelings directly influence each other's responses. Ideally, interdependence involves a sort of team spirit that places a high value on cooperation and flexibility. Although one partner may sometimes need more attention, caring, or support, neither one does all the giving while the other only takes. This type of relationship adapts to the varying emotional needs and external stresses each partner faces.

People go through varying stages of neediness. When under stress or depressed, someone can be described as dependent. When feeling more comfortable and experiencing less stress, the same person may be described as independent. Couples may fall into one of four *fluctuating* stages of independence and dependence outlined by Kathy Weingarten in the book *Working Couples*. Truly interdependent couples can tolerate all of the following four stages:

    independent-dependent
    dependent-independent
    independent-independent
    dependent-dependent

This last stage, however, is often a stressful one for a relationship. Both partners look to each other for support and sometimes neither one can deliver. For example, Paul was recently competing at work for the right to represent a prestigious new client. Even though he had received favorable reviews of his work in the past, he knew his current perfor-

mance was being closely watched and evaluated by his su-
periors. Meanwhile, Andrea had just been given a new boss,
one who had a reputation for being both sexist and overly
demanding.

At the end of each day, Paul and Andrea would drag themselves home, each hoping the other would be waiting to listen,
be supportive, and even take care of most of the household
responsibilities. In reality, neither partner could be supportive
since they were both stressed out, and maybe even a little depressed.

When couples are in this dependent-dependent stage, sexual frequency will often drop. However, some couples develop
more significant sexual problems. One partner or both may feel
angry, hurt, or abandoned when the other cannot provide support. These types of feelings often cause people to pull away
physically and ISD can result.

Partners who are interdependent can weather the stressful
dependent-dependent stage more successfully and can see that
it's only temporary. These partners remember easier times and
know that at some point in the future things will change: They'll
go back to taking turns giving and receiving, or both will be
more independent at the same time, or one dependent partner
will manage to give the other a bit more. Thus, they can tolerate
the temporary discomfort of a dependent-dependent state.

Other Trouble Spots

Other areas that often create or contribute to problems in intimate relationships include:

- demonstrating your mutual love, respect, and understanding of one another
- maintaining your independent identities and accepting
  each other as separate individuals with personal goals,
  aspirations, needs, strengths, weaknesses, and preferences
- handling each other with care and making a commitment *not* to exploit each other's weaknessess, aim for

each other's sore spots during arguments, or otherwise use what you know to hurt or manipulate one another
- trusting each other
- agreeing to have or *not* to have children
- agreeing on how to divide child care responsibilities
- controlling the lingering effects of past experiences that get reenacted in your present-day relationship or influence your feelings about yourself, your partner, or sex
- giving each other enough personal space and privacy, including some separate interests and/or friends
- negotiating a "sexual contract" that merges the desirable elements of your individual sexual scripts and defines the agreed-upon rules and your partner's role in your sex life
- meeting the many demands of your separate and shared lives, coping with stress and emotional depletion, and managing your time
- making the commitment to tough it out together, to do what is necessary to nurture your relationship during both the good times and the bad—especially when it would be easier for one of you to run at the first sign of trouble

While all of these trouble spots are likely to be encountered by any two people who embark upon an intimate relationship, they seem to be even more troublesome for two people who try to excel in their careers and in their intimate relationship *simultaneously*.

DOUBLE TROUBLE—THE DUELING LIFESTYLES OF DUAL-CAREER COUPLES

"Just what are you saying?" Judy glares at her husband, Howard. "Are you telling me to quit my job, to give up everything I've worked so hard for? Is that your idea of a solution to our problems? Maybe that's what you wanted all along, a little stay-at-home wife who irons your shirts and organizes PTA bake sales and worships the ground you walk on. Well, you married the wrong woman, pal."

"Now, Judy," Howard says softly and a little too sweetly, "have I ever asked you to give up your career?"

"No, of course not," Judy retorts sarcastically. "You just expect me to do everything as if I didn't have a career!" She takes a deep breath, her hands shaking with fury and frustration.

Like many of the sessions we have with Judy, a thirty-five-year-old hospital administrator, and her husband, Howard, a forty-year-old city planner, this one starts off by going around and around the same issue—Judy's resentment about having to do more than her "fair share" on the home front.

Like Andrea and Paul, Judy sets exceptionally high standards for herself. She views anything less than perfection as equivalent to failure and expects to be a consummate career woman, a loving mother to her two young daughters, an efficient household manager, a gracious hostess, a devoted wife, and, of course, a sexual superstar. She has taken on more roles than it is humanly possible for one person to handle adequately, no less perfectly. She has literally set herself up to fail on a regular basis and indeed goes through each day feeling extremely anxious and inadequate. And angry.

Judy sincerely believes that she could successfully "do it all" if only her husband would contribute more to their marriage and family life. She is angry at him for "never doing anything without being asked two dozen times and then doing it so half-assed that I have to do it over anyway." She is intensely angry because she believes that she is constantly sacrificing her needs to meet his. Day in and day out her outrage simmers inside her until she can no longer contain it and she explodes.

Howard always remains calm and unemotional. "She's very high-strung," he told us during one of their therapy sessions. "You really can't take her little tantrums too seriously." Of course, not taking Judy's concerns seriously has only made her more furious. And at some level, Howard knew that. By minimizing and placating and playing the patient, long-suffering husband of a "hysterical female," he was passive-aggressively expressing *his* anger. You see, under that calm, laid-back exterior lived a very insecure, needy man who wasn't getting the reassurance and unconditional emotional support he required from the person he believed should be providing it—his wife.

"I try to help," Howard sighed, "but nothing I do is good enough. And believe me, she never lets me forget it. Lots of guys don't do half as much as I do, but Judy doesn't appreciate anything, so what's the point of trying to please her?"

Judy is also more successful professionally than Howard. While she has climbed steadily up her career ladder and now holds the top administrative position at a major medical center, Howard has made only lateral career moves for the past seven years and he cannot forget that Judy "completely deserted" him when he was vying for the position of executive director at a prestigious city-planning firm. "I really wanted that job," he said. "I needed to talk about it and get Judy's feedback on how I should handle the interview, but she was too busy. We were invited to a cocktail party the board gave to get to know the prospective candidates and their wives, but Judy forgot about it. She called a hospital staff meeting and wouldn't reschedule. I had to go to the party alone and probably looked like a real wimp who couldn't even get his wife to go anywhere with him. Needless to say, I didn't get the job."

In her defense, Judy reported that she had just accepted her top-dog position and was overwhelmed by her new, as yet unfamiliar responsibilities. She wanted to "start out on the right foot," and felt she could not do that without giving the job priority over her husband, no matter how much he might have needed her at the time. "Maybe I should have handled things differently," Judy sighed. "But Howard wasn't exactly Mr. Sensitivity when I was going after my job." In fact, from Judy's point of view he had been particularly insensitive and demanding, especially about sex.

And indeed, he had been, because Howard, like Barbara and other people we have previously discussed, increased his sexual demands to boost his decreasing sense of self-worth. He always made more sexual advances and was more interested in having sex when he needed any kind of reassurance. "Every time I turned around, he was pressuring me to have sex," Judy recalled. "He expected me to drop everything and hop in the sack."

As Howard felt increasingly inferior, Judy's sexual rejection left him feeling disappointed—but sexually superior to his wife. At the same time, Judy felt like a sexual failure. By using sex, Howard had evened the score. Unfortunately, both were losers.

A "persist-resist" battle began, but it appeared to end when Judy felt more comfortable in her new job and Howard seemed to have recovered from not getting the job he wanted. However, each time work-related pressure diminished Judy's sexual desire, the battle began again. Acting out his anger instead of expressing it in words, Howard would make sexual overtures when he knew Judy was too emotionally depleted to respond. He would conveniently "forget" to do household chores. Furious, especially after she took on the additional burden of being the "perfect mother," Judy lost all interest in sex.

By the time we met Judy and Howard, their marriage was a wreck and their sex life was nonexistent. Not only had they failed to negotiate the trouble spots any couple faces, but they had fallen victim to several of the relationship dilemmas that are unique to dual-career couples.

Dilemmas for Dual-Career Couples

Identity dilemmas are psychological and/or relationship conflicts arising from discomfort with who you are, who you "should" be, or what you are becoming. Identity dilemmas are sometimes experienced by men who doubt their masculinity after assuming responsibilities they consider to be typically female. Howard was struggling with an identity dilemma when Judy asked him to take the kids to the doctor. "How can I tell my boss that I have to leave work early to take my kids to the pediatrician?" Howard asked. "A woman might do that, but a man never would, not one who has any self-respect anyway."

Role-cycling dilemmas accompany new responsibilities

that must be carried out and decisions that must be made at various stages of a dual-career couple's relationship; often included is the question of whether and when to have children, as well as when work should come before the relationship and vice versa. Although too much stress and too little time played the most significant role in Andrea and Paul's sexual desire problems, this dilemma was what pushed Paul over the edge.

"We somehow managed to have sex and enjoy it, right up until the first time I mentioned having a baby," Andrea explained. "Suddenly Paul was a whole lot busier than he had been before, way too busy to have sex with me." It took Paul a while to acknowledge the connection, but eventually he said, "I just wasn't ready. I didn't know if we could handle the added pressure of having a family when I was dealing with so much at work. When things started going sour because of our sex life, it seemed to prove my point. We were just balancing too much. I am not going to step back from my job responsibilities to help care for a child. The timing just isn't right."

Social life dilemmas involve sacrificing personal friendships and "economizing" by restricting your social circle to mutual friends who are often part of your work world as well. This reduces potential emotional support from people other than your partner. As a result, your partner is sometimes responsible for meeting *all* your needs. Limiting outside relationships makes it more difficult to separate your work and private worlds. In addition, some friends and family members may become angry because you're always "too busy" to see them.

Inequity is what Andrea experienced several years ago when she was being considered for a prestigious position with a New York–based public relations firm. "I didn't go looking for it," she explained. "They found me and asked me to interview. I was really flattered. But the first thing Paul said when I told him was 'You aren't going to take it, are you? We can't move to New York when I may soon be offered a partnership in the law firm.' Then I knew for sure that no matter how equal Paul *said* things were, they really weren't." This sort of inequity in a dual-career marriage often creates conflict and causes the "less equal" partner to harbor resentments that can get acted out in the bedroom.

Competition was certainly a problem for Judy and Howard, in particular because of Howard's need to prove that he was at least as good as his wife. Howard was feeling this need all the more acutely because Judy was succeeding in her career while he was floundering in his. As often happens when a competition cannot be decisively won in the boardroom, Judy and Howard moved theirs into the bedroom, where they both used sex as a weapon.

Trying to serve too many masters may be the most common dilemma of them all. To derive maximum total satisfaction from your nontraditional lifestyle, you may compromise the areas of your life that seem to be the least important. And since sex does not provide the tangible rewards your career does, it may not seem as important in the long run as child rearing or physical fitness or finishing graduate school. As a result, sex is one of the first things to be sacrificed when other, ostensibly more important areas of your life require your time and attention.

As dual-career relationships are becoming increasingly common, more and more couples are finding out the hard way that trying to serve too many masters invariably ends in failure.

Married with Children: Family Expansion Dilemmas for
Dual-Career Couples

With the arrival of children, you must make room in your already overcrowded lifestyle for 2 A.M. feedings, schedules disrupted by childhood illnesses, plans ruined by unavailable babysitters, and guilt—most acutely felt by mothers who worry that their children will be scarred for life because they do not spend enough time with them, or who are plagued by doubts about their ability to live up to their own or society's standards for "good" mothers.

Even though you and your partner have chosen a nontraditional lifestyle, you were influenced by traditional values earlier in your life. Among other things, you were raised with traditional sex role stereotypes that portrayed men as productive and women as nurturing. In simple terms, women were expected to devote more emotional energy to their families than to their careers, while men's priorities were expected to be exactly the opposite. Even if you and your partner managed to overcome these stereotypes before your children were born, chances are you reverted to them afterward, with child rearing becoming primarily the wife's responsibility.

If you are the female partner in a dual-career couple, you had to make a choice. You had to either discontinue or decrease your involvement in a career so that you could be a full-time parent, or attempt to achieve superwoman status and "do it all." Either option could create relationship problems, including sexual ones.

For instance, Leslie, a thirty-two-year-old mother of two young sons, gave up a promising career on Wall Street so she could stay at home to raise her children. "Don't get me wrong," she says. "I love my boys. They're more important to me than any job could ever be. But still, sometimes I wonder where I might be now if I hadn't gotten pregnant when I did. How far could I have gone? Would I have made it out there in the jungle? I wonder if I had what it takes to get ahead in my field and now I'll never know."

She admits she sometimes feels jealous of her husband, Doug, who continues to move steadily upward in the same firm where she was once employed. "It doesn't seem fair that he got to have children and a career, to have his cake and eat it too, so to speak."

Since she lost a major source of self-esteem and stimulation, it is not surprising that Leslie wakes up on many mornings feeling "like half a person." At first, we mistakenly thought that the low-grade depression she'd suffered since her second son was born was the only reason for Leslie's ISD. But then we leaned that although she has "absolutely no interest" in having sex with Doug, she frequently has sexual fantasies about "being my old self again, having some man walk into my office and doing it with him right there on the floor." Clearly, Leslie's "old self," the self-confident career woman who throve on power and excelled under pressure, was someone who could feel sexual desire. But she had given up that role to become a full-time mother, and apparently she had given up her sexual desire as well.

On the other hand, if you opt for "superwomanhood" or "supermanhood," you are apt to experience **role overload,** the end result of trying to be all things to all people, as Judy did. This inevitably leads to physical exhaustion, emotional distress, feelings of inadequacy about your own capabilities, and feelings of resentment toward your often less-than-helpful partner.

What's more, dual-career couples also encounter the intimacy, relationship, communication, and other trouble spots that can create conflicts for any couple. As a result, they may find that they are indeed in double trouble and, as you know by now, that trouble may include ISD.

HOMOSEXUAL RELATIONSHIPS

We have found that lesbian women and gay men in ongoing intimate relationships who suffer from ISD and desire discrepancies generally do so for the same reasons as heterosexual men and women. If you are involved in a homosexual relationship, your relationship, like all intimate relationships, may include some nonproductive conflicts, intimacy and communication problems, power struggles, and sexual script incompatibility, which can lead to sexual desire difficulties. If yours is also a dual-career relationship, then you are subject to the same added stress and strain that is experienced by any two people attempting simultaneously to pursue active careers and a family life.

However, the trouble spots that come with the territory of all intimate relationships may cause you and your partner a bit of additional trouble because you may not have as many reasons to stay together as heterosexual couples do. Society does not sanction your relationship and your family may not support it. Indeed, your parents and other people who think they have your best interests at heart may actually try to undermine it. No legal contract binds you to your partner, and the prospect of complicated and emotionally draining divorce proceedings will not serve as a deterrent to dissolving your relationship. Your household may not involve children, and therefore you cannot justify staying together for the children's sake. Indeed, your only reason for being in the relationship may be your emotional commitment to your partner—a bond that may be deeply threatened by the negative feelings stirred up by any kind of relationship conflict. As a result, each trouble spot you encounter may have a more dramatic impact on your relationship and your sex life than it would for a heterosexual couple.

Homosexual and heterosexual relationships are more alike than different. However, lesbian couples and gay male relationships are both subject to certain unique influences that sometimes increase the probability that one partner or both will suffer from ISD or will react drastically to even slight drops in sexual activity or desire.

Lesbian Couples

Lesbian women in intimate relationships tend to be less sexually active than either gay male or heterosexual couples, which has more to do with their·socialization as women than with their lesbianism.

Women are socialized to avoid, smooth over, and deny conflict. Until relatively recently, women have been taught that sexual desire and sex itself were more important to men than to women. Regardless of your sexual orientation, if any aspect of your sex life provokes anxiety or appears to have the potential to cause conflict, your first inclination may be to circumvent the problem by avoiding sex, suppressing sexual urges that you have consciously or subconsciously labeled dangerous because they might lead to humiliation or conflict. Logically, if both partners in a relationship, being women, have been "trained" to take this approach, sexual avoidance and ISD are more likely to occur.

Because traumatic past sexual experiences are twice as common in women as in men, they are more often a major barrier to sexual adjustment in women. As mentioned earlier, one in four adult women experienced sexual abuse during childhood and too many others have been raped, have encountered sexual harassment at work, or have had anxiety-provoking early sexual experiences. Thus, when two women embark upon an intimate relationship, one or sometimes both partners may bring this sort of unfinished business with them.

Then there is the fact that you, like many other women, may have learned only one reason to be sexual—to achieve intimacy. The romance and excitement of a newly developing relationship may activate or spark your sexual desire. However, after this initial stage, your basic intimacy needs may be met by the increased closeness or emotional sharing of the longer-term relationship. Thus, sex drive and sexual activity in general may decrease as your intimacy needs are being met through the overall relationship, rather than through sex alone.

Finally, while intimacy can be a trouble spot for any couple, it presents a common dilemma for lesbian couples, which sometimes become so enmeshed that individuality and separate identities become blurred or lost. As Denise put it, "Sometimes I'm not sure where I end and Linda begins." You and your partner, like Denise and Linda and many, many other lesbian couples, may share all social and recreational activities, friends, professional services (including the same psychotherapist), and even the same employer. Even if you do not work together, you may call each other throughout your work day so that you rarely spend more than a few hours on your own. You may share all of your belongings, including your clothes, and assume that you also share all the same thoughts, feelings, and values.

On a conscious or subconscious level, this fusion may make sex extremely anxiety provoking, since during sex there is no "distance" at all. This may mean that the slightest effort your partner makes to assert herself or act independently will trigger your underlying fear of rejection or abandonment—as it did in Denise's case. And, like Denise, you may subconsciously use ISD as a buffer against rejection or losing yourself completely.

Since your identity and your partner's may be defined by your
involvement with each other, you will do whatever you can to
maintain that involvement—avoiding any and all potential
sources of conflict, including sexual ones.

Gay Male Relationships

Gay men grew up under the influence of the same messages
about what was and was not acceptable masculine behavior that
their heterosexual counterparts received. Unfortunately, what
they absorbed during childhood and adolescence included a
great many negative attitudes about homosexuality.

If you are a gay male, chances are you originally learned
that homosexual sex was unnatural and immoral. If other people picked up on the fact that you did not fit the stereotypical
male mold, you may have been ridiculed and humiliated by
your peers and subtly or not so subtly rejected by your parents.
You may have gone out of your way to prove that you could not
possibly be gay, doing all sorts of macho posturing, getting into
fistfights to prove how tough you were, and even having sex
with as many women as you could seduce. Your self-esteem
suffered from the effects of both trying to be something you
were not and being unable to accept who you really were. More
often than not, you internalized the homophobic attitude that
prevailed all around you. Even after you acknowledged your
homosexuality and adopted a homosexual lifestyle, these old
negative attitudes lingered in your subconscious mind where
they continued to whittle away at your sense of self-worth,
sometimes wreaking havoc on your relationships and your sex
drive.

Subsequently, you may have come to rely on external
agents to help you feel good about yourself. If those external
agents include alcohol or other drugs, you run a very high risk
of physically inhibiting your sexual desire and functioning. If
one of those external agents is sex itself, getting involved with
someone whose sex drive is noticeably lower than your own can
lead to persist-resist battles that make Barbara and Dan's con-

flict look like child's play. In addition, if your self-esteem is dependent upon sex, you may be prone to abuse sex (which can be downright dangerous), overreact to even infrequent periods of going without it, and overwhelm an intimate relationship because of your dependency on sex.

But more important, a positive sense of your own identity and self-worth is a prerequisite for intimacy. Like lesbian couples, you and your partner, because of both traditional male conditioning and unsteady feelings about yourself, are prone to have intimacy-related problems, which, as you know, are a common cause of ISD.

Unfortunately, any progress you may have made toward feeling better about yourself as a person or as a man who is homosexual may have been challenged in recent years. The current nightmare of the AIDS crisis may have further hampered your ability to feel good about your sexuality. In addition to reviving your internalized negative attitudes about your sexuality, AIDS has likely caused you to suffer many losses. You have probably lost at least one friend, if not many. Indeed, it may seem as if hardly a week or a month passes without news that someone else you know has died. You want to grieve for those losses, but like all "real men," you may be conditioned not to show your feelings. If you do, in fact, suppress feelings of sadness, anger, or fear, you will often inadvertently suppress your sexual desire as well.

What's more, your sexual functioning and sexual desire are bound to be affected by *fear* of AIDS, which is sometimes accompanied by general anxiety, panic attacks, preoccupation with your physical health (especially any symptoms that might remotely resemble those linked to AIDS), depression, and obsessive worrying—especially about your own or your partner's past unsafe sex practices.

Fear of AIDS limits the range of safe sexual behaviors available to you and removes the option of engaging in sex outside your relationship to cope with relationship problems, desire discrepancies, or other sexual problems. Indeed, the fear of AIDS may convince you to "tough it out" and make your relationship work—no matter what. Unfortunately, like Kevin and Carl, you and your partner may have a decidedly limited amount of experience in resolving day-to-day relationship conflicts and find yourself at a complete loss when problems dissolve the sexual glue that held your relationship together. All of these factors can inhibit sexual desire and, in fact, have significantly increased the number of gay male patients who seek our help for sexual desire problems.

Now that you know a great deal about the physical, psychological, and relationship causes of ISD, it's time to find out how you can get past them and begin to reignite your sexual desire. Whether you are homosexual or heterosexual, married or single, you cannot expect desire to return magically of its own accord. You will have to build the fire and strike the match, by using the self-help measures you will find in the next three chapters and, if need be, by seeking professional help.

CHAPTER SIX
Setting the Stage for Change

THE INFORMATION AND EXERCISES you will find in the remainder of this book are not a magical, money-back guaranteed cure-all. They depend on your own and your partner's *willingness and commitment to change* yourselves, your relationship, elements of your lifestyle, and your sex life.

Making those sorts of changes is never easy and the fact of the matter is that few of us embrace the prospect of change with open arms. It makes us uncomfortable at best. And for some of us, the thought of changing ourselves or our relationships—especially when we cannot know in advance how our efforts will turn out—is truly terrifying.

REASONS TO CHANGE

Perhaps you have heard the joke that asks, "How many therapists does it take to change a light bulb?"

The answer: "One, but the light bulb really has to want to change." Part of what makes people laugh at a joke like this is the element of truth in it. When it comes to ISD, the truth is that you and your partner must really want to rebuild your sexual relationship in order to attempt the effort that will be asked of you.

Some of our patients—like Wendy, whose interest in sex

had not bounced back two years after her husband's death, and Larry, who had felt no sexual desire since suffering a heart attack—are painfully aware of their own ISD and its impact on their lives. They know that they want to restore their sexual desire. You may fit this description as well. Other patients—like Andrea and Paul, who were dissatisfied with the frequency and quality of their lovemaking, and Bobby, who was baffled by his complete lack of interest in sex—have struggled to integrate sexuality into their lives and relationships. They want to change so that sex can be a pleasure rather than the void it now is. That may be what you want too.

On the other hand, like a significant number of our patients, you may not be committed to reigniting sexual desire per se. For instance:

- You may be reading this book because your higher-desire or more sexually interested partner insisted upon it. After months or even years of listening to pleas and demands that you get help, you gave in—to please or appease your partner. This was certainly the case for Barbara and Dan. And Kevin agreed to enter sex therapy only to "settle the matter once and for all so Carl will get off my back."

- Like many men and women with low desire, you may want to change because you are afraid of losing your partner. Perhaps your partner is actually threatening to leave you. Or, the two of you may not have actually discussed the problem, but you assume that it is only a matter of time until your inability to develop interest in sex will irreparably damage your relationship or drive your partner to seek sex elsewhere.

- You and your partner may have already made a commitment to change and may even be receiving therapy for marital problems that you initially insisted had nothing to do with sex. But now, having discovered that sex or the lack of it is, in fact, another source of conflict in your relationship, you may be motivated to reignite sexual desire because you are already working to improve other aspects of your life together.

- If you are a single, divorced, or widowed man or woman—like Rachel and other individuals we have described—you may be more concerned about your single status than your sex drive, worrying that you will never be able to attract a suitable partner or maintain a relationship because you avoid social and sexual situations.
- Like Al, who came to us because he could not maintain an erection, perhaps you have a sexual dysfunction other than ISD but suspect that a desire problem may be causing or exacerbating your condition.
- Or, like Janet and Tim, you may want something—most often to have children—that ISD prevents you from getting.

Even a reason like wanting to get your partner off your back can stir up enough emotional discomfort to push you in the direction of help. You simply must have *some* reason to change or you will not make the effort, and the suggestions and exercises that follow will be of little value to you.

Obviously, it helps to know that your problem is ISD or linked to ISD, and actually to want to reignite sexual desire. If you do, you have an advantage over many of our patients. When you opened this book, you acknowledged that you or your partner *might* have a sexual desire problem, and by reading this book you gathered a great deal of information about ISD. Unfortunately, your willingness to learn and what you learned will not necessarily exempt you from encountering certain obstacles that can prevent you from improving your sexual relationship.

BARRIERS TO CHANGE

No matter what ISD has taken from you—closeness, sexual pleasure, a source of relaxation or stimulation, self-confidence, or positive feelings about your partner—you may have also *gained* something from it. You may wonder what you could gain by losing interest in sex. What good could possibly come from something that has probably driven a wedge between you and your partner; that has saddled one or both of you with hurt, angry, or resentful feelings; that has left you anxious, insecure, or feeling inadequate, and wreaked havoc on your self-esteem and your relationship? The answer is that ISD may help you avoid situations that you find more threatening than your present circumstances.

The 10 Percent Payoff

If you want to find out what ISD may be protecting you from, simply ask yourself: *What negative outcomes might result from increasing my or my partner's interest in sex?"*

Could your relationship be getting too close for comfort, suffocating you, or paving the way for your partner to make more demands than you could meet—as Dan feared Barbara would? If your partner becomes more interested in sex, will you have to face your own performance anxieties and sense of inadequacy? If you start to feel sexual desire, what will you have to give up in order to find time in your overcrowded schedule to have sex? And if you are often pushed around by a domineering partner, what will you have left to help you even the score or reassure yourself that you have some power in your relationship? Not having ISD could mean the loss of a powerful bargaining tool that helps influence or control your partner's behavior. These are the kinds of consequences that many of our patients fear *more* than those of having ISD or relating to a partner who has it.

Hidden Relationship Problems

A serious but *hidden* relationship problem may also present another barrier to change. Camouflaged by a litany of minor conflicts and small complaints—like those Kevin and Carl presented—more fundamental and frightening issues may stand between you and a more satisfying sex life. These include lack of trust, fear of intimacy or rejection, old anger and resentment, or unfinished business from your past. You maintain the smokescreen of arguments and minor skirmishes, both because the underlying problem is affecting your feelings about yourself or your partner, and because one or both of you fear that acknowledging the underlying problem will ultimately destroy your self-esteem or your relationship. If this is the case, you may resist *any* effort to change.

In addition, since focusing on your sexual problems may be one way that you avoid dealing with underlying issues, hidden relationship problems can sabotage any progress you do make toward reigniting sexual desire. If you increase your sexual intimacy, the feelings and problems you and your partner have buried may begin to rise to the surface, creating anxiety, pain, or confusion that you were previously able to avoid. As you may recall, this is precisely what happened to Ellen and David, who had convinced themselves that Ellen's back pain and ISD were the real problem in their relationship. Once they began to work on those problems, however, they discovered that the bigger problem was the inequity in their relationship and Ellen's resentment about being forced to move when David decided to look for a job in another part of the country without consulting her.

Because David and Ellen were in therapy, they were able to confront and deal with those problems immediately. On the other hand, you may *feel the effect* of underlying issues without quite knowing what they are. Because this happens so often, we will discuss some common signs of resistance to change or sexual sabotage and ways to handle them. However, if you find that you cannot get moving again after getting stuck, we recommend that you seek professional help in the form of marital counseling or sex therapy or both. In Chapter Eight, we'll discuss how to decide if professional help is necessary and how to find it if it is.

Believing That ISD Is Only a Medical Problem

Another barrier is assuming that your sexual problem is a medical one and that, as a result, there is nothing you can do about it. While some sexual disorders, including ISD, are caused by physical factors or medical conditions, this is not a conclusion you should draw prematurely or without professional advice. If you suspect that there is a connection between ISD and a physical problem, a medical evaluation—including a thorough physical examination and laboratory tests—can confirm or rule out your theory. If your assumption proves incorrect, as it did for Larry, who believed his heart attack had altered his body chemistry and destroyed his sex drive, you will need to confront the emotional and interpersonal barriers that are currently blocking your sexual desire.

If there is a medical reason for your sexual problem, there may be a medical treatment for it as well, and even if there isn't, you can still learn to engage in satisfying sexual activities and improve your sexual relationship. A physical condition, no matter what it is, may limit the range of what you can do sexually, but it does not mean you cannot be sexual at all.

Too Much Anger

One of the barriers that we often encounter with our ISD patients, and that you probably noticed in our description of Barbara and Dan's persist-resist battles and most certainly in the caustic crossfire between Frank and Liz, is *too much anger*. There is a good chance that this barrier is operating in your relationship if:

- Your attempts at communication quickly lead to knockdown, drag-out fights with a lot of yelling, screaming, criticizing, or even throwing things.
- The angry feelings you or your partner express are out of control or an overreaction to the situation at hand.
- Bitter, hurtful arguments are repeated time and time

again but never seem to resolve the problems that lead to them.

- Resentful, hurt, and angry feelings linger long after the argument itself ends.
- One partner's *passive* anger blocks communication. More difficult to identify than the explosive fury we just described, quiet anger takes the form of withdrawal, "forgetting," coldness, being subtly uncooperative or blatantly doing the exact opposite of what is asked, walking away from a conversation, or otherwise creating a silence that cannot be broken. Howard, for instance, acted out his anger in this way each time he made light of Judy's concerns, did a chore in what she called a "half-assed" manner, or completely ignored what she was saying to him.

Regardless of the form it takes, if you and your partner cannot get beyond your anger, you will not be able to solve your sexual problem—and on some level you will not want to. You may have to work through the relationship problems—perhaps with the help of a psychotherapist—before you can tackle the sexual ones.

Denying That a Problem Exists at All

Finally, a barrier we often observe in one partner is the tendency to avoid admitting you really do have a problem. You may believe that acknowledging sexual problems of any kind, and sexual desire disorders in particular, is an admission of personal failure and inadequacy.

ISD and the conflicts it causes will not go away just because you don't pay attention to them, however. In fact, your own or your partner's distress and dissatisfaction will probably escalate—until you can no longer ignore them because you are in too much pain. We can only hope that while reading this book, you have decided to stop burying your head in the sand and are willing to take steps to solve your problem *now* rather than waiting for a severe crisis to force you to change.

GETTING STARTED:
PREREQUISITES FOR REKINDLING SEXUAL DESIRE

Before you actually attempt the self-help exercises we have
provided, there are several steps you must take to create a
climate that is conducive to change. The ability to express your
needs, thoughts, and feelings without blaming or attacking your
partner, to listen attentively and confirm that you understand
what your partner is saying, to respond without becoming defensive, and to negotiate differences of opinion effectively is
essential for solving day-to-day problems. These skills will also
help you broach the subject of ISD to your partner. Consequently, we would like to offer you the following tips and guidelines:

1. Recognize that both you and your partner have the
right to express your needs, thoughts, feelings, and concerns. However, this right brings with it the *responsibility* to
present your point of view in the manner that is least likely
to hurt or provoke the other person.

2. Say what you mean. Express yourself clearly and
directly. Do not beat around the bush, say one thing when
you mean something else, or water down your feelings
(saying you are "a little concerned" about your sex life, for
instance, when you are actually extremely upset about it
and frightened that your relationship is coming to an end).
Do not expect your partner to play detective and figure out
what is really going on inside you. Clearly identify your
feelings, explain what you are thinking, specify what is
bothering you, and let your partner know what you need as
directly as possible. This is vital when discussing ISD. While
saying, "Our sex life stinks and you can either shape up or
ship out, buddy," is definitely direct, it is neither specific
nor helpful. "I'm unhappy having sex only once a month
and I'd like to talk about what we could do to have it more
often than that" is both more to the point and more likely
to pave the way for a productive discussion.

3. Use "I" messages to express *your* feelings, beliefs, needs, and wishes. For example, say, "I get upset when I find dirty dishes in the sink," or "I need you to help me by cleaning up the kitchen after you get a snack," instead of "You are a hopeless slob," or "You like making messes for me to clean up, don't you?" "I" statements will express what you are feeling while breaking the pattern of making accusations or generalizations. Make a concerted effort *not* to begin conversations or statements with "You always" or "You never." Such generalizations are rarely true and they only invite a counterattack. For instance, when discussing ISD, you are much more likely to make progress by saying, "I feel pressured and frustrated when you come on to me at the end of a rough day, and I wish you could be more sensitive to how stressed out I am sometimes," than if you say, "You're a selfish, insensitive bum who never stops to think about how I'm feeling before you demand that I drop everything and have sex with you."

4. Listen attentively. Focus your attention on what is being said to you, not on what you are going to say in response.

5. Listen *actively*. After your partner finishes speaking, *reflect* the message you heard, summarizing or paraphrasing what you think your partner said. *Clarify* by asking if that is what your partner meant and if you might have missed anything. *Respond* by expressing your feelings about your partner's message as well as your ideas about the topic being discussed.

6. Remember that neither of you is a mind reader. Do not *assume* that your partner understands your point of view or that you understand your partner's thoughts or feelings. You should also definitely avoid voicing your partner's thoughts or feelings—as in "You think that my job isn't as important as yours," or "You're not really angry about the dirty dishes. You're still trying to make me feel guilty about stopping to have a drink with the guys on my way home from work."

7. When communicating in general or for the purpose of solving a problem, making a decision, or negotiating a compromise:

    a. Make sure you have enough uninterrupted time to discuss the matter thoroughly.

    b. Be specific about what the problem or subject under discussion is.

    c. Discuss one topic at a time, focusing your attention on that area and how it affects each of you here and now. Do not kitchen-sink, bringing up other current problems or old business and unresolved feelings from previous conflicts.

    d. Skip the question of whose fault it is that the problem exists. Blaming your partner and justifying or defending your own behavior *will not* help you resolve your differences. In fact, you should try to acknowledge your own part in the situation and identify what *you* are willing to do to resolve it.

    e. Move toward a win-win outcome, one in which both of you get at least some of what you need, rather than having one partner's needs met at the other's expense.

8. If communication between you and your partner has been strained and ineffective in the past, practice this new approach with topics that are relatively easy to discuss before tackling the emotionally charged issues that have led to angry confrontations in the past.

9. Effective communication is *not* restricted to discussing problems and airing grievances. Ideally, you would use these methods in all of your interactions to express appreciation, affection, and positive regard, as well as distress and dissatisfaction.

These communication skills are so important because talking together about your sexual concerns is the only reasonable starting point for improving your sexual relationship.

Typically, one partner is more aware of and disturbed by sexual desire difficulties than the other. Since you are reading this book, it is probably safe to assume that *you* are aware of the problem, whether your partner is or not. If so, it's your responsibility and your right to voice your concerns. You should not do this, however, by insisting or by attempting to shame your partner into changing. Demanding that changes be made rarely if ever creates an environment in which positive change will actually occur.

Dos and Don'ts for Discussing Sexual Desire Problems

1. DO remember that you are having a discussion, not a fight or a debate. DO think about what you want to say and how to say it. Toward this end, you may want to run through your part of the conversation ahead of time, identifying the points you want to make and coming up with ways to phrase your concerns so that they will be less likely to put your partner on the defensive. DO take a direct approach.

2. DON'T criticize, attack, or blame your partner. You may be completely convinced that every single snag in your life and your relationship is entirely your partner's fault, but saying so will solve absolutely nothing. A counterproductive conflict will ensue and neither of you will be better off than you were before.

3. DON'T hit and run. This is not a discussion you should have in bed, just before bed, during a five-minute drive to your in-laws' house, ten minutes before one or both or you must leave for work, or when your kids are likely to interrupt you. If you will not have enough time to really discuss your concerns, or if you are angry, in the middle of an argument about some other issue, or have just had a sexual overture rebuffed, DON'T start a discussion about working on your sex life. Wait until a more appropriate time.

4. But DON'T postpone the discussion indefinitely either. If you wait until you are truly "mad as hell and not going to take it anymore," you eliminate any possibility of talking about the topic rationally or negotiating any sort of agreement to work together.

5. DO make sure that your partner understands that you want to work together to have a sex life and a relationship that will be better for *both* of you. Refer to the conflict as "our" problem. Acknowledge anything you might be doing to contribute to the problem—saying, "I know my timing isn't always the greatest," for instance, or "I guess it must seem like I'm asking for a lot from you sometimes." Admit that talking about the rough spots in your sex life is a difficult thing for you to do and say you can understand that your partner might feel threatened or anxious by the topic. But most of all, let your partner know that you are not asking for change for your sake alone, and that you hope both of you can change together to get more of what the two of you want from each other, your relationship, and your sex life—even if you want different things.

6. DON'T settle for Band-Aid measures. It is not uncommon for couples to go directly from this type of discussion into the bedroom. They have sex and the partner who was worried about their sex life thinks, "Gee, this was easy. All I had to do was speak up and now everything's okay again." If ISD or desire discrepancies were involved in the first place, everything may seem okay, but it really isn't—which the temporarily placated partner soon discovers. Resolving sexual desire problems takes time and effort. *One discussion rarely, if ever, resolves the problem on a long-term basis.*

7. DO keep bringing up the topic if you don't reach an agreement the first, second, third, or twentieth time you discuss it. When you let things slide, you, your partner, and your relationship will eventually experience so much tension and dissatisfaction that it will be too late for repair.

If Your Partner Continues to Resist Change

Even if you follow the guidelines we offered, there is no guarantee that your partner will agree to work on the problem or even admit that there is a problem. In fact, your partner may steadfastly refuse all suggestions for change. If this occurs, you may feel hurt or angry, or you may jump to the conclusion that your partner simply does not love you and wants your relationship to end. But this is only sometimes the case. So, before you let your imagination run away with you, try to put yourself in your partner's shoes, considering the possibility that one of the previously described barriers to change may be making it hard to face the situation.

More often than not, we find that resistant partners, especially if they are the ones with ISD, are acutely aware of the problem and feel terrible about it. Unfortunately, they are either convinced it cannot be fixed or they are frightened that trying to change will reveal aspects of themselves or their relationships that they will be unable to handle.

We suggest that you give your partner time to think about the situation and your requests, especially if your concerns come as a surprise. Perhaps you could give your partner this book to read. Then, in a few days or a few weeks, try again to start another discussion and see if some change can occur.

If your partner continues to resist, you will eventually have to confront the consequences of *not* working together to improve the situation. You might say something like "If we can't work together to solve this problem, then I can't feel good about you or our relationship. It makes me wonder what our relationship means to you and maybe I have to rethink my commitment to the relationship too. I'm not sure what sort of answers I'll come up with, but if we can't agree to do something together, I'm going to have to find a solution I can live with."

You may have to present more specific consequences as well, letting your partner know that if you cannot work things out between you, then you want to get into therapy together, or separate temporarily or get divorced. DO NOT make threats you do not intend to carry out, however, or hurl ultimatums that will do more harm than good. Many higher-desire partners have vowed to have an affair and have even gone through with it, only to discover that they are even further from a resolution to their marital and sexual problems.

Realize as well that if your partner will not change and you cannot learn to live with the situation as it is, separation or divorce may, in fact, become a realistic alternative. However, this rarely occurs because of a sexual desire problem alone.

In addition, although it won't necessarily change your relationship or your sex life, until your partner is ready to work with you, you can work on changing yourself, improving your self-esteem and increasing your options for the future.

Deciding What You Really Want—and Can Realistically Get

While you are coming to terms with your sexual problems and your need for change, you and your partner must individually and jointly set goals for yourselves. You need to clarify what you want from each other, your overall relationship, and, specifically, your sex life—and your goals in all three areas must be reasonable. They must take into consideration the realities of your lifestyle as well as your partner's needs and wishes.

The following exercise can help in this area. It will also allow you to establish a mutually agreeable contract for change.

GOAL-SETTING STRATEGY

You will need at least one hour's worth of time per partner, possibly spread over several days, to clarify and set your own goals individually, and as much time as it takes to agree on mutual goals.

PART ONE
What do you want *more* or *less* of in your sex life? In your relationship? From your partner? Working

alone, you and your partner should make separate lists answering these questions for yourselves in a general way. For example, answers might include frequent sexual interactions, more sex play before intercourse, more variety during sex, less pressure to have sex, more communication, more help around the house, bringing less work home from the office, more time for just the two of you, and so on. You need not complete the list in one sitting.

Next, choose the two or three items from each category that are most important to you. Then, for each item or goal you have chosen, write specific examples of:

1. What you would *ideally* want in that area
2. The bare *minimum* you would accept in that area

State these goals in the most precise terms possible, with your ideal reflecting how things would turn out under the best of all possible circumstances. This is your "wish list" and does not have to reflect the realities of your current lifestyle.

Your minimum expectations should be somewhere between where things are now and your goal. Your minimum should represent the *least* amount of change you would settle for and should also be very specific.

For example, Barbara, as you might expect, wanted to have sex more often. Her *ideal* was "To be able to have intercourse whenever I am in the mood for it." Her *minimum* was "To have intercourse at least three times a month." Her husband, Dan, on the other hand, and also rather predictably, wanted less pressure to have sex. His *ideal* was "No sexual pressure from Barbara. She would let me decide when to have sex." His *minimum* was "She could ask for sex whenever she felt like it, but would be more accepting of me when I wasn't in the mood."

To give you another example, Judy, the would-be superwoman who was suffering from role overload, wanted Howard to help more around the house. Her *ideal* was "We would divide household responsibilities between us equally and Howard would do his tasks without being asked and the right way." Her *minimum* was "I could ask Howard to do something specific, like put the clothes in the dryer, and he would do that without fussing, forgetting, or screwing up." Howard, of course, had some wishes of his own. He wanted Judy to be more supportive. *Ideally*, "I would have time every day to talk to Judy about my day or things that were bothering me, and at least 50 percent of the time she would choose to go places and do things with me instead of putting work commitments first." *Minimally*, "Judy and I would spend two hours a week together and compare schedules at the beginning of the week so that her work wouldn't conflict with doing things together."

As you can see from these examples, and probably from your own list as well, ideal goals tend to be unrealistic in light of the actual circumstances of your life and your partner's needs, which are likely to be somewhat or very different than your own. Yet, the bare minimum may not be enough to satisfy you. Consequently, neither end of the spectrum reflects both what you want *and* what you can reasonably expect to get—and therefore neither should be used as a goal for your change effort.

Set a reasonable standard to work toward—*by identifying a goal that falls somewhere between your ideal and your bare minimum*. Barbara's goal, for instance, was to have intercourse once a week, while Dan's was to be approached for sex no more than twice a week, not to be approached when Barbara knew he was under work pressure, and to retain the right to refuse Barbara's sexual overtures whenever he wanted to.

PART TWO

In this part of the exercise, you and your partner must negotiate and compromise to establish goals that you can both comfortably and willingly agree to work together to achieve.

Once you have set your own realistic standards, sit down together and compare lists. Try to find a middle ground on similar goals. For instance, Barbara and Dan compromised in this way by agreeing to work toward having sex three to four times a month. Barbara agreed to make sexual overtures only when she felt a very strong desire to have sex, while also considering how much stress Dan might be under at the time. Although Dan retained the right to refuse any sexual invitation, he agreed to tell Barbara why he was refusing and to work on stress and time management so that he could be more receptive to her advances.

Negotiate trade-offs—giving your partner something he or she wants in exchange for something you want—even though one goal may have nothing to do with the other. Judy and Howard negotiated this sort of exchange. She agreed to spend a minimum of three hours each week with Howard. During those times he could request whatever kind of support he needed, and if the request was one she could fulfill, she would. They would agree on their together times in advance, and for the moment, having sex would *not* be one of his requests—although working on sexual self-help exercises could be. In exchange, at least three times per week Howard would be responsible for household management. He would prepare or purchase dinner, do the dishes, get the kids ready for bed, straighten up before going to bed, and arrange for the house to be presentable before leaving for work in the morning.

He did not have to do all of those things on the same day, but he agreed to do each of them at least three times a week.

Considering the complexity of such agreements, four points are worth making. *First,* negotiating your contract for change will take some time and effort and will require you to follow the discussion guidelines we presented earlier. *Second,* although your agreement is not carved in granite and can be renegotiated at any time, you will find it helpful to write down what you have agreed to do. *Third,* if you find your partner does not follow through part of the bargain, we recommend that you follow through on your part anyway. If you withhold your negotiated contribution, the process of change might stop. To continue the process, you and your partner must discuss what obstacles got in the way of keeping your agreement. *Finally,* both of you must recognize and accept that you will not reach your goals immediately. Look for progress, not overnight turnarounds. As long as both of you are working toward those goals, you are sticking to your contract. However, if either or both of you behave in ways that clearly keep you from moving toward your goals, you must discuss the situation right away and, if necessary, get outside help.

This strategy, like others you will find in the remainder of this book, reflects the obvious but so often overlooked reality that both partners in an intimate relationship will *get* more of what they want if each is willing to *give* the other more of what he or she wants. And that is something we hope you will keep in mind throughout your effort.

MAKING TIME TO CHANGE

Andrea and Paul, Judy and Howard, Barbara and Dan, and Kevin and Carl, as well as other couples and individuals we have introduced to you, suffered various negative consequences because they wanted to have sex more frequently and derive more satisfaction from it *without* giving it a higher priority in their lives. Indeed, they wanted a fulfilling sex life and a healthy relationship, but left themselves literally no time to accomplish these feats. And they discovered, as you probably have as well, that *if there is no good time to have sex, then sex is unlikely to be good.*

Finding the time to work on your sex life and your relationship, as well as assigning sex and intimacy a higher priority than you have given it in the past, is absolutely essential for reigniting sexual desire. None of the exercises or guidelines we offer you will work if you frantically squeeze them into your life between myriad other activities. And they certainly can't help you if you repeatedly put them off because everything *but* sex seems more important at any given moment. You simply cannot follow the same hectic timetable and wait for the magic to happen.

You will need to allocate at least three hours per week for working together to revive sexual desire, preferably in the form of 3 one-hour blocks of time. Of course, at this point, you may be unable to imagine finding that much time in your jam-packed schedule. Andrea and Paul claimed they couldn't. It was absolutely out of the question, they insisted. But *we* insisted that if they hoped to achieve their goal of having intercourse two or three times a week, they would have to find that much time eventually—and so will you. By rearranging your schedule *now* and devoting three hours per week to sexual self-help exercises, you will develop a positive habit that will serve you in the future—when your interest in sex has been restored.

Obviously, you may have to let go of something else in order to make the time for these things. You may have to spend less time at work or give up some of the time you spend with friends. You may have to work out at the gym three times a week instead of four, or let the dinner dishes sit in the sink overnight, or send the kids to Grandma's for a few hours on Saturday afternoon. In short, you must rearrange your priorities in order to get the benefits a better sex life offers you, including closeness, physical pleasure, relaxation, stimulation, and much more.

Of course, you always have the option of accepting that you just don't have enough time and energy to maintain your present lifestyle and be sexual or intimate as well. You can decide that it is completely impossible to devote three hours a week to improving your sex life. But then you must also accept the fact that your sex life and your relationship are not going to get any better than they are now.

But before you do that, we advise you to take a closer look at *why* you have not found time for sex in the past and *why* you may feel unwilling to make time for it now. Ask yourself: Am I really too busy or am I too anxious, frustrated, or angry? Is there really no time in my life for sex and intimacy or am I just not ready to work on this problem yet? Is an overcrowded schedule standing in my way or have I encountered some other barrier to change?

You may discover that having too little time is an excuse for not facing or taking action to change your present circumstances. If so, we encourage you to review the previously discussed barriers to change and use our suggestions to break through them.

As long as we're on the subject of time, let's address a concern we suspect you might have—how long it will take to get positive results. Although we would like to tell you—and you would no doubt like to hear—that you will be able to reawaken sexual desire and create a more satisfying sex life after a specific amount of time, we cannot give you an exact time frame. How long it takes for change to happen depends on why you or your partner suffer from ISD, how willing both of you are to work together, and your diligence in working on the problem even when you do not immediately see a dramatic improvement. We can tell you, however, that if you devote three hours per week to reigniting desire and improving your sexual relationship, and if you see *no* change whatsoever in yourself, your partner, or your relationship after two months, you should consider seeking professional help. But please, if this should happen to you, don't think that you or your partner have failed in any way. You have simply encountered a barrier or a problem that you cannot understand or overcome without the assistance of an objective and professionally trained expert.

SETTING THE STAGE FOR CHANGE

Before we move on to the specific ways you can strengthen your relationship, feel better about yourself, and improve your sexual relationship, we would like to suggest some ground rules for working together to reignite sexual desire. They will help you set the stage for change, enabling you to pursue your goals more comfortably and willingly. Unlike the self-help exercises, following these ground rules does not require you to set aside specific blocks of time, but you should try to incorporate them into your lifestyle and relationship.

1. Use the strong, positive areas of your relationship as building blocks. When rearranging your schedule to make time to change, try not to let go of the activities that help you and your partner enjoy each other or feel close emotionally. In fact, try to increase these behaviors, focusing as much as possible on your own and your partner's good points.

2. Whenever possible, avoid distancing behaviors such as pouting, criticizing, giving each other the silent treatment, losing your temper, walking away from your partner in the middle of a conversation, and so on. These are probably old, familiar habits and you may be unable to eliminate them completely, but you can try to catch yourself as soon as you start to do them and change your negative pattern of relating.

3. Put day-to-day problems and minor conflicts on hold while working on self-help exercises or spending intimate time together. Some of the things that get on your nerves or need to be settled can certainly wait an hour or two before being discussed. An hour of intimate, positive time together may make it easier to deal with the problems the two of you must confront later.

4. Try to increase physical contact in general. Do more touching, hugging, and handholding. Scratch his back, massage her hands or head. Simply enjoy being physically close for its own sake, *not* as a prelude to sex.

5. Add a bit of romance to your lifestyle. Have special dinners, remember special days, dress up and go out to dinner even if you're only going to the local pizza parlor. Leave notes, send cards, give gifts, bring home flowers just for the joy of it. Get away once in a while, whether to a romantic Caribbean island or to a motel three miles from your home. Create a romantic environment for the self-help exercises and when having sex. Try candlelight, music, silk sheets, exotic fragrances, and so on.

6. Be playful and creative. Do something surprising, like wearing a sexy new outfit or making an erotic telephone call to your partner at work. Come up with imaginative ways to spend time together. Do things together that you did when you first dated. Stir up some nostalgia by looking through old photographs or visiting the places you frequented while you were dating. Eat dinner on the living room floor instead of around the kitchen table. Forget about mowing the lawn or cleaning out the hall closet and take a drive in the country. Try some activity together that you've never tried before. You'll find that putting the adult in you on hold for a bit can be beneficial for both your relationship and your sex life.

7. Don't take this change business too seriously. Keep your sense of humor, have fun, and play during the self-help exercises.

8. Don't let your roles as parents prevent you from being physically close. Allow yourselves to express affection in front of your children and take measures to ensure that you get privacy when you need it. Lock your bedroom door and instruct your children as to what does and does not constitute a legitimate reason to interrupt you. Get a babysitter or let children spend the night with friends or relatives when you want to be alone together, and even consider taking brief vacations without your children.

9. BE PATIENT. You did not get where you are overnight and you will not instantly reignite sexual desire or improve your sex life and relationship either. Look at the steps you are taking now as an investment in a better future; like a monetary investment, this effort will need time to accumulate "interest" and make a "profit."

CHAPTER SEVEN
Making Personal and Relationship Changes

As you now know, in order to experience sexual desire and feel free to act upon your sexual urges, your personal conditions for satisfying sex must be met. Of particular importance are:

- feeling safe and comfortable with, as well as attracted to, your partner
- feeling secure and positive about your relationship
- communicating with your partner in general and about sex in particular
- having a positive self-image, including feeling comfortable with your body and your sexuality

No matter how many sexual self-help exercises you try or how diligently you attempt to revive sexual desire, without these ingredients, your recipe for satisfying sex will produce disappointment instead of desire, and frustration instead of fulfillment.

So, if enhancing your sexual relationship is your goal, you must begin your change effort by reinstituting the conditions that improve your chances of enjoying and looking forward to sex. You need to work on your *non*sexual relationship and feel better about yourself *before* rushing full speed ahead.

In other words, *foreplay begins long before you reach your bedroom.* It includes almost everything that goes on between you and your partner and in your own mind. By offering strategies and suggestions for enhancing your relationship and feelings about yourself, including your sexuality, this chapter teaches how to engage in a less obvious, but very important type of foreplay that will ultimately help you to have better sex.

STARTING WITH YOUR RELATIONSHIP

If you are married or involved in an ongoing intimate relationship, try as you might, you cannot perform a "sexectomy" that removes your sex life from the context of the relationship in which it occurs. In fact, you could be the world's greatest sexual partner and have a truly impressive repertoire of techniques, but still have a sexual relationship that is mediocre at best. You may also have a partner who seems not only unimpressed by your prowess, but completely uninterested in being sexual with you. To understand how such a thing could happen, you must thoroughly evaluate the state of your relationship, paying particular attention to sources of conflict, as well as what you and your partner do when conflicts occur. You must then take steps to strengthen your relationship by communicating more effectively, building trust and intimacy, resolving conflicts constructively, becoming more skillful at time and stress management, and understanding what each of you needs from each other. Then and only then will you have a sturdy foundation upon which to build a satisfying sexual relationship.

If you are not involved in an intimate relationship at the present time or are just now embarking upon one, the strategies and suggestions in this section can still be beneficial to you. They can help you clarify what you want from a relationship and teach you skills that will help create that relationship once you do meet someone with whom you would like to become intimately involved.

EVALUATING YOUR RELATIONSHIP

As you may recall, disagreements, anger, miscommunication, distrust, power struggles, or lingering resentments can easily cause one partner or both to lose interest in sex or to withhold it as a punishment. There is a clear connection between relationship conflicts and sexual problems. If you are not aware of the ways your relationship affects your sexual desire and satisfaction, or if you know something is amiss but are not sure what it is, the following self-test can help you pinpoint your trouble spots and direct you to various exercises that specifically address them.

RELATIONSHIP TROUBLE SPOT SELF-TEST

Think carefully about your relationship and answer the following questions. If your answer reveals a trouble spot, as indicated by the discussion following each question, you can use our suggestion to begin resolving that particular problem.

1. Do you and your partner AGREE on (a) your respective roles in your relationship, (b) what you each expect to get from and give to each other and the relationship, (c) who is supposed to be in charge of taking care of your home, raising the children, arranging your social life, managing your finances, and so on, and (d) whose job is more important and who is expected to do the caretaking in your family?

If you answered "no" or "not sure" to any of the above, there may be a conflict over who is or is not doing a fair share of work in your relationship, and one or both of you may feel overburdened and resentful.

SUGGESTIONS: Try the Goal-Setting Strategy (page 194) to establish a mutually agreeable relationship contract; develop communication skills (page 210) and follow rules for "fair" fighting (page 218) to resolve conflicts constructively.

2. Are you and your partner facing one or more stressful events or life transitions, such as pregnancy

or childbirth, job changes or promotions, increased travel or relocation, recent entry into the job market, or illness of a partner, a child, or elderly parents?

If you answered "yes" to any of the above, you may be experiencing excess stress, anxiety, depression, and emotional depletion. Sex and intimacy may have dropped to the bottom of your list of priorities, at least temporarily, and many stay on the back burner until one or both of you can emotionally and/or physically refuel.

SUGGESTIONS: Try tips for better time management (pages 198 and 226), stress reduction (page 227), and reducing role overload (page 221).

3. Have you and your partner found ways to cope when you both simultaneously feel needy, dependent, or overstressed?

If you answered "no," you may be suffering guilt, resentment, conflict, emotional distance, sexual withdrawal, and excess stress. Sexually, this is most troublesome when one partner uses sex to relax or feel less needy but the other cannot develop interest in sex when feeling tense or emotionally depleted.

SUGGESTIONS: Establish terms in your relationship contract to cover such situations—see Goal-Setting Strategy (page 194), tips for better time management (pages 198 and 226) and stress reduction (page 227), and the Basic Conditions Exercise (page 265).

4. Are you, your partner, or your interactions adversely affected by unfinished business from the past? Do you experience the lingering effects of childhood experiences, sexual traumas, old relationships, or old problems in your current relationship?

If you are not sure how to answer those questions, ask yourself instead: **Do you or your partner react to situations or respond to each other in ways that make little sense or seem to be out of proportion to the issue at hand?**

If you answered "yes" to any of the above, unresolved feelings and unfinished business from the past
may be causing one or both of you to consistently overreact or say and do things you yourself cannot fully
understand. This may create conflicts or cause you to
withdraw emotionally and physically. This is most
likely to occur if one or both of you:

- have been sexually abused
- previously were emotionally or physically bat-
  tered spouses
- were recently widowed or divorced
- are adult children of alcoholics or were raised
  in dysfunctional families
- had a series of unpleasant past sexual or relationship experiences
- are recovering from an addiction

SUGGESTIONS: Try tips for talking back to old
tapes (page 229), the Thought-Stopping Technique
(page 232), and tips and exercises for improving communication (pages 188–191 and 210). In addition, the
following can be useful: psychotherapy, participation
in a self-help or support group, and bibliotherapy
(reading about your problem area and what to do
about it).

**5. Do you and your partner solve problems, make
decisions, and communicate effectively?**

If you answered "no" to any of the above, you may
have a relationship that is characterized by numerous
unresolved conflicts, hurt and resentful feelings, minor differences that turn into major arguments, and
instances of acting out negative emotions instead of
expressing them—including sexual sabotage and withholding sex.

SUGGESTIONS: You need to develop better
communication skills (page 210), agree to follow the

same ground rules for fair fighting (page 218) and practice the Talking and Listening Exercise (page 210) and those exercises designed to improve sexual communication (starting on page 248).

6. When you and your partner disagree, does tension remain in the air after the argument itself has ended? Do either of you stew, sulk, leave the house, slam doors, or otherwise indicate that the battle may be over on the outside but is still raging under the surface? Do either or both of you withhold sex after an argument—especially if you were the "loser"?

If one of you answered "yes" to any of the above, you may have a bigger problem that is hidden by a smokescreen of smaller ones, or accumulated anger that neither of you can get beyond.

SUGGESTIONS: Review "Barriers to Change" (page 183) and the Caring Days Exercise (page 212), as well as the other intimacy exercises found in this chapter, particularly the section on improving communication (page 210). You need professional help if you get stuck.

7. Do you and your partner feel close, trust each other, and comfortably share your thoughts and feelings with each other? Have you found your intimacy comfort zone and do you generally stay within its boundaries?

If you answered "no" to any of the above, you may have persist-resist battles—a yo-yo relationship in which one partner tries to get closer while the other attempts to maintain distance, distrust, or power struggles.

SUGGESTIONS: Try the Talking and Listening Exercise (page 210) as well as Caring Days (page 212) and all the other exercises in the section of this chapter called "Building a More Intimate Relationship" (page 212).

You may want to take some time now to make a list of the self-help exercises that apply to your situation.

As you may have noticed, many of the relationship trouble spots highlighted in the previous exercise involve miscommunication, no communication, or ways of communicating that only escalate conflicts.

IMPROVING COMMUNICATION

A good starting point for reconnecting is the following exercise, which will help you understand who your partner is, how he or she feels, and what is going on in your partner's life.

TALKING AND LISTENING EXERCISE

1. Select two periods of an hour each during the upcoming week and agree to spend them together *without interruption*—no phone calls, no kids, nothing else, period.

2. Both you and your partner will have an opportunity to talk and to listen. Flip a coin to see who talks first.

3. For thirty minutes, the partner who won the coin toss talks while the other partner listens attentively *but makes no verbal response whatsoever*. When the first half-hour ends, the partners switch roles—the listener talks and the talker listens.

WHEN IT IS YOUR TURN TO TALK, you are to talk *only* about yourself as a separate person—the things you think about; the joys and sorrows in your life; *your own* needs, wishes, frustrations, fantasies, worries, and so on. You are *not* to say anything at all pertaining to your partner or your relationship. If you talk second, you are *not* to comment on what you heard; like the first speaker, talk about yourself.

AS THE LISTENER, you are to listen attentively *without* commenting. Do not interrupt and try not to signal disapproval or dismay through your facial expression or in other nonverbal ways. You can show that you are listening by looking at your partner and nodding occasionally. If your partner gets stuck and does not speak for a few minutes, do not rush in to fill the silence with words of your own.

4. When both of you have taken your turns as talker and listener, the exercise is complete. You are *not* to discuss anything that you said or heard *for at least one day.* Please adhere to this rule, because the fact that you and your partner cannot immediately respond to each other is part of what makes this exercise work.

The preceding exercise, which was developed by Richard Stuart and adapted from *Intimate Partners* by Maggie Scarf, presents a challenge to partners who have spent so many years defining themselves as half of a couple that they have lost touch with their own independent identities. It is also difficult for partners who are especially insecure and find themselves trying to read between the lines or becoming anxious about what their partners might be implying. Whether or not you encounter these problems, if you follow the directions and *repeat this exercise for several weeks,* it will get easier.

By making you listen to each other and breaking your habitual pattern of communication, the Talking and Listening Exercise increases the likelihood that each of you will feel better understood and the two of you will feel more connected. It also forces you to face the fact that, even though you are involved in an intimate relationship, you and your partner are separate people with your own unique ways of viewing the world.

BUILDING A MORE INTIMATE RELATIONSHIP

If you and your partner have been experiencing sexual problems or dissatisfaction, and if you are being afflicted by one or more relationship trouble spots, chances are that you do not feel as close to each other as you once did. You may be engaging in power struggles and adding distance to your relationship by withdrawing, arguing, or withholding sex. In fact, you may have completely lost sight of each other's positive qualities and the good things you do get from your relationship. This negative perspective makes you feel like you're not getting enough, and so you're likely to give less. And as you give less, your partner is likely to respond in kind. This leads to a downward spiral that leaves both of you feeling deprived.

The first step toward restoring intimacy is rediscovering the up side of a relationship that may have been going downhill for quite some time now. This may be difficult for you to do at first, because conflict, bitterness, anger, and pain are fresh in your mind. The following exercise gives you and your partner an opportunity to pay more attention to the positive elements and potential of your relationship. It asks you to take small, specific steps toward increasing the pleasure of intimate exchanges. Those steps will pave the way for the more difficult steps you may have to take later.

CARING DAYS EXERCISE

If you have been experiencing sexual or nonsexual problems and escalating conflicts, you may have some serious doubts about whether you and your partner still care about each other. Indeed, you may need to be reassured that both of you do care in order to willingly work together to solve your problems. Although you cannot make yourself or anyone else *feel* more caring, you can ask yourself and your partner to do more to *show* caring.

Of course, all of us have our own personal ideas about what caring behaviors are. The first step in this exercise, which was developed by Richard Stuart, asks you to identify exactly what *you* think those behaviors are.

PART ONE

1. Ask yourself: Exactly what could my partner *do* that would show me that he or she cares?

2. Separately and without consulting each other, you and your partner are to list twelve acts that the other person could perform to show caring. Make sure each item is:

> **a.** Positive and constructive ("Ask me how I spent my day," rather than "Don't ignore me so much.")
>
> **b.** Specific and easily understood ("Clear the table and do the dinner dishes," rather than "Help around the house.")
>
> **c.** A small act that will not consume a great deal of time and could be done on a daily basis
>
> **d.** Nonproblematic (something that has not been the subject of recent conflicts; for instance, if you have been arguing for months about helping around the house or parenting, any requests, even very specific ones, for that sort of help may be misinterpreted and should *not* be included)
>
> **e.** Nonsexual—for now, none of your requests or rewards should involve sex. Do not confuse sex and affection, however. "Have intercourse with me" is off-limits but hugs, massages, and "Kiss me goodbye before leaving for work in the morning" are not.

3. If you have trouble thinking of twelve caring behaviors, here are some examples to get you started: Ask about my day; give me a hug when you get home from work; call during the day; bring me flowers or a little gift; send me a card or leave me a little note saying something positive; fold the laundry; rub my neck; make a dinner or dessert I really like; ask me what restaurant or movie I want to go to; bring me a cup of coffee to drink while I get ready for work; play with the kids when I get a phone call or one of my friends drops by; tell me I look pretty or attractive.

4. When both of you have completed your lists, share them and negotiate. Each of you has the right to refuse to do something that makes you uncomfortable or that you think asks too much of you. *However,* you and your partner must come up with an alternative so that there are twelve do-able items on each of your lists.

5. Post your lists on the refrigerator door or the bathroom wall or anyplace else where they can easily be seen.

PART TWO

1. Do four items from your partner's list *every day* (and your partner should do four items from your list). You can do more than four caring behaviors if you want to, but *not* to one-up your partner. This is not a contest to see who cares more.

2. To break the habit of acting positively only *after* your partner has done something positive, do these things whether or not your partner makes similar gestures. Don't wait to see who goes first. Take responsibility for what you do, not what your partner doesn't do.

3. Do them without expecting to be thanked, rewarded, or even acknowledged each time you show that you care.

4. Do them even if you do not *feel* caring. We are not asking you to be dishonest. We recognize that you may feel a good deal more hurt, anger, and resentment than positive regard right now. Nonetheless, this exercise asks you to act *as if* you care, to give and receive positive gestures so that you can once again become aware that there is more to you, your partner, and your relationship. than the problems you have. The final step of this exercise enables you to pay more attention to those positives.

PART THREE

1. Keep a record of the caring that you *receive*, not to keep score, but to remain aware of—and acknowledge—the caring things your partner does for you each day. Use a sheet of ledger paper or draw a chart that lists the caring behaviors you requested in the left-hand column and has narrow columns filling the remainder of the page. At the top of each column write the date, and then check off each of the ways your partner has shown caring that day. You can do this at the end of the day, although at first you may want to mark your chart throughout the day.

2. Once a week or so, look over your record to remind yourself of what your partner has done to show caring, and take note of any items that may have been overlooked. You are *not* to compare what you have done to what your partner has done. However, if there is some caring behavior you really want to see but have not been getting, you are responsible for asking—in a gentle, nonaccusatory way—if there is a reason that item has been neglected and if your partner could try to do that particular behavior during the upcoming week.

The Caring Days Exercise can produce an immediate change in the emotional ambience of your relationship. It may not be a dramatic change. It probably won't solve all your problems. But after injecting caring gestures and positive behaviors into your daily interactions, you will notice shifts in attitude that pave the way for the change effort that lies ahead.

Cooperating Instead of Competing over Intimacy

If you and your partner have a tendency to engage in power struggles over anything from child rearing to who initiates sex, if you feel that there is an imbalance of give-and-take, or if you frequently find yourselves in a closeness-distance tug-of-war, this next exercise may help change things. It teaches you how to share power and control in an intimate relationship by allowing you to take turns being the ultimate authority—on alternating days of the week.

But more important by far, it enables you to become more comfortable with your need for closeness, identify how you want that need met, communicate your intimacy needs to your partner, make requests, and experience the positive aspects of both giving and receiving.

ODD DAY/EVEN DAY EXERCISE

1. Divide the days of the week between you. One of you gets Monday, Wednesday, and Friday, while the other gets Tuesday, Thursday, and Saturday. Sunday belongs to no one. On Sunday you are free to relate to each other in whatever way you'd like. On your days, you are in charge of the intimacy in your relationship and you are to make *one intimacy request,* which your partner must satisfy. On the other days, your partner makes the request and you fulfill it.

An **intimacy request** is something that you and your partner can do together or that your partner can do for you and that allows you to feel close and emotionally connected to each other. The request must, of course, be *specific and reasonable.* For instance, asking your partner to "adore" you is obviously too general. It is also unreasonable, since no one should be expected to produce an internal emotional state like adoration upon demand. More appropriate requests might be:

spending an hour talking about something that is troubling you, going for a walk together, helping you decide how to handle a problem co-worker, letting you plan where to go and what to do during an evening on the town, or going to the mall with you to pick out new curtains for the living room.

2. Your intimacy request for the day should be identified as such so that your partner knows that is is the one he or she has agreed in advance to fulfill. This is nonnegotiable.

The person in charge *must* make that one request on that day. We emphasize this point because "distancers" and traditionally less powerful partners may "forget" or resist doing it.

Regardless of whose day it is, you or your partner can make other intimacy requests. *However,* neither of you is obliged to respond positively to those other requests.

3. ADDING REQUESTS: Once you get used to making and fulfilling one intimacy request a day, you can add requests, with the person in charge making more than one request per day. These requests must still be identified as such and be satisfied by the person who is not in control on that day. Other requests can be made by either partner, but need not be honored.

There is no upper limit to the number of requests you can make. However, we advise you to:

- become comfortable with the Odd Day/Even Day process before increasing requests
- discuss and agree on increasing requests
- keep those requests specific and reasonable
- remain sensitive to the timing and phrasing of your requests. If you ask for intimacy at a time when your partner cannot comfortably oblige, or ask in a way that provokes anger, guilt, or resentment, you are not doing this exercise in the spirit in which it was intended to be done

LEARNING TO SAY NO

While focusing on the positive, asking for and receiving caring gestures, and sharing responsibility for getting closer are all essential to building an intimate relationship, there are still going to be times when one partner wants and needs to say no. Unfortunately, most people (women in particular) find it difficult to do that—especially in sexual situations. In fact, as we pointed out previously, ISD may be how one of you avoids unwanted sex or intimacy without having to assert yourself.

Whether in the bedroom or outside of it, being unable to communicate openly and effectively your desire *not* to do something can lead to resentment, anger, anxiety, and other negative outcomes. If you can't assert your thoughts, feelings, and needs in your relationship, then you won't feel safe in it. What's more, when you or your partner cannot say no, you will find other ways not to do what is being requested (or to do it but punish your partner for making the request you could not refuse). You may instigate arguments, sulk, do tasks in a careless manner, explode over unrelated issues, or harbor resentments that you feel or air during every conflict. Needless to say, none of this will help you feel good about yourself or your partner, nor will it in any way enhance your sex life.

FAIR FIGHTING

To enhance your relationship and protect the intimate feelings that will rekindle sexual desire, you must begin to reduce counterproductive, win-lose and lose-lose conflicts.

You will never eliminate *all* conflict from your relationship. No one ever does. Working on your relationship will not change that reality. However, you *can* learn to prevent minor arguments from turning into full-scale battles. In short, you will still fight, but you can fight *fair*.

You are fighting fair when you both know what your are fighting about, when you have identified a specific issue and focused your discussion on that issue and that issue alone.

You are fighting fair when you employ the communication skills we described earlier in this chapter.

You are *not* fighting fair when you begin a discussion by attacking your partner or attempt to "win" the conflict at any point. For instance, if you were to say, "You don't care about anyone but yourself," your partner would probably feel compelled to point out all the things he or she has ever done for you to counter your blanket indictment. Your partner might reply, "I do plenty of things to show I care. The real problem is that you're never satisfied. You never appreciate anything I do." Getting off the track in this way will get you absolutely nowhere except more deeply embroiled in conflict. Remember, when you attack, you invite counterattack.

You are definitely *not* fighting fair if violence of any kind occurs or is threatened. When actual battering of either partner takes place or objects are thrown or shattered, an unhealthy, counterproductive, and downright dangerous conflict is occurring. Verbal abuse like name calling is also against the rules for fair fighting. If your fights involve violence or invariably degenerate into verbal abuse, you should seek professional help.

Whether or not you are aware of it during the actual argument, a fair fight has *not* taken place if the problem was not really resolved or if either partner feels cheated or resentful.

A fair fight:

- ends with each partner having a better understanding of the other's feelings and point of view
- leads to a negotiated compromise in which both partners get some of what they originally wanted or needed
- moves partners closer to solving the problem instead of attempting to bury it or deal with it in a way that hurts one of them

You will be more likely to fight fair if you think before you speak, asking yourself:

1. What is *really* bothering me? (And is it something other than the issue I was about to raise?)

2. How do I *feel* about this situation?

3. What do I want to accomplish? (And what am I willing to give in order to get more of what I want?)

4. What is my part in this problem? What have I contributed to this situation?

5. Is there anything my partner can actually do about this situation? (If not, there may be no point in arguing about it.)

6. Is this a good time to discuss it?

7. Have we discussed this before? And if we have, what can I do differently this time so that we won't have to go through this again?

8. Do I really want to solve the problem or do I just want to fight or hurt my partner? (*And if the latter is true, go back to the first two questions and figure out what is really going on.*)

By going through this process rather than simply launching into an argument, you and your partner will discover that your discussions are less emotionally charged, more likely to result in win-win outcomes, and unlikely to escalate or be repeated over and over again.

DEALING WITH DYSFUNCTIONAL AND DUELING LIFESTYLES

Role overload, feeling there are more demands on you than time to meet them, stress, and high expectations are facts of life for dual-career couples and career-oriented individuals. As you may recall, these factors increase the likelihood that these driven and often emotionally depleted couples will experience sexual problems, including ISD. We will discuss each of these factors below, but first please accept the fact that if you are part of a dual-career couple, your sex life simply will not improve until you establish a compatible, cooperative lifestyle to replace the dysfunctional one you now have. Many of the suggestions and exercises we have already provided can help you do that, but we encourage you to take advantage of other resources as well. These include individual and marital therapy, stress management courses, relaxation training tapes, parenting classes for dual-career couples, and books, such as those we recommend in the Bibliography as well as the many self-help texts on stress and time management.

The following guidelines and exercises are specifically for dual-career relationships. However, they can all be applied to more traditional relationships (with one breadwinner) and other relationships that would benefit from stress reduction, role overload reduction, better time management, and learning how to say no.

Role Overload

Both partners in a dual-career relationship wear many hats, attempting to meet the demands of a number of different roles. Although these roles may or may not conflict with each other, they almost always *compete* for a "fair share" of your time and attention.

The primary roles assumed by members of dual-career couples are:

- a work/professional role
- parent
- home life manager (including housekeeper, cook, etc.)
- socializer
- partner in a relationship
- individual (with independent interests and needs for time alone)

You may play other roles as well. You may be a student, for instance, or you may devote a portion of your time to caring for an aging parent. Regardless of the specific roles you play, what percentage of your time do you devote to each of your roles?

For the next weeks, keep a diary—jotting down what you

do and how much time you spend doing it. Once you have a general ideal of how you actually use your time, create a pie chart by drawing a circle and dividing it into sections that represent the portions of a "typical" day that you devote to your various roles. Here is the pie chart Judy drew.

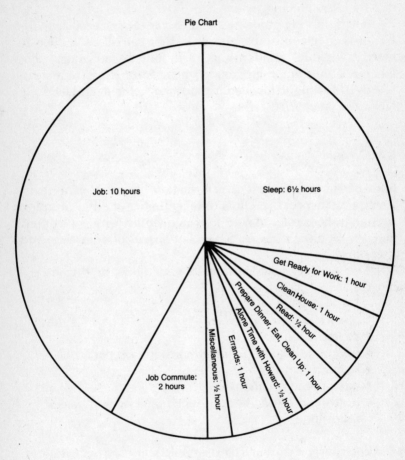

Pie Chart

Job: 10 hours

Sleep: 6½ hours

Get Ready for Work: 1 hour

Clean House: 1 hour

Read: ½ hour

Prepare Dinner, Eat, Clean Up: 1 hour

Alone Time with Howard: ½ hour

Errands: 1 hour

Miscellaneous: ½ hour

Job Commute: 2 hours

As you can see, Judy devoted a minuscule percentage of her time and attention to her role as Howard's partner and no time at all to herself. This is quite typical for members of dual-career couples. You may have noticed it in your own pie chart as well.

In order to improve your relationship and your sex life, you will have to change your priorities and find time for these roles, because they are the ones that have the greatest impact on sexual desire and satisfaction. Since adding more hours to the day is not an option, the only way you will be able to pay more attention to your partner and yourself is to pay *less* attention to something else.

Chances are that your first reaction to that statement is to gasp, "But how can I do that? Everything I already do is important too!" We do not deny that. However, we firmly believe that if you take a closer look at how you spend your time, you will discover that you actually can let go of or share some of the responsibilities that accompany your roles, both reducing the strain of role overload and freeing up time to devote to yourself and your relationship.

FINDING TIME EXERCISE

1. List each of the roles you play on paper, leaving approximately ten lines of space after each role.

2. Now, under each heading, list the tasks and demands that go along with that role and that are now your responsibilities. If you need more space, use the back of the page or another sheet of paper.

For instance, under "home life manager" you might list: preparing meals, grocery shopping, doing the laundry, paying household bills, mowing the lawn, and so on—if these are jobs you actually do. If "home life manager" is a secondary role for you, try not to pad your list with references to helping your partner with his or her responsibilities. Household chores that you do only when asked and not on a regular, voluntary basis do not cause role overload. Indeed, you may have to do *more* in these areas in order to have more time with your partner.

3. Go back over your list and *check off* the items that *you and only you* must do. These should be the tasks you would not consider asking anyone else to do or help you do.

If you check off every item, something is wrong. Go over the list and ask yourself *why* this task has to be your responsibility alone. Look for excuses that are maintaining your role overload—like "I'm the only one who does this the right way," or "A good mother, (breadwinner, etc.) does these things," or "People would think less of me if I didn't do this." Unless absolutely no one else in the entire universe could handle this demand, or unless you would feel dreadful about giving it up or sharing it (spending an hour before bedtime with your children might fall into that category), erase your check mark.

4. Write the letter *P* next to any responsibility that your partner could assume or share with you at least some of the time.

5. Place the letter *O* next to any task you could delegate to someone *other* than your partner, ask for anyone's assistance with, or pay someone to do. Then write that person's name or job title (e.g., cleaning lady, gardener) next to that item.

6. Finally, place an *X* beside any checked or unchecked item that would consume less time and energy *if you lowered your expectations* about how the demand gets met. For instance, you might buy time if you stopped expecting to spend every waking weekend hour with your children or if you gave up the self-imposed demand to clean the house the night before your cleaning lady is supposed to come in. You might find time if you did not feel you had to work out *every* day in order to stay physically fit or if you accepted the fact that you could be just as successful if you spent eight or nine hours a day at work instead of ten or twelve.

7. Now, with these ideas in mind, list seven role-strain reduction efforts you would like to try during the next few months. You can get some ideas from this list, which Judy made:

- I will be responsible for cooking dinner no more than three nights each week.
- On the nights I cook, I'll ask Howard to do the dishes—and promise not to criticize the way he does the job.
- At least two nights each week, I will not bring work home.
- I will send Howard's shirts to the laundry instead of trying to wash and iron them myself.
- I will do the weekly grocery shopping and let Howard be responsible for picking up anything we need or run out of during the week.
- I will let the children spend two Saturday afternoons each month with their grandparents (one with my parents and one with Howard's).
- I will have our cleaning lady come in twice a week instead of once and let her clean instead of doing it myself the night before.

8. After you make your list, figure out how much time you will save and decide how you will use it, preferably for yourself and your relationship.

9. Then draw up another pie chart, representing the way you now *want* to allocate your time. Remember that you will not make these time and role changes overnight and that this pie represents the goal you will work toward.

At least some of the changes you would like to make will require your partner's cooperation. We recommend that you

and your partner share and discuss your present pie charts and
the ones you would like to work toward. Pay particular attention to the differences in your priorities, especially if one of you
wants more partner time than the other. Try not to use your pie
or your list of responsibilities as ammunition against a partner
who is obviously not doing a fair share in some area. Instead,
use the Goal-Setting Strategy found in the last chapter as well as
your newly developed communication skills to make exchanges
and reach compromises. If you get stuck—either because your
partner will not cooperate or because you are unwilling to let go
of various role demands—get help.

Additional Time Management Tips

1. Watch out for perfectionism. You must recognize
that thinking, "If I want something done right, I have to do
it myself," adds to your role overload. It is less indicative of
reality than of your need to maintain control, since what
you may really be saying is "If I want something done *my
way*, I have to do it myself." What you give up in quality
pays enormous dividends in time and emotional energy.

2. Prioritize. Many of us tend to consider all of our
responsibilities to be of equal importance, when in fact they
are not. There is invariably at least one task we could let
slide without suffering dire consequences. On a daily basis,
when you list the things you want to accomplish, give them
A, B, and C ratings, with A's restricted to the demands you
absolutely must meet before the end of the day, B's going
to tasks you would like to accomplish (but the world would
not end if you did not get them done), and C's to items that
could easily be done another day. And don't sabotage yourself by giving everything an A rating.

3. Set limits for the amount of time you will spend on
things like housecleaning, ironing, reading professional
journals, balancing your checkbook, yard work, visiting
your in-laws, and other B and C tasks. When that time is
up, stop. But more important, let go of that task psycho-

logically. Tell yourself that you did as much as you could during the time you had, and then *stop thinking about it.*

4. Learn and employ specific time-saving techniques. If you already use these measures in the workplace, you can simply incorporate them into the rest of your life. Or you can turn to the many books, magazine articles, and seminars on this topic, which are readily available.

Stress Reduction

In addition to creating conflict and emotional depletion, role overload and ineffective time management can also add to the stress dual-career couples already experience. And as we have pointed out in several other chapters of this book, the higher your stress level, the lower your sexual desire and satisfaction are likely to be. Therefore, it makes sense to reduce stress. To do this, we recommend that you:

1. Develop outside support systems. Expecting your partner to be there for you and single-handedly replenish the emotional energy you expend meeting the many demands in your life is unreasonable, especially if your partner is pressured and exhausted too. When you need someone to listen, commiserate, offer options, cheer you up, or otherwise provide emotional support, consider turning to friends, relatives, colleagues, support groups, or professional therapists—at least some of the time.

2. Try to pinpoint what you actually need whenever turning to another person for support, and especially when you want emotional nourishment from your partner. The more specific you are, the more likely you will get that kind of support without overburdening your partner or another support resource. Types of support include physical help (with chores, transportation, child care, and so on), active listening and the opportunity to air your feelings, encouragement, positive statements about your good qualities and reminders of your past successes to boost your self-esteem and self-confidence, information and ideas, guidance, and a collaborative effort to solve a problem.

3. Develop and engage in transition activities that enable you to switch gears when you switch roles. For instance, your mindset or behavior in the workplace is *not* the same one you need to relate to your children or partner. Yet none of us can effectively change our focus instantaneously. There is no switch we can flip to go directly from driven professional to patient parent to caring partner and so on. Consequently, anything that you can do—taking a walk, reading the newspaper, listening to music, meditating, sitting quietly over a cup of tea, or working out—before putting on a hat that is distinctly different from the one you were wearing earlier will reduce the stress associated with thoughts from one world bleeding through into another.

4. Exercise. This not only allows you to release tension physically, but actually creates a biochemical change that leads to an overall sense of relaxation and emotional well-being.

5. Employ specific relaxation techniques like deep-muscle relaxation exercises, meditation, biofeedback, visualization, and others that you can learn from self-help books, audio tapes, and stress management courses—all of which are readily available.

Finally, you can reduce stress by developing a more positive self-image, which can be done by taking steps to cut down on negative self-talk. Pay more attention to your good points and revise your expectations for yourself, your body, and your sexuality so that you no longer think you have to be perfect in order to be good enough. Those steps, which are vital to reigniting sexual desire and improving your sexual relationship, are the subject of the next section of this chapter.

FEELING BETTER ABOUT YOURSELF

Before and after you and your partner begin working together to improve your relationship, you may need to work on yourself as well. You will need to take the necessary steps to reinstitute your personal conditions for sexual desire and satisfaction, including feeling good about yourself and your body. Just as your relationship must be stable and strong enough to support and integrate the changes that the sexual self-help exercises in the next chapter will create, your internal psychological state must be one that is likely to accept and seek out positive change.

Shedding Old Ideas About Yourself to Make Room for New Ones

Some of the greatest obstacles to positive feelings about yourself are the negative thoughts you think, the negative self-talk you bombard yourself with, and the "old tapes" that you replay in new situations. We have already explained how this negative thinking works. You have even eavesdropped on people like Rachel, who talks herself out of sexual desire by telling herself that sex is not worth the hassles that come with it. Then there's Al, who both increases his anxiety by reminding himself of his past sexual failures and shuts down sexual desire by distracting himself with extraneous thoughts; and Ed, who found that intrusive thoughts about aging and his wife's body automatically drained him of sexual desire.

We all are plagued by similarly negative and self-defeating thoughts from time to time and in situations other than sexual ones. Whether you think, "I'll never get the promotion I want," or "I hate my thighs," or "I'm not capable of making it on my own, so I'll just have to stay in this marriage no matter what," the negative things you tell yourself about yourself:

- chip away at your self-esteem
- keep you from noticing or appreciating the positive aspects of who you are
- increase anxiety and fuel your fears, convincing you to avoid countless situations—which could actually prove that you are more lovable and capable than you think
- convince you that you don't deserve a better relationship

or sex life; that you are stuck with the problems you now have and that they are, in fact, your just desserts for somehow being deficient in the first place.

The most important thing to recognize about negative self-talk is that it was not *created* by you, but it is *probably* sustained by you. It may represent some aspect of reality. For instance, most of us really won't be asked to appear on the cover of *Vogue* or a body-building magazine. Or your self-talk may represent an old reality—something that was true when you were a child or in previous relationships. Or it may have nothing to do with reality at all, like believing that people will reject you if they discover you are not as independent as you seem, or that your spouse's ISD is a sign of an affair. Regardless, you take whatever "facts" you do have, distort them, and use them against yourself. *You do not have to do that.* In fact, you should and can stop doing it right now.

Begin by identifying your own negative and self-defeating thoughts. Although your self-deprecation may be worded in many different ways, you can start to pinpoint your negative thinking by writing a dozen sentences beginning with:

I AM NOT. . .

You can write more than a dozen if you get on a roll. But don't go overboard, depressing yourself with all that negativity. Address general issues as well as sexual ones, but make sure that some of your sentences are aimed at your body image, sexuality, and ability to get involved in or maintain a satisfying intimate relationship.

Then look at the value judgments you make—the standards of comparison that you use to condemn yourself or that increase your anxiety in various situations, including sexual ones. This time write six to twelve sentences reflecting your own beliefs and beginning with:

"GOOD GIRLS" DON'T . . .
"REAL MEN" DON'T . . .

Figure out where these perceptions originated. Nine times out of ten, negative self-talk and inhibiting moral judgments reflect messages you once received from other people, messages that you internalized and now tell yourself. It is as if you recorded certain ideas that other people presented to you and now replay that old tape over and over again—whether or not it actually applies to the realities of your life today.

Whose voices are on your tape? Is it your mother saying, "That's dirty and disgusting—don't ever touch yourself down there"? Is it your father saying, "You idiot, if you can't do it right the first time, don't do it at all"? Your teachers saying, "You're not trying hard enough; your laziness is going to be your downfall"? Your priest warning you that "lust is the deadliest of the seven deadly sins"? An old lover who told you, "You're a sorry excuse for a lover. I've never in my entire life met anyone who is as uptight as you are"? Or media images reminding you that you are not as sexy, macho, organized, or in control as you are supposed to be?

With these examples in mind, go through your list and jot down the source of your negative self-talk and your rigid moral standards, including messages you heard in the past and images that come to mind when you consider these aspects of yourself.

Now, here are some provocative thoughts for you to consider: You are not the person you were when you received those messages—not only are your circumstances different than they were then, but you have also grown and changed as a result of your life experiences. Those messages may have been inaccurate or completely untrue when you received them, and even if they were true then, they may not apply to you now. YOU ARE AN ADULT and you can *choose* what to believe about yourself and your sexuality. You can give yourself permission to *talk back to your old tapes.*

Take some time to do that now. Choose a few "I am not . . ." or "Good girls/Real men don't . . ." statements and, in your mind or out loud, *talk back* to them. For instance, you might say, "Mom, I know you probably meant well when you told me good girls (or boys) don't touch or look at their own or other people's genitals because they're disgusting and dirty, but that was never really true. I don't want it to be a part of my sexuality now. There is really nothing wrong with touching or having someone touch my genitals. In fact, if I didn't keep thinking about what you said, it might even feel good. I have the right to feel good. . . ."

Actually contradicting your negative self-talk or rejecting the ideas found on your old tapes may make you nervous or uncomfortable at first. In fact, you may find it difficult to believe your own words. But keep practicing and you will discover that those self-defeating attitudes no longer have so strong a hold on your self-esteem or your sexuality.

In the meantime, we suggest that you try the following technique to cut negative self-talk off at the pass, especially if negative thoughts and images intrude upon you at inopportune moments—including sexual ones.

THOUGHT-STOPPING TECHNIQUE

This technique is based on the simple and logical principle that none of us can consciously focus on more than one thought at a time. You may be well aware of this already, since *negative* thoughts have been interfering with your positive ones or intruding when you start feeling sexually aroused—preventing you from responding to sexual cues or paying attention to pleasurable sensations. The Thought-Stopping Technique allows you to reverse that process, by saying or thinking "STOP!" or visualizing a stop sign when unwanted thoughts come to mind.

TRY IT OUT

Focus your attention on a self-defeating or unproductive thought. You can use one of the sentences from the previous exercise if you'd like. Once that thought is clearly in your mind, imagine a voice shouting "STOP!" or say it out loud. Then close your eyes and take a deep breath. Consider conjuring up an image of someone or someplace that makes you feel calm and secure.

Open your eyes and focus your attention on something else. Write a letter, read a magazine article, do a household chore or a work-related task, balance your checkbook, or make a phone call. If the negative thought returns, start over, beginning with "STOP!"

USE IT WHEN YOU NEED IT

The more you practice this technique, the more adept you will become at using it. At first it will seem awkward, even weird to you. Soon enough, however, you will be able to use it to silence recurrent self-defeating or intrusive thoughts. Allow yourself to silence them by softly whispering "Stop," or visualizing a stop sign.

Self-Affirmations: How to Think More Positively

Finally, your mind may be full of negative thoughts because you have too few positive ones. You have spent so many years viewing your cup as half empty that you don't notice that it's also half full. Indeed, you may have convinced yourself that you have no positive attributes or very few of them, when in fact you have merely been overlooking them. Just as you cannot focus on the word *stop* and continue thinking the same thought, you cannot think positively and negatively at the same time. The trick is to accumulate an ample supply of positive *affirmations,* which you can use to counter or replace negative thoughts when they appear in your mind.

Identify your good points. Chances are that this will be considerably more difficult to accomplish than listing your negative perceptions of yourself. But give it a try. Write twenty—yes, twenty—sentences describing your positive attributes. These need not be major accomplishments, saintly qualities, or outstanding physical features. In fact, to get yourself started you may even have to come up with characteristics that you think are "not bad." These sentences might even start with "I am a good. . ." (for your general effectiveness) or "I have attractive or acceptable. . ." (for your body image).

Hang on to this list. You may even want to make copies of it, so that you can post them in your home and your office as well as carrying one with you.

Review your list. Every morning before you begin your day or every evening before you go to sleep, read the entire list. Read it slowly and thoughtfully so that each sentence can really sink in. If you receive compliments or achieve successes during the day, use these experiences to add to your list. You may even want to read these self-affirmations out loud. If you start trying to contradict your affirmations, use the Thought-Stopping Technique to clear your mind before you focus on your positive traits again. In addition, you may want to review your list or repeat specific affirmations whenever you are feeling down or to boost your confidence before entering an anxiety-provoking situation.

If you follow the suggestions and practice the exercises included in this chapter, you and your partner will build a solid foundation for reigniting sexual desire and improving your sexual relationship. What's more, you will develop skills and attitudes that will enable you to complete and benefit from the sexual self-help strategies that you find in the next—and final—chapter of this book.

CHAPTER EIGHT

Reigniting Sexual Desire: Sexual Enhancement Exercises for Individuals and Couples

IN THIS CHAPTER, you will find self-help strategies for increasing both sexual desire and sexual satisfaction. Many of these exercises are the tried and true components of sex therapy—the homework assignments that sex therapists give their patients. Of course, you do not have to be receiving treatment from a sex therapist in order to benefit from the techniques.

However, there are certain advantages to having a competent therapist work with you as you complete these exercises, especially if one or both partners do not "follow directions" or become anxious or otherwise emotionally distressed. A therapist would then be able to help individuals or couples explore the reasons for their reactions, often discovering the underlying causes of ISD in the process. We will cite some of the pitfalls you may encounter while doing certain exercises, explaining what specific adverse reactions might mean and recommending alternative courses of action. However, if you get stuck and are unable to get past an obstacle even after several attempts, we advise you to seek professional help. Please realize that encountering tenacious obstacles or needing professional assistance does *not* mean that you failed. In fact, you might say you succeeded in revealing the fire burning behind the smokescreen, but need help putting it out.

And while we are on the topic of success and failure, let us emphasize that it is *imperative* to look upon all of the following exercises as *opportunities to learn* rather than as tests you must pass or goals you can achieve or fail to achieve. Please keep in mind that you are not doing the sexual enhancement exercises in order to collect trophies or get an A on some imaginary report card. You are, we hope, gathering information that will help you and your sexual relationship flourish.

SEXUAL SELF-AWARENESS

Because of early prohibitions, chances are that you never had an opportunity to become familiar and comfortable with your own body or to discover what feels good sexually. If you can begin to do that now, you increase the likelihood of feeling secure and comfortable during sex with a partner.

To begin this process, we suggest that you start by taking a close, objective look at your genitals in the privacy of a comfortable, well-lit location that is warm enough for you to be able to recline nude or seminude. With the aid of a hand-held mirror, examine your genitals, looking at them from various angles. Women will have to use one hand to part the outer vaginal lips, exposing the parts of their anatomy that are usually hidden from view. Both men and women may want to refer to the drawings on pages 285 and 288 in order to locate the various parts labeled on the drawings.

You may wonder why anyone in his or her right mind would want to do this. The answer is really quite simple. Your genitals are a part of you. They are as much a part of you as your eyes, your teeth, your hair, or any other part of your anatomy that you look at every day. Yet you may—thanks to your past programming—perceive your genitals as mysterious, baffling, bothersome, unattractive, repulsive, or as if they were not really part of you at all. When such an attitude carries over into sexual situations, as it so often does, you are more likely to feel "disconnected" from sexual activity or anxious and uncomfortable during sex.

Your genitals are neither dirty nor disgusting and you have a right to know exactly what they look like. But you probably received messages to the contrary, and when you so much as think about looking at your sexual organs, old prohibitive messages are likely to echo in your head. If this happens to you, we encourage you to talk back or use the Thought-Stopping Technique described on page 232.

It's important to examine your genitals visually in order to accept finally that *your* sexual organs are good enough the way they are. Just as having a big nose or a small one does not affect your breathing or your sense of smell, the different ways genitals look do *not* affect what they can do or the pleasurable sensations they can produce. And the simple truth is that although everyone has the same parts, each person's genitals look different.

If you are a man, you have probably spent a lifetime being victimized by your ideas about what constitutes "good" genitals and a "good" penis in particular. You may find your penis lacking because of its length, width, angles—you name it. But none of these things makes any real difference to your sexuality, especially when you recognize that the size of an erect penis, regardless of its size when not erect, varies little from man to man. Don't create problems by worrying needlessly, stirring up anxiety, and giving in to negative self-talk that says your penis, for one reason or another, is not good enough the way it is. Accept the fact that you can't change it, nor do you need to, because it wouldn't change you or your sexuality. What you see really is good enough just the way it is and can provide you with a great deal of pleasure.

To increase sexual self-awareness, you will need to do more than look at your genitals, however. Even if you have been sexually active for decades, you will have to train yourself to focus on pleasurable sensations and learn more about what *your* sexual arousal feels like. To date, you may have engaged in

sexual activity without fully tuning in to the pleasurable sensations it produces. Indeed, you may be convinced that the only
significant sexual sensation is an orgasm, but actually there is
much, much more to feel than that.

To become more aware of your sexual responses and the
types of stimulation you most enjoy—without feeling pressure
to perform or please a sexual partner—self-pleasuring is recommended. Set aside some time—at least thirty minutes—and
then:

1. Undress and get comfortable in the privacy of your
own home.

2. Relax and get in the mood through fantasy, by re-
membering pleasant sexual experiences, or by using erotic
books, pictures, or films.

3. In whatever way pleases you, stroke and caress your
body, focusing on the pleasurable sensations you feel and
noticing any increases in sexual arousal. Allow yourself to
touch areas of your body that have previously received
little, if any, attention.

4. Then touch, stroke, and stimulate your genitals. A
lubricant might enhance your exploration. Lubricants include massage oil, baby oil, saliva, or, for women, the natural lubrication of the vagina. DO NOT USE products that
are not water soluble, such as Vaseline, or products that
contain alcohol. Both types can be irritating and harmful.

5. TAKE YOUR TIME. Experiment with different
strokes, pressures, speeds, and areas of your body. *Pay
attention to what you feel at each moment.* Do not think ahead
or push yourself to reach orgasm.

In fact, you do not have to have an orgasm at all. If you are
approaching orgasm before the end of a thirty-minute self-
pleasuring session, we recommend that you stop stimulating
yourself until your arousal has diminished. There is no pressure for men to have erections or for men or women to have
orgasms, although you can if you want to. Try to think of
self-pleasuring as a way to learn what feels good to you and to

tune in to different levels of sexual arousal, so that you will ultimately become an expert on your own sexual pleasure. You can both enjoy that expertise alone and share it with your partner to increase your pleasure.

The first obstacle you are apt to encounter when attempting to increase sexual self-awareness through self-pleasuring is negative self-talk, yet again. This is especially likely if you have deeply held religious convictions or old tapes of negative self-talk that prohibit masturbation. If you can't reconcile those old messages with your desire for sexual growth and learning, skip the self-touching exercise.

Let us assure you, however, that by encouraging you to touch your genitals we are not trying to tell you that your beliefs about masturbation are good or bad, or that masturbation itself is necessarily good for you. We are simply offering you a way to learn how your body responds to sexual stimulation.

Once you permit yourself to engage in self-pleasuring, you may encounter other barriers. For instance, you may get bored, frustrated, or anxious, especially if you have never masturbated before or expect intense sexual arousal instantaneously. Don't give up if you are initially disappointed. Focus on the pleasure you did experience and build from there. Remember, this is a learning and growth process, not a test. If you experience negative reactions or thoughts, try thought stopping or relaxed breathing, or focus on a soothing fantasy. If you become extremely anxious or upset, discontinue the exercise and try again another day.

If you are a woman who has not had orgasms in the past or has not reached orgasm through self-stimulation, you may stop stimulating yourself just before you reach orgasm because you get "jumpy" or feel "different" physical sensations. In many instances, you are experiencing sensations that are actually intense arousal—and you can simply practice self-pleasuring so that you can become more comfortable with and accepting of this new, unfamiliar feeling. If you feel physical pain while masturbating, you may not have sufficient lubrication or you may be providing too much stimulation to sensitive areas, such as your clitoris. Switch your touching to another area of your body and vary the stroke. Intense stimulation can also cause the clitoris to become numb. Again, touch another area of your body and clitoral sensation should return.

If you consistently feel physical pain, we advise a gynecological exam to determine if some sort of physical problem exists. And if you feel no physical sensation (other than the clitoral numbness described above), you may want to seek the assistance of a sex therapist, who, upon hearing a description of how you self-stimulate or what you think while masturbating, may be able to suggest specific steps for you to take.

For both men and women, actually feeling nothing at all is uncommon. But many people do feel disappointed because "the earth didn't move" or "there weren't any fireworks." Such disappointment is simply the price you pay for lofty expectations rather than a sign of sexual problems. If you find yourself feeling disappointed, the next time you do this exercise try thinking more about what you *are* feeling instead of what you think you are *supposed to be* feeling.

It's not unusual to find your attention wavering during your early attempts at this exercise. When you catch your mind wandering, simply bring your attention back to your genitals and your bodily sensations. However, if your mind wanders to thoughts that dramatically reduce your arousal or replace good feelings with anger, anxiety, fear, or disgust, try the Thought-Stopping Technique on page 232.

And finally, if you are too tense and hurried to get into the exercise, we recommend doing some work on stress and time management. This should include engaging in transition activities so you can switch gears *before* you begin self-pleasuring.

To further increase sexual self-awareness, you may want to improve your understanding of male, female, and partner sexuality in general. We believe that as long as you are careful not to use new information as another way to pressure yourself to be a sexual superstar, the more sexual knowledge you have, the better off (and less anxious) you will be. There are numerous helpful books available at your local library or bookstore, including three we often recommend to our clients: *Male Sexuality* by Bernie Zilbergeld, Ph.D., and *For Yourself* and *For Each Other* by Lonnie Barbach, Ph.D.

REIGNITING YOUR SEXUAL DESIRE

In addition to becoming more aware of how you feel when you are turned on, being able to identify *what* turns you on will benefit you and your sex life. The following exercises can help you discover what ignites your sexual desire and how to fan the flames of your sexual excitement.

As Lonnie Barbach points out in her book *For Each Other,* "If you can ascertain what activities or circumstances *do* stimulate your sexual desire, you are in a position to capitalize on these occurrences—and even plan for them." With this goal in mind, the next exercise asks you to take notice and keep track of the sexual thoughts, feelings, and urges you do have—and what instigates them.

SEXUAL DESIRE DIARY EXERCISE

Like most of our ISD patients, because you do not feel *enough* sexual desire to motivate you to seek out, become receptive to, or engage in sexual activity, you may assume that you really do not have sexual thoughts, feelings, or urges at all. This almost never proves to be true. If you pay close attention to your emotional state, you will discover that throughout any given week, you do indeed think about sex, feel sexual urges, or experience sensations that could be transformed into sexual arousal—from exhilaration after exercising to longing to be held and comforted. Time and time again, we have observed that if you look for signs of your own sexual desire, you will find them.

This exercise is also beneficial for higher-desire partners, who often learn that at least some of the time, their sexual desire is triggered by nonsexual needs that could be met in nonsexual ways. This reduces the pressure they place on their lower-desire partners, as well as reducing their own feelings of rejection and anger when sexual advances are rebuffed.

For at least one week, keep a sexual desire diary. Purchase a pocket-size notebook, carry it with you, and make a note in it each and every time you feel the slightest spark of sexual interest. Record sexual thoughts no matter how fleeting, sexual urges no matter how feeble they might seem, and any pleasurable sensations that you can in any way associate with sex.

Each entry should include the date, the time of day, what sparked your sexual desire, and how strong your sexual urge was on a scale of 1 to 10—with 1 indicating almost no excitement and 10 a very high degree of excitement. The following entry from Maggie's sexual desire diary will give you an idea of what we are asking you to do.

Wednesday, February 12

11 A.M. Watching photo shoot for tropical getaway feature. Lots of men in shorts and swimsuits—5.

Thursday, February 13

1 P.M. Heart and pulse racing, sweating after aerobics class—4.

3 P.M. Michael stopped by office, looking and smelling great, saying he missed me—7.

7 P.M. Candlelight, music, dinner waiting when I got home—6.

Friday, February 14

8 A.M. Michael walking around the bedroom naked—3.

10 A.M. Cocky young writer flirts with me—4.

noon Michael calls, talks dirty—3.

5 P.M. Get prints from Wednesday's photo shoot—2.

8 P.M. Steamy love scene in video we watch—6.

9 P.M. Michael suggests we reenact steamy love scene—4.

After faithfully keeping track of your sexual desire for at least one week, review your entries, asking yourself: What sorts of cues turn me on? Which trigger the highest level of sexual desire? How can I get the maximum benefit from the stimuli that excite me the most? How can I re-create these feelings or make sure these cues are there when my partner is present and interested in sex?

Your answers to these questions reveal the directions in which you can go to reignite your sexual desires.

Although by keeping a sexual desire diary you may find that you feel sexual urges and respond to sexual cues more often than you thought, you may also realize that you feel sexually excited *less* often than you would like to, respond to only a limited number and kind of cues, or barely register above a 2 or 3 on the scale of sexual interest. To increase your sexual desire, you must learn to tune in to more cues and to up the intensity of the desire you do feel. One way to do this is to conjure up and enjoy sexual fantasies.

Sexual Fantasies

If you have ISD, chances are that you rarely if ever indulge in sexual fantasy. If you learned that fantasizing about sex was bad or felt guilty when you thought about certain sexual activities, situations, or partners, this avenue for activating sexual desire may have been unavailable to you throughout your life. Or you may have stopped fantasizing at about the same time that you first experienced a dramatic drop in sexual interest. In either case, allowing yourself playfully to explore sexual fantasies helps you re-create in your mind the cues and circumstances you already know arouse you, as well as offering you new images and ideas to spark your sexual interest.

You may feel anxious or guilty about having sexual fantasies. Let us assure you that research has shown that fantasizing about sex—including fantasies about activities you do not want to carry out in real life or about people other than your partner—is not only a normal practice, but also a very common one. Imagining yourself having sex with a rock star or a magazine centerfold model or your best friend's spouse does not mean that you are betraying or feel less in love with your partner. You are simply being imaginative and playful. If you actually acted out your fantasies with these other partners, it would be a different story.

However, fantasizing about something is not the same as doing it or actually wanting to, and it does not even mean that you would act it out if you had the opportunity. All of us fantasize about things that we would never actually do—from quitting our jobs and running off to live on a deserted island, to punching out the boss or in-laws the next time they criticize us, to having sex on a train with a total stranger or being raped. In each and every instance, we control our fantasies. They do not control us.

In addition, you may tell yourself, "If anyone knew what I was thinking, they'd lock me up (or at the very least, think less of me)." But the truth is that no one does know what you think about when you fantasize, and no one can find out unless you talk about it. One of the most enjoyable aspects of fantasies is that they are private. There is no need to worry about being "good enough" in your fantasies, no one to please but yourself, no pressure to perform like a sexual superstar, and no one to judge you in any way.

Like some of our patients, you may worry that fantasizing will become so pleasurable and enticing that you will become "addicted" to what goes on in your own mind. While we cannot say that this *never* happens, the chances of it happening to you—or anyone with ISD—are extremely remote. Besides, we are not encouraging you to live in a fantasy world or use fantasies to *replace* sexual activity. Instead, we are giving you permission to use your imagination, to experiment with *ideas* and be playful.

Finally, if you have not fantasized in the past or your fantasies tend to be vague or unexciting, you may need a few ideas to get yourself started. Our patients have found it helpful to "borrow" the fantasies that appeal to them in Nancy Friday's books *My Secret Garden, Forbidden Flowers,* and *Men in Love,* as well as Lonnie Barbach and Linda Levine's *Women's Sexual Experiences* and "Penthouse Forum" in *Penthouse* magazine. If you consult these resources, please remember that they do not offer advice, but are simply collections of other people's fantasies intended to stimulate your imagination.

SEXUAL FANTASY EXERCISE

On at least five days this week, take two 5-minute breaks at some point during the day to fantasize about sex.

Do this in a location that feels safe and offers you privacy. Breathe deeply, relax, and clear your mind of other thoughts, shutting your eyes if you want to.

Then conjure up any sexual images that you find pleasing. Feel free to fantasize about anyone: your spouse or lover; someone you saw on TV, on the way to work, or at your office; or someone you used to date. You can imagine doing things you've never done, would never do, did when you were younger. You can drum up memories of past sexual experiences. You are limited only by your own imagination.

You may get sexually aroused by your fantasy or you may not. Either way, it's okay. And if you do become aroused, you need not do anything about it, other than allow yourself to enjoy the feeling.

After your five-minute fantasy is complete, if you found it pleasurable or arousing, make a mental note of it. You may want to explore it further the next time you fantasize, or recall it the next time you are in a sexual situation and want to increase your sexual desire.

New Sexual Stimuli

If you find it difficult to experience sexual desire spontaneously, you can increase sexual excitement and reawaken sexual desire by using such stimuli as sexually explicit books, magazines, films, and videos. This recommendation may seem to contradict what we said in earlier chapters about the unrealistic expectations and misconceptions you absorbed from romantic and erotic films and fiction. However, we are not suggesting that you use these materials as role models or idealized images of beauty or sexual adequacy. Instead we are offering you another source of sexual stimulation and arousal, and encouraging you to feel free and enjoy it.

In fact, you might look upon the use of sexual stimuli as an experiment, a pseudoscientific quest to figure out what sexually arouses you. Not everything you encounter will be appealing to you. Some things will stimulate minor sexual interest, while other visual representations or written descriptions will be highly arousing. As the subject of your own experiment, you are the only one who can decide what turns you on and what does not.

Of course, you may be repulsed by the very thought of watching a sexually explicit film, embarrassed by the prospect of purchasing a sexually explicit magazine, or unwilling even to consider reading erotic fiction. If this is the case, you may be listening to those old tapes again, the ones that tell you that good girls and boys don't look at "dirty pictures." You can choose to talk back to those tapes. On the other hand, you may be afraid you will get "hooked" on these materials. While people who have serious preexisting emotional problems or sexually addictive tendencies can become preoccupied with pornography, the vast majority of research on this subject shows that sexually explicit materials simply increase sexual desire and sexual activity *without* compelling people to engage in the behaviors they see or become obsessed with sex.

As you experiment with various sexual stimuli—which can include sexy lingerie, silk sheets, new settings, exotic fragrances, and oils, as well as sexually explicit materials—if you discover cues that are indeed arousing for you, enjoy them, and incorporate them into your fantasies. Then consider using them to trigger or intensify desire in real sexual situations, perhaps by reading or viewing sexually explicit material alone or with your partner prior to having sex.

SEXUAL ENHANCEMENT FOR COUPLES

Once you and your partner have agreed to work together, and you have already worked on feeling better about yourself, your body, and your sexuality, you are ready to participate in the following series of sexual enhancement exercises for couples with sexual desire difficulties.

However, you must first agree to a *ban on intercourse,* which is to last until you have completed the third exercise in this sequence (Sensate Focus II). Since your goal is to increase sexual desire and frequency of sex, why, you may ask, would you want to avoid intercourse? A ban on intercourse will:

- decrease the pressure to perform—which so often means pushing yourself to have an orgasm or valiantly trying to ensure that your partner has one
- decrease frustration with sexual activity (since there is no goal to achieve, you need not fear that you will fail to achieve it—which is the definition of frustration)
- result in a mutually agreed-upon truce in the persist-resist, pursuer-distancer battle that has been raging in

your relationship (both partners benefit from this truce, since the lower-desire partner will not be pressured to engage in intercourse and the higher-desire partner will not feel the sting of rejection that so often accompanies a sexual refusal)

- enable both you and your partner to focus on the exercises themselves. Since they are not tests that you can pass or fail, you are free to experience them, instead of worrying about success or failure. You and your partner will be able to focus on areas of your bodies that have been ignored or never fully explored.

Sensate Focus Exercises

Adapted from the ground-breaking work of Masters and Johnson, the following exercises enable couples to touch and be touched, discover what they enjoy giving and receiving, communicate their preferences, and respond to the feedback they receive—all of which are vital to sexual satisfaction.

Masters and Johnson originally developed two exercises—Sensate Focus I and II—but we have found that even Sensate I, with its nongenital focus, may be too anxiety provoking for partners who are extremely anxious about sex, who have been avoiding sex for a long time, or who have a good many conflicts and arguments about their sexual relationship. If you fit into one of these categories, or simply would like a warm-up exercise to ease into the sensate focus process, we offer the following modified Tame Touch Exercise.

TAME TOUCH EXERCISE

The purpose of this exercise is to use thirty minutes three times a week to become comfortable touching and being touched. This will begin the process of physically connecting or reconnecting with your partner in a nonsexual, nonthreatening way.

Before you begin, mutually agree upon the three times this week when you will do this exercise. Choose a setting that is as relaxing and comfortable as possible. We recommend wearing as little clothing as possible during this exercise, but also as much clothing as you need to feel comfortable. You can undress completely or wear undergarments or a robe.

Flip a coin to determine who will "give" first. You will switch after fifteen minutes and the giver is responsible for timekeeping.

The receiver tells the giver exactly which body parts he or she wants massaged. We recommend initially giving and receiving head, hand, foot, or back massages. The giver agrees beforehand to touch only those areas defined by the receiver.

The giver caresses and massages the specified body parts, experimenting with different types of strokes and pressures. The receiver tells the giver what feels good, what would feel better, what the receiver wants more or less of, and so on. The giver responds to this verbal feedback by doing what is asked.

We recommend three different ways for the receiver to let the giver know how the touching feels. The first way is with an "I" statement. The receiver starts each statement with the word "I," as in "I like a lighter touch on my back." If a certain touch is *not* enjoyable, the receiver should *redirect* the touching by saying something such as "I don't like that heavier touch; I like the lighter touch better." By doing this, the giver is provided with an alternative or another direction to explore, rather than simply being informed that something isn't working.

The receiver's second way to communicate is to place a hand over the giver's hand and guide it. This way, the receiver can show the giver the locations and types of pressure or stroking that are most enjoyable. If, because of the position your body is in, this is awkward, use another way of communicating.

Finally, there is also the "numbers system," which works well for partners who find it awkward to verbalize or guide by hand. Using this method, the receiver simply responds to each touch with a rating of 1 to 10, 10 being the most pleasurable.

There is no "best" way to communicate how touching feels. The receiver should simply choose one or more types of communication that feel comfortable. Partners do not have to choose the same style.

After fifteen minutes, partners switch roles and repeat this process with the giver now receiving and the receiver now giving.

During the exercise, while both giving and receiving, focus on how it feels to be touched, to give pleasure to your partner, to tell your partner what you like, and to make or fulfill requests.

You or your partner may become sexually aroused. However, that is not the purpose of this exercise and you should not act on your sexual feelings during the exercise or with your partner afterward. If you want to masturbate to orgasm *after the exercise is completed,* you can.

After both of you have given and received, using effective communication skills, discuss your feelings about and reactions to the exercise.

Do this exercise at least three times before proceeding to Sensate Focus I. If you need more time to feel comfortable, continue with it for several weeks longer. If you or your partner become anxious or distressed during the next exercise, return to this one.

SENSATE FOCUS I

The purpose of this exercise is to use one hour, two or three times per week, to give and receive *nongenital* touching without leading up to intercourse and to focus on the sensation of being touched, rather than sexual goals. In both parts of this exercise you and your partner will have an opportunity to get and give a body rub involving different types of touching, stroking, and massaging. In the second half of the exercise you will get a chance to teach your partner what you enjoy and how you want to be touched. You will also learn about your partner's preferences and how it feels to give physical pleasure. In both parts of the exercise, touching is to be an end in itself and not a prelude to intercourse or anything else. The goal is to feel comfortable giving and receiving physical pleasure, *not* to produce sexual excitement or orgasm.

Before you begin, agree on a time for this exercise. Two 30-minute blocks of time during the same day are suggested. They can be back to back, but because the receiver may not immediately be ready to give, you may agree to schedule an hour break before switching roles. As always, plan the session for a time when you will not be interrupted and choose a location that is warm and offers both privacy and comfort.

PART ONE

Flip a coin to determine who will *receive* first. Both giver and receiver undress and the receiver lies face down (but will turn over midway through the receiving half hour). If the receiver wants to try it, a lubricant such as hand lotion, massage oil, or baby powder may be used. The giver touches, strokes, and rubs the receiver's body, doing whatever the *giver* thinks of trying. Although there is a lot of leeway to try different types of touching, when you are the giver, keep your touch relatively light, avoiding the heavy kneading of deep muscle massage, which could cause discomfort.

The giver is *not* to touch the receiver's genitals or breasts, or his or her own. The giver is to focus on touching, exploring the receiver's body, and discovering what the *giver* likes to do.

The receiver is to focus on the sensations created by the giver's touches, noticing what is particularly pleasurable, neutral, or unenjoyable. The receiver should use the ways of communicating described in the last exercise to provide the giver with feedback on the experience of being touched. This feedback is important and will enable your partner to touch you in the most pleasing way in the future. The receiver should remember to turn over, in order to receive touching on both sides of the body.

After thirty minutes, partners switch roles. When both have taken their turns as giver and receiver, the exercise is over. Partners should then take some time to discuss their feelings and reactions, including what they thought about remaining passive while receiving and being "in control" while giving.

REMEMBER—even if you become sexually aroused, you and your partner are not to have intercourse, nor should you attempt to have orgasms during the experience.

PART TWO

After you and your partner have repeated Part One of this exercise twice—alternating who receives first—you can move on to Part Two.

Do exactly what you did in Part One (including not touching genitals or breasts), only this time the *receiver* is in complete control, instructing the giver on where and how to touch. The giver simply follows these instructions.

The receiver should use this opportunity to find out what feels enjoyable, giving in to any curiosity about being touched in certain ways or in certain places that do not usually get touched. It is the receiver's responsibility to make sure that they get touched the way desired, even if this means repeating instructions several times. Hand guiding, described in the last exercise, may be useful, especially if it's hard to verbalize at first.

The giver should do everything asked unless the request causes special discomfort.

Again, switch roles after thirty minutes and discuss the experience afterward, especially your reactions to giving and following instructions, being in charge, or doing what was asked of you.

After you have done both parts of this exercise twice without encountering problems, you can proceed to Sensate Focus II.

SENSATE FOCUS II

This exercise is identical to the previous one, with one exception—this time genital and breast touching is included.

Again, with your only goal being to learn for yourselves and teach each other what feels good, you and your partner will take turns touching and stroking each other's body *as well as* your own genitals or breasts.

As in Sensate Focus I, the first two times you do this exercise the *giver* will be in charge. As the giver, you should explore, caress, stroke, and "play with" your partner's body in any way you desire. Try to figure out what pleases you. As the receiver, unless your partner does something that hurts you or makes you very uncomfortable, you are to remain passive, focusing your attention on your own responses. If both of you feel comfortable with it, the giver can use mouth as well as hands on any part of the receiver's body.

After you have done the exercise twice with the giver in charge, it is time to turn over the controls to the receiver. As the receiver, you will tell your partner where and how to touch you, as well as indicating how you are responding to different touches. As the giver, you will do what your partner asks of you, unless you feel uncomfortable with the request.

Following each Sensate Focus II session, after both of you have given and received, discuss your experience—recognizing that more intense feelings are likely to come up now that you are experiencing genital and breast touching.

IMPORTANT POINTS TO CONSIDER BEFORE BEGINNING

1. If you become *extremely* uncomfortable or anxious when you look at or touch your partner's genitals, we encourage you to seek professional assistance.

2. Touching and exploring each other's genitals is *not* to be your sole focus, and so you shouldn't start there. Do not rush over the other parts of the body. *This isn't a race and genital touching is not the finish line.* In fact, the anticipation of genital touching can be quite pleasurable itself—for both the giver and the receiver. And finally, once genital touching begins, do not ignore the rest of your own or your partner's body. Your old routines may have involved concentrating all of your attention on your genitals once you got there. However, one of the many benefits of this exercise is learning that returning your attention to other types of touching on other areas of your body actually enhances pleasure.

3. Becoming sexually aroused or arousing your partner is *not* the purpose of this exercise. Learning about and teaching your partner about your body is. You are not to push yourself to feel sexually excited. You are to allow yourself to focus on whatever you are feeling and learn from that. If you don't get an erection or lubricate, that's fine. If you do, that's okay too. But, during the exercise, you are *not* to do anything with your arousal and should *not* expect or ask your partner to stimulate you to orgasm. Even after the exercise is over, *intercourse and other types of partner sex leading to orgasm are still off-limits.* You can masturbate to reach orgasm if you wish—but only after the exercise has been completed.

Once you and your partner have completed this exercise three times without encountering any of the problems we are about to describe, you can proceed to other exercises and the ban on intercourse can be lifted, if it's mutually agreeable.

Possible Problems and What to Do About Them

Following is a brief discussion of common problems couples encounter when they attempt any or all of the three exercises we just described, what those problems may mean, and several alternatives for resolving them.

Possible Problem 1:   You and your partner cannot find or agree on a time to do the exercise, "forget," or are "too busy" to do it. This may mean that one or both of you feel ambivalent or anxious about reconnecting physically and want to avoid the anxiety-provoking exercise, or that you are overwhelmed with stress. Or it may mean that there is a deeper relationship conflict that needs to be resolved.

Suggestions: (1) Talk about your anxiety or ambivalence, expressing your feelings and negotiating a compromise. (2) Actually schedule the exercises, writing down dates and times in your appointment book or on a calendar. (3) Employ time management techniques (see tips on pages 198 and 226). If the exercises still are not occurring, you should explore the possibility of a deeper relationship conflict, perhaps with the help of therapy.

Possible Problem 2:   One partner feels anxious about giving feedback or making specific requests, so you don't do it at all or as much as you could. This may mean that you are hearing old, negative tapes telling you not to talk about sex, that you are not entirely sure you deserve pleasure, or that you have trouble being assertive.

Suggestions: (1) As a temporary measure, give feedback after you finish the exercise. (2) Give nonverbal feedback by guiding your partner's hands—putting your hands over your partner's while you are receiving, and placing your partner's over yours while you are giving. (3) Use numbers instead of words, letting your partner know what feels good on a 1-to-10 scale, as described on page 250. (4) Get as much practice as possible before trying Sensate Focus II, since giving feedback about genital touching is most difficult.

Possible Problem 3: One or both of you get sexually aroused and push for orgasmic sex of one kind or another. This may mean that you are subconsciously sabotaging the exercise because of an underlying fear or anxiety, that you have not yet learned to control your sexual urges sufficiently, or that you are unwilling to share the control in your relationship or sex life.

Suggestions: (1) Discuss your agreement *not* to have orgasmic sex and commit yourselves to it once again. (2) Discuss controlling the urge to have orgasmic sex now in order to change your sexual relationship for the better in the long run. (3) Take advantage of the option to masturbate *after* the exercise has been completed.

Possible Problem 4: One or both partners become so anxious that the exercise must be discontinued. This may mean that one or both of you believe that it is not okay to "lie back and do nothing" but receive pleasure. One or both of you may also fear intimacy or be reacting to unfinished business. Or one or both of you may be experiencing performance anxiety and worrying about "doing it right."

Suggestions: (1) Return to the Tame Touch Exercise (page 248) and stick with it until you are less anxious about moving on. (2) Talk with your partner about your anxiety, trying to explore it and find mutually agreeable ways to feel safer. (3) If suggestions 1 and 2 do not work, seek professional help.

Possible Problem 5: One or both of you feel angry while giving your partner pleasure. This may mean that there are unresolved conflicts in your relationship and old hurts or unforgiven acts that are rising to the surface during the exercises.

Suggestions: (1) Return to the relationship exercises, working especially on Talking and Listening (page 210) and Caring Days (page 212). (2) Discuss your anger with your partner, using effective communication skills and without attacking. (3) Postpone doing the exercises until the conflicts in your relationship have been dealt with constructively, and perhaps get marital counseling to help you work through them.

BREAKING OLD HABITS AND CREATING NEW ONES

Once you and your partner have reconnected physically and built a foundation for sexual communication and satisfaction, you can begin to replace old sexual behaviors and attitudes with new ones. If you truly want a more comfortable, satisfying sex life, the first thing that must go is the misguided notion that orgasms are the most important part of sex (and thus your goal), and everything else that happens between you and your partner during sex is just a means to that end.

Stepladders and Circles: Two Approaches to Sexual Interaction

Most couples we treat, and indeed most couples in general, tend to approach sex in a very rigid, routine fashion—as if it were a stepladder they must climb in order to get to the erections or lubrication and orgasms that wait at the top. Not only do they move toward their goal in a step-by-step fashion, but quite often they also take exactly the same steps every time they have sex. First they touch. Then they kiss. Then they spend a few minutes petting—stroking the same areas of the body in the same way they have stroked them countless times before. Some stimulation of each other's genitals follows. Then they have intercourse. They repeat this same pattern time and time again—even though one partner or both may be bored with it.

These couples tend to divide their sexual interactions into two stages, calling everything that comes before intercourse "foreplay." Often, they look upon foreplay not as a pleasurable process in itself, but as an obligation before "real sex." Of course, this view prompts these couples to do only as much as is absolutely necessary to "get on with it." This approach, which places an enormous value on intercourse and orgasms while *devaluing* all else, increases any pressure to perform that they already feel. It makes every moment leading up to the achievement of their goal an anxious one (which, of course, reduces the likelihood of getting the erections or having the orgasms for which they so intrepidly strive).

In place of this largely unsatisfying and self-defeating approach to sex, psychologists Richard Timmons, Lloyd Sinclair, and Jane James have proposed an alternative that we have adapted to our own work. We encourage people to think of their sexual interactions as a circle instead of a stepladder. Since circles have no beginning or end, your sexual encounters have no fixed starting point and no prescribed ending either. You can start anywhere and go in any direction—including having pleasurable and satisfying sex *without* having intercourse or orgasms. What's more, with this approach, you always succeed— since your goal is *pleasure*, not performance. You do what feels good for each of you at that time, rather than inattentively doing what you have to do in order to get to the top of the stepladder where pleasure may or may not be waiting.

When you and your partner use the circle approach to sexual interactions, you may or may not have the same goals for that sexual encounter. One of you may want to have an orgasm while the other one wants to cuddle and kiss. However, YOU BOTH GET WHAT YOU WANT and boredom becomes a thing of the past because you have more options available to you, more directions to go on your circle than you did on your stepladder. You can kiss and cuddle, give or receive a back rub, kiss and cuddle some more, stroke various parts of each other's bodies, stimulate one partner to orgasm manually or orally, kiss and cuddle some more, and so on. And you can even do things the "old way" occasionally, if that is what both of you agree to do. In fact, the old way will then seem new and interesting again, since it isn't the *only* way to have sex anymore.

However, to derive pleasure and satisfaction with the circle approach to sex, you must first understand each other's sexual preferences—which the next exercise helps you to do.

CIRCLE EXERCISE

As a result of this exercise, you and your partner will have a clearer understanding of each other's sexual preferences and a larger repertoire of pleasurable behaviors to include in your sexual interactions.

Separately and without consulting each other, you and your partner are each to take out three sheets of paper and draw a large circle on each page. Label one page "Do Now and Enjoy," the second page "Don't Do Now but Would Like to Try," and the third "Don't Do Now and *Don't* Want to Try."

Being as specific and creative as possible, fill up your circles by listing behaviors or activities that fit the labels. Since it is a broad category rather than a specific behavior, sex play should *not* be listed as a separate item, but broken down into actual acts such as back and/or neck rubs, head massages, foot massages, shoulder massages, hand caresses, kissing lips, kissing ears, kissing feet, kissing breasts, fondling breasts, stroking thighs, performing oral sex, being masturbated, and so on. In other words, break down general behaviors into the smallest possible components.

Here are a few examples to help you list behaviors you do not do now and may or may not want to try:

- having your genitals orally stimulated
- orally stimulating your partner's genitals

- having your clitoris directly stimulated
- receiving or giving anal stimulation
- being on top or having your partner on top during intercourse
- new ways of letting each other know you want to have sex (e.g., leaving a note, wearing a specific article of clothing, leaving a sexy negligee laid out on your bed, etc.)
- talking about your fantasies during sex
- wearing different clothing during sex (sexy lingerie, your husband's shirt, etc.)
- using fragrances or oils
- being sexual in new locations, times, or positions
- reading or viewing sexually explicit materials
- masturbating your partner or holding your partner while he or she masturbates

Of course, there are more options than these, and while making your lists you should try to come up with as many as possible—regardless of which circle you list them in.

The second circle—things you don't do now but would like to try—is perhaps the most difficult to fill. In fact, you may feel quite anxious or embarrassed about acknowledging interests and preferences that you have not actually engaged in at all or not with your current partner. It is okay to feel that way. However, you must still try to list these behaviors, recognizing that writing them down does not commit you to actually doing them. In addition, the fact that you would like to try them does not mean your partner will agree to engage in them. Your partner can flat out refuse, or try the behavior once and decide not to engage in it again.

After your lists are complete, and still without consulting each other, rate each item using the following 1-to-10 scales:

For circle 1: 1 = little pleasure; 10 = "ecstasy"
For circle 2: 1 = a little interested; 10 = very interested and would like to try
For circle 3: 1 = some room for negotiation; 10 = absolutely no way you will agree to do this

After both of you have completed your lists and rated all the items, exchange lists. This should be done when you both have the time and energy to discuss the lists. It should not be attempted when either or both of you are preoccupied with other matters, or feeling angry or hurt because of a recent conflict.

Give each other all three circles. After you have read each other's lists, discuss your reactions to various items, without attacking, criticizing, or saying things like "That's disgusting," or "How perverted." Ask questions about items that you don't understand.

Then, with your lists spread out in front of you, begin discussing the possibility of incorporating new behaviors into your sexual encounters. A good place to begin is to look for items in circle 2 that both of you have in common. Next, talk about making even trades, exchanging items in your partner's "want to try" circle for items in your own—as long as those behaviors are not the ones you have rated 5 or above in your third circle. *Neither partner should even consider coercing the other to engage in behaviors the other clearly does not want to do.*

You can consider the Circle Exercise a success if you come away from it with a better understanding of your own and your partner's individual sexual preferences, as well as the ones you have in common. Of course, you will benefit even more, if—by mutual agreement—you begin to incorporate these new behaviors into your sexual interactions and try the circle approach to sex instead of staying stuck on the same old stepladder.

In many cases, the desire to try new behaviors raises another anxiety-provoking question. During sex or immediately beforehand, how do you let your partner know that you would like to try something new or do something differently than you have done it in the past?

Sexual Assertiveness

The closest thing to a universal obstacle to satisfying sex—one that almost everyone experiences—is the inability to convey your sexual preferences to your partner, especially during sex. This obstacle can be the result of assuming that your partner likes what you like or that your partner will know what you like without being told (which we stubbornly continue to believe in spite of repeated proof that it isn't true). Or you may be hearing old tapes that say you are supposed to *have* sex, not *talk* about it. Finally, plain old anxiety about asking for what you want may be getting in your way. Regardless of the specific reason you encounter this obstacle, you must take steps to dismantle it in order to enjoy sex enough to reignite your interest in it. In short, you must learn to assert yourself sexually. The following exercise offers you a method to let your partner know that you would like to try a new behavior during sex. In addition, it divides sexual assertiveness into stages that can reduce your anxiety about asserting yourself.

SEXUAL ASSERTIVENESS EXERCISE

The purpose of this exercise is to learn to assert yourself so that you can try a new activity or type of stimulation during sex.

PART ONE
Sit quietly and think about the types of activities that are sexually arousing for you. Think of the be-

haviors you listed in circles 1 and 2 of the previous exercise or new ideas that you have recently encountered in adult films or erotic literature. You might think about things that you have done in the past with other partners and would like to try with your new partner. Choose one that you would like to try the next time you have sex.

We recommend initially choosing something that doesn't provoke much anxiety. Since you are likely to experience some anxiety about being sexually assertive in the first place, choosing a relatively nonthreatening behavior guards against adding to that desire-inhibiting emotional state.

Never choose a behavior that your partner has indicated he or she does *not* want to try. You would be setting yourself up for trouble if you chose an activity that aroused you but turned off or repulsed your partner. Having completed the Circle Exercise, you know what your partner likes and does not like, so keep your choice within that range of behaviors. However, your partner need not be as interested in that behavior as you are and can, in fact, have no feelings about it one way or another.

PART TWO

Shut your eyes, take several deep, relaxing breaths, and imagine starting the activity you have chosen. Think about how and when during sex you would initiate the activity. Mentally experiment with different approaches—guiding your partner's hands with your hands, moving his or her body with your hands, moving your body to a new position, waiting until the time feels right and then slowly and gently beginning a behavior, verbally asking or instructing your partner, and so on. When you imagine making a verbal request, think about what you would say, the tone and volume of your voice, and whether you want it to sound playful, seductive, passionate, or otherwise. Explore as many alternatives for sexually asserting yourself as you can think of. Then choose the one that feels right for you.

If you notice your anxiety level increasing when you consider certain approaches, eliminate those options for the time being. If every alternative makes you feel anxious, choose the one that provokes the *least* amount of anxiety.

This time, focusing on the alternative you have chosen, mentally rehearse the situation again, imagining it in greater detail. If you want to, you can run through this scenario in your mind several more times over the next few days before moving on to the next step.

PART THREE

Actually assert yourself and initiate or request the activity during sex. Your partner may be surprised at first—but then you will be too the first time your partner wants to try something new. If your partner registers a stronger and more negative reaction or if you feel anxious or uncomfortable with the behavior (or satisfied that you have tried it and can thus move on), you can discontinue it. On the other hand, if your partner does not seem to mind and you are enjoying the new behavior, go on with it as long as you like.

You and your partner may find it beneficial to discuss your feelings about the experience immediately afterward or at some other time. This is particularly important if one or both of you had a negative reaction to either the behavior you initiated or your sexual assertiveness.

PART FOUR

After you have successfully asserted yourself and added a new element to sex once, keep doing it, trying at least one new behavior each time you have sex.

Sharing Sexual Conditions

As you know, sexual desire and satisfaction are based upon more than what you and your partner do during sex. In fact, you will not even get that far if the setting and circumstances for having sex do not meet your expectations or match the conditions for satisfying sex found in your sexual script. Thus, to rekindle sexual desire and improve your sex life, you and your partner must clearly and specifically identify what your own conditions are and communicate expectations to one another.

Of course, clarifying and sharing your expectations does not mean that each and every one of your conditions will be met each and every time you have sex. However, by completing the following exercise, you can take steps to ensure that the absolutely essential elements are present before engaging in sexual activity. This will increase feelings of interest, stimulation, closeness, safety, and comfort, which will, in turn, increase pleasure and desire.

BASIC CONDITIONS EXERCISE

The purpose of this exercise is to help you and your partner specify, discuss, and attempt to meet each other's basic requirements for the mood, setting, and circumstances that lead to comfortable and satisfying sex.

1. Separately, make a written list of the ingredients that increase your sexual comfort and pleasure. As comprehensively and specifically as possible, address each of the following areas:

TIME: For example, before 11 P.M., after 6 A.M., when we have at least forty-five minutes to ourselves.

PLACE: Bedroom only, bedroom or living room, anywhere but outdoors or in public, etc.

SOUND: Music, little talking, lots of talking, etc.

LIGHTING: Complete darkness, candlelight, bright light, etc.

FEELINGS: Not after an argument, when I don't have work to worry about, when I need some TLC, etc.

PRIVACY: When the kids are asleep, when the kids are not home, not when we have guests who might overhear us, not in other people's homes, etc.

MOOD: Relaxed, romantic, playful. Not when sad, stressed, preoccupied, etc.

OTHER: Certain types of clothing, looking at sexually explicit materials, "talking sexy," etc.

PROCESS: Who initiates, how, how much advance planning, amount of affection beforehand, amount of sex play before intercourse, cuddling or talking or going right to sleep afterward, etc.

2. After you make your list, code it—writing the letter *E* beside elements that are *absolutely essential;* the letter *P* next to those you *prefer, but would not feel especially uncomfortable doing without;* and the letter *X* next to those that are *extras and would be the easiest to give up.*

3. Rank your *E* conditions, assigning a different number to each, with 1 for the most important condition, 2 for the next most important, and so on.

4. Place an asterisk (*) beside any *P* items that particularly enhance your feelings of comfort, relaxation, and enjoyment.

5. After you both have individually completed this task, schedule some uninterrupted together time to share, compare, and discuss your lists. Negotiate compromises on *E* items that conflict, and establish your bottom line for conditions under which you will be completely *un*willing to have sex. Be sure to use effective communication skills and, if possible, make a commitment to be more sensitive about checking out the circumstances before making sexual overtures.

Sharing and taking steps to ensure that your own and your partner's minimum requirements are met serve two purposes. First, both of you will be more comfortable and relaxed during sex. It's also likely that this type of discussion will reduce the number of conflicts you have about when, where, and how to have sex. While this is in itself a significant accomplishment, you can go several steps further—increasing sexual desire and enhancing sexual pleasure—by enhancing the mood, setting, and circumstances for sexual activity. You can do this long before you get to your bedroom by:

- physically expressing affection throughout the day—and not necessarily as a signal that you want to have sex
- wrapping up other obligations at a predetermined time so that day-to-day worries don't accompany you into the bedroom
- planning ahead, selecting a time to be together and doing whatever is necessary to ensure that your minimum requirements will be met at that time
- devoting at least a few minutes of every day to fantasizing or daydreaming about sex

Then you can create special conditions, settings, moods, and circumstances that go beyond the bare minimum for comfort and add variety, romance, excitement, and a bit of playfulness to your sex life. You can try different types of lighting, locations, music, and sensory experiences—like silk sheets on your bed. Or you might dress differently than usual, forgoing the flannel pajamas for sexy lingerie, wearing an article of your partner's clothing (like a shirt or sweater) or fantasy costumes. You may want to experiment with sexual accessories including vibrators, erotic literature, adult films, massage oils, powders, fragrances, edible underwear, and so on—always agreeing on what to try and never forcing your experiments on an unwilling partner. Many couples enjoy bathing or showering together, as well as fantasizing individually or sharing their fantasies with each other. In fact, you might even try acting out some of your "safe" fantasies. For instance, you might go to a bar, where, pretending to be a stranger, one partner "picks up" the other. You could pretend to be having an illicit affair, with one partner checking into a hotel room and the other arriving later. One of you could play a delivery person who comes to the door and ends up having sex with the man or lady of the house. As long as both of you agree to participate, neither of you is hurt or degraded by it, and the playacting does not mirror the problem areas of your relationship, living out your fantasies is an excellent way to stir up sexual interest and enhance sexual pleasure.

BRIDGING DESIRE DISCREPANCIES

A desire discrepancy, the difference between your level of sexual desire and your partner's, is inevitable when one of you has ISD. But it can also occur when one partner's sex drive is naturally higher than the other's. In fact, we treat as many couples in which partners have normal but mismatched levels of sexual desire as couples in which one partner has ISD. For both types of couples, we would like to offer a few suggestions and exercises that can reduce conflicts about sex and enable both partners to get more of what they want or need from their sexual relationship.

First of all, we would like to emphasize and encourage you to accept the fact that *you* are responsible for your own sexual desire. Regardless of any preconceived notions you might have, when you got married or romantically involved, your partner did not agree to be interested in sex as often or whenever you were. Sexual desire is an internal psychological appetite, and just as two people need not be hungry for food at the same time, they need not—and generally do not—have the same appetite for sex. You do not get insulted, feel rejected, or believe you are somehow deficient when your partner is not hungry for food, and if you are the higher-desire partner in a couple with desire discrepancies, you need not feel that way when your lower-desire partner is not interested in sex. What's more, you do not hold anyone else accountable for your hunger, expecting your partner to feed you and eat with you whenever you are in the mood for a meal or a snack. If you are not hungry, you do not expect your partner to give up eating or feel no hunger until *your* appetite returns. Yet, these are precisely the expectations couples with desire differences have about their sexual appetites. For your own peace of mind and the health of your relationship, you must change those expectations.

If you are the higher-desire partner, you must stop expecting your partner to be interested in sex whenever you are, and stop misinterpreting low interest as a personal rejection or attack. You must stop believing that your partner is responsible for your sexual desire. There are two specific steps you can take immediately. One is to consider and perhaps take advantage of the option to satisfy your sexual urges through self-stimulation. Yes, you may have strong negative feelings about masturbation in general or about "having to" masturbate when you are involved with a partner who is physically capable of having sex with you. You will simply have to weigh the consequences of each alternative. Is getting past your mental block about masturbation and using it to satisfy your sexual urges worse than engaging in an endless persist-resist battle that threatens to destroy your relationship altogether? When examining the alternatives, we think self-stimulation has some benefit, but you will have to decide for yourself.

The second step you can take is to identify the needs you try to meet through sexual activity and then find other ways to meet those needs. For instance, if you use sex to relax, perhaps you could work out instead, or learn deep muscle relaxation techniques, or meditate. Or, if you use sex to affirm your self-worth, you might consider looking for reassurance and recognition in other ways—by joining a support group, doing volunteer work that is truly appreciated (like being a Big Brother or Big Sister, reading to hospitalized children, befriending a senior citizen), returning to the work force, or going back to college. If sex is what you want when you are bored, develop other interests. If sex gives you a feeling of being attractive or loved, there are many other things your lower-drive partner can do to provide those feelings. However, you must let your partner know about these needs in a calm, productive discussion.

Of course, not every need you use sex to fulfill can be satisfied by other means, but some can. Sex may still be your first choice to relieve tension, insecurity, or boredom. However, if it is no longer the only choice you will consider, you will become less dependent on sex and less wounded when your partner rebuffs your sexual advances.

Please do not think that we are trying to make higher-desire partners the "bad guys" or that we are saying they must give up hope and accept the circumstances that desire discrepancies create. We are simply saying that because your past efforts to pressure your lower-desire partner into being more interested in sex have not worked, you must take some of the pressure off while the two of you *work together* to bridge the gap between you.

If you are the lower-desire partner, for your own sake and the sake of your relationship you must find out if you have ISD and are consciously suppressing or subconsciously inhibiting your sexual urges. If this turns out to be the case, we urge you to take the steps we have outlined in this book—contracting with your partner to work on the problem together, with or without the assistance of a sex therapist. Even if you don't have ISD and are simply less interested in sex than your partner is, you have certain responsibilities. Just as your higher-desire partner cannot expect you to have sex whenever he or she is in the mood, you cannot expect your low desire to dictate all the terms for your sex life and your relationship. If nothing else, you must come to accept the fact that your partner has a right to feel sexual desire more often and more urgently than you do and that unwelcome sexual overtures may not necessarily be designed to negate, pressure, criticize, or humiliate you.

In addition, while your higher-desire partner is making an effort to cut down on sexual demands and find nonsexual ways to meet unfulfilled needs, you can be making similar efforts. You can learn to respond to more external cues, discover more psychological wants and needs that sex could fulfill, and work to intensify the sexual excitement you do feel—using many of the exercises in this book. As a result, you and your partner will spend less time pulling each other in opposite directions and instead move closer to a more comfortable middle ground.

Finding the Middle Ground

Chances are that you and your partner have not yet been able to bridge the emotional and sexual gap between you because you have previously viewed your circumstances in black-and-white terms. One of you wanted sex and the other one didn't. Each time a sexual overture was made, it was assumed that the only options available were to have intercourse or not to have intercourse and the only possible answers to the invitation were yes or no. This made every sexual situation a win-lose proposition. The only possible outcome was for one partner's needs to be met and the other's negated. This book has provided countless examples of the disastrous consequences of such an approach, but it has also given you enough insight and information to be ready to try a different approach—negotiating exchanges of sexual and nonsexual gifts.

Before we explain how to do this, let us return to the hunger analogy we used earlier. Let's say that you're famished and want to eat a five-course meal. In fact, you've been fantasizing about that meal all day, planning a menu that includes all of your favorite foods and imagining how each morsel will taste. In your fantasy, your partner eats and enjoys that meal with you. However, after you get home and prepare the meal, it turns out your partner is not hungry. Does that mean that your only option is not to eat? Of course not. You could eat by yourself. Your partner could sit with you while you eat. Your partner could eat just one course while you eat all five, or nibble at a favorite food. Or, while you are getting what you want—to satisfy your hunger by eating a five-course meal—your partner could be getting something else—like time to talk with you, or having you listen to the speech he or she has to make, or help with the difficult clues in the Sunday crossword puzzle. The point is that, in this situation and in sexual ones, there are always more options than all or nothing. What's more, you and your partner can discuss the available options and negotiate a deal that allows you to get some, if not all, of what you want in exchange for giving your partner something (which can be entirely different).

SEXUAL CARING DAYS EXERCISE

1. Ask for what you want. The partner who is interested in sexual or intimate activity is responsible for expressing that interest. You are not expected to read each other's minds. Make a request in a nondemanding way. If possible, the request should be specific and can be anything from wanting a hug to needing to talk, from wanting to have an orgasm to engaging in sexual intercourse.

2. Respond to the request. The partner who has received the request is responsible for conveying how interested he or she is in that specific request, and how willing to fulfill it. Although you are not obligated to do exactly what the initiator asks, you must be willing to do something that allows the initiator to get some of the expressed needs met.

If you are both willing and interested, you can say yes to the request.

If you are not interested in that activity, you are to offer an alternative from the initiator's "Do Now and Enjoy" or "Don't Do Now but Would Like to Try" circles (see page 259). For instance, if your partner wants to have intercourse and you are not interested in doing so, you might offer to stimulate your partner to orgasm manually or orally, hold your partner while he or she masturbates, watch an adult film together, give a back rub, or do something else.

Clearly, some negotiation will be necessary in order to arrive at the alternative that allows the initiator to get some needs met without requiring the other partner to do something objectionable.

3. Discuss *how much* **you are willing to contribute to the activity.** On occasion in the past, you or your partner may have made a sexual requests when the other partner did not have the physical or emotional energy to fulfill it. One of you may have been too tired, stressed, preoccupied, or depressed to give 100 percent to that activity. Since you could not give it your full attention or develop *as much* interest in it as your partner seemed to have, you did not engage in it at all. But the truth is that you do not have to devote 100 percent of your energy to the activity for it to be satisfying, especially when you are fulfilling your partner's request rather than initiating sexual activity yourself.

Whether you say yes to the initiator's request or offer an agreeable alternative, let the initiator know how much energy you are willing to put into the activity. Use a 1-to-10 scale, with 1 indicating that you want to be relatively passive and devote very little to the activity and 10 indicating that you are willing to go all out, doing whatever is necessary to make the activity pleasurable and satisfying.

The initiator should then honestly appraise how much energy to put into the activity and use the same rating scale.

Then add your two ratings together. If the combined total is 10 or above, you will be able to engage in that activity. If it comes to less than 10, neither of you is willing or able to give enough to make the activity satisfying and you must renegotiate. Sometimes this will involve choosing a less strenuous activity. Sometimes the initiator will have to change a rating in order to engage in the activity requested. And sometimes the situation can be resolved by postponing the activity until later when one or both of you will have more energy for it.

4. Engage in the agreed-upon activity. Don't feel obliged to contribute more energy than you originally agreed to or lay a guilt trip on yourself because your partner is engaging in the activity for your benefit—and might not have offered to do it if you had not asked. In other words, receive your gift graciously. As the gift giver, give graciously. If you followed directions earlier, you should not be doing anything you do not want to do or expending more energy than you said you would. And just because you are doing something for your partner, it doesn't mean you can't enjoy it yourself. Just as someone who was not hungry may regain an appetite after seeing the meal his or her partner has prepared, you may become interested in and excited by the activity once it begins—although you are not obligated to.

5. The gift exchange. The next day, the partner who received the request and gave the gift is to make a request for a sexual or nonsexual gift, which the other partner is to fulfill—using the same negotiation and energy rating process.

6. It is likely to take several weeks of practicing this exercise for you and your partner to become comfortable with the gift exchange process and iron out any problems you encounter. However, you can continue the exercise as long as you wish, and better yet, incorporate elements of it into your overall lifestyle—generating alternatives and negotiating compromises instead of viewing sex and life as all-or-nothing propositions.

IF YOU GET STUCK:
WHEN AND WHERE TO GET HELP

Although we would not have written this book if we did not sincerely believe that comprehensive information about ISD and solid self-help strategies could help you revive sexual desire and improve your sex life, it is possible that a self-help approach may not be enough to accomplish those goals. As you know by now, ISD is an exceedingly complex problem, so much so that a one-size-fits-all remedy simply does not exist. If the ideas and exercises you find in this book do, in fact, have positive results for you, enjoy them and your newfound sexual desire and satisfaction. If you get stuck, however, don't give up. Get professional help.

Needing help is not a sign of weakness, inadequacy, or failure. Instead, it's an indication that you are wise enough to recognize your own limitations, self-respecting enough to do what is best for you, and committed to making your relationship work. You are most likely to need professional assistance of some kind if:

- Either partner or both are experiencing severe, persistent depression, including two or more of the symptoms listed on page 114.
- Severe marital conflicts are occurring, including physical abuse, arguments that do not ease tension or solve problems, frequent discussions about separation or divorce, discussions of one or more topics—including sex—that always lead to fights, or a general long-term sense of unhappiness or dissatisfaction with the relationship.
- Either or both of you have alcohol or drug problems—whether the user thinks substance abuse is a problem or not.
- Either or both of you have significant unfinished business, especially if you have been the victim of sexual assault, child abuse, a bitter divorce, or an alcoholic or otherwise dysfunctional family.

- Your sexual difficulties have persisted over a long period of time. This includes a sexual relationship that has never been satisfying or that did not bounce back within a reasonable amount of time after a relationship crisis or a stressful time in your life.
- Other sexual problems, especially sexual avoidance and phobic reactions, are affecting your sex life along with ISD.

How to Select a Therapist

At the present time there are no academic or professional standards someone must meet in order to claim the title of sex therapist legally. Unlike psychologists, social workers, and psychiatrists, sex therapists do not have to be licensed or certified in most states. As a result, you must be careful to choose a truly qualified sex therapist.

Your best bet is to look into sex therapy programs that are affiliated with large hospitals or medical schools where therapists are carefully screened and closely supervised. In addition, you have a right to inquire about the therapist's background; a qualified person will usually be quite willing to answer your questions about college degrees, years of experience, and sex therapy training. You may also want to find out about the therapist's affiliations with professional organizations or associations—which may not license sex therapists but do have specific criteria for membership. The better-known organizations qualified sex therapists belong to include:

- The American Association of Sex Educators, Counselors and Therapists (AASECT)
- Society for Sex Therapy and Research (SSTAR)
- American Psychological Association (APA)
- The Society for the Scientific Study of Sex (SSSS)
- American Association for Marriage and Family Therapy (AAMFT)

Because sexual problems in general and ISD is particular are often reflections of relationship problems, you should look for a therapist who has experience in marital counseling as well as sex therapy. Unless you are already in couples therapy for marital problems, rarely will you want or be able to afford to see separate sex and marital therapists, who may or may not coordinate their treatment efforts. Also, because the complexity of sexual desire disorders means that no single therapeutic technique works all the time for any patient, eclectic therapists—those who use a number of different approaches to therapy—tend to have the most success with ISD patients.

Any program or therapist qualified to treat ISD will do an extensive "intake" evaluation that includes a medical history and sometimes referrals for physical exams and lab tests as well. If the therapist you choose launches right into treating your problem *without* this physical, psychological, and relationship assessment, you have probably chosen the wrong therapist.

Finally, the acid test is how you *feel* about the therapist after your first session. Taking account of the fact that everyone is somewhat uncomfortable talking about sexual problems when first visiting a therapist, try to ascertain whether or not this new therapist:

- seems comfortable with the topic of sex
- seems involved, listening attentively to what you are saying and asking questions that show an attempt to understand you
- is someone you find likable
- gives you input (unlike some other types of psychotherapists, a sex or marital therapist both listens and talks, giving instructions and often pointing out patterns of interaction)
- behaves in a professional manner. If there is any suggestion that you will be asked to have sex while the therapist watches or *with* the therapist, he or she is *not* practicing in a professional or appropriate manner. Discontinue treatment and find another therapist.

Please do not feel disconcerted if your first attempt to find a suitable therapist does not work out for you. In fact, it may take several tries to find the right match. It is worth the effort, however, because a solid, trusting relationship with a qualified therapist can work wonders for your sexual desire and satisfaction.

APPENDIX

Body Basics:
A Quick Biological Tour
of Sexual Functioning

THE BASICS OF HUMAN SEXUAL RESPONSE

What happens during sex? Thanks to the groundbreaking scientific research conducted by Masters and Johnson, we can answer that question accurately, at least concerning how your body responds physically. In recent years, many experts in addition to Masters and Johnson have proposed various conceptualizations of what happens during sex. The one we will refer to here is Helen Singer Kaplan's tri-phasic model, which divides the human sexual response into three separate but interlocking stages—desire, excitement, and orgasm. The following summary of what happens during each stage may help clear up some misconceptions about sexual functions that are affecting your feelings about and interest in sex.

Desire

In the desire stage, you become interested in having sex, feeling an urge to engage in sexual activity, which you consciously or unconsciously choose either to act upon or to suppress. In short, you feel turned on or "hungry" for sex. Governed by nerve centers in your brain and chemicals called neurotransmitters,

sexual desire is activated by anything you consciously or unconsciously interpret as having sexual meaning. Various physical conditions or emotional states can interfere with or
completely block the transmission of sexual messages, dimin-
ishing sexual desire or preventing you from feeling it at all.
However, if an opportunity to have sex is available, and if no
external circumstance or element convinces you *not* to have sex
at that particular time with that partner and under those specific circumstances, you reach a state of readiness that enables
you to proceed to the next stage.

Excitement

The excitement stage includes the physical and emotional responses you experience once sexual activity of any kind begins.
Sexual excitement is created and enhanced by physical and
emotional stimulation—touching, fondling, rubbing, kissing,
pleasant fantasies, and mental images of sexual pleasure. While,
for most people, the external sexual organs (the man's penis
and the women's clitoris) are the parts of the body most sensitive to physical stimulation, many other areas respond to sexual
touch, contributing to and increasing sexual arousal.

When, where, and how you like to be stimulated is very
much a matter of personal preference. Each time you have sex,
the stimulation you give and receive has the potential to increase excitement, detract from arousal, or have no significant
effect at all—and the same sort of physical contact does not
always have the same effect. In fact, what aroused you yesterday may turn you off today, since responses to sexual stimulation are influenced by any number of physical and emotional
factors—from "feeling fat" to having had a trying day at work.
Familiarizing yourself with your own and your partner's preferences and expectations, and knowing how to communicate
these preferences as well as tuning in to your body and mood,
can enhance sexual excitement or even enable you to experience it in a positive way for the first time.

Barring any physiological complications during the excitement phase, men who are sexually aroused get erections and women lubricate, making it possible for the penis to enter and thrust into the vagina. Throughout this stage, excitement tends to increase steadily, although it can be reduced to lower levels by various distractions including loud noises, physical discomfort, anxious or distracting thoughts, or actual interruptions. In addition, to prolong the sexual experience, partners may intentionally lower their level of arousal by slowing down, discontinuing certain kinds of stimulation, or taking a break to talk. However, excitement can eventually build to the point where it carries sexual partners into the next stage of the sexual response.

Orgasm

An orgasm occurs as a reflex response to high levels of sexual excitement. Orgasms are often accompanied by feelings of warmth and relaxation, as well as a wide variety of pleasurable sensations.

What does an orgasm feel like? There are probably as many answers to that question as there are people engaging in sexual activity. However, we can safely say that the way orgasms are described in popular fiction is an exaggeration of actual experience and that you are setting yourself up for disappointment if you expect the earth to move every or *any* time you are sexual. We can also assert that for the most part orgasms feel good, although there is a wide range of possibilities for how they feel good and how good they feel. Sometimes orgasms feel terrific and other times merely good. Sometimes orgasms help you relax and nothing more. Sometimes they hardly seem worth the effort. That's the way orgasms are.

Not having an orgasm is neither debilitating nor dangerous. Although many men grew up believing that if they did not ejaculate or have an orgasm, they would suffer dire consequences including extreme pain, the truth is that sexual excitement without ejaculation and orgasm is not particularly painful. Although it will leave some men feeling irritable, it does not

cause any lasting physical damage. Most men experience this at
least once during their lifetimes and usually quite a few times.
Although wanting to ejaculate and reach orgasm but being unable to on a regular basis constitutes a sexual problem, which we
discuss in Chapter One, sex without orgasm is not physically
dangerous.

Unlike men, women often learn that it is not necessary for
them to have orgasms and that perhaps they would be better off
expecting *not* to have them. In the not too distant past, being
nonorgasmic, rarely having orgasms, or barely noticing when
they did occur was considered the norm for women. But that is
no longer the case. Nowadays, most women do indeed expect to
have orgasms and feel disappointed or worried about themselves when they do not. They may strive to have multiple
orgasms—a sexual response that was sensationally publicized
during the sexual revolution.

However, there is no evidence that having a series of orgasms is better for you than having just one. In fact, the dogged
pursuit of multiple orgasms or mutual orgasms or any other
ultimate orgasmic experience can actually diminish sexual satisfaction instead of enhancing it. For one thing, it tarnishes the
pleasure you do feel during the orgasms you do have. That was
good, you think, but was it good enough, could it be better? If
you think orgasms should be better, you and your partner are
bound to get caught in the "trying harder" trap we described
earlier.

And the fact of the matter is that most women do *not* have
orgasms each and every time they have sex, and just because
some women have multiple orgasms some of the time, it does
not mean that all women can have them or that any woman has
them all the time. Indeed, all those shoulds and supposed tos
can create as many problems for women—and men—as not
having an orgasm in the first place.

In fact, the sexually scripted belief that orgasms should be
the goal every time you have sex, and that kissing, touching,
and other forms of foreplay are only means to that end, plays
a major role in sex lives that are often too goal oriented, pressured, and unfulfilling. Sex is not a business deal or a career

move where you set a goal, plot the most direct route to reach it, and surge ahead, letting nothing slow you down. Pushing for, rushing toward, thinking of nothing but orgasms is decidedly counterproductive. This will cause you to spend too little time experiencing sexual pleasures other than orgasm, increase the pressure you feel to perform, and often inhibit the very orgasm you are so intent on achieving.

After Orgasm

After having an orgasm you may feel both physically and emotional relaxed or even exhausted. But then again, you may not. Some people fall asleep instantly, while others want to engage in postcoital cuddling and intimate conversation. But more important, contrary to what you may have learned from film or novels or other sources, many people are not ready, willing, or able to get sexually aroused again immediately after they have an orgasm.

MALE SEXUAL ORGANS

Contrary to common folklore, which states that there are far more differences than similarities between men's and women's bodies, there are not. In fact, there are far more similarities, including some between the actual sexual organs and how they work.

The reality is that the differences in genitals that distinguish men from women appear in the fetus approximately two months after conception has occurred. Prior to that time, there are *no* differences. While in the uterus, the male fetus is exposed to androgens. Then the anatomical differentiation between males and females with which we are all so familiar begins to occur. While these eventual differences are obvious, they should not be exaggerated. Many men and women come to us with the assumption that the other sex's genitals are like alien beings. From such a perspective, they are unable to comprehend the sensations felt by and the responses of the opposite sex's genitals. Understanding what your partner is experiencing helps develop a comfortable, satisfying sexual relationship. Therefore, it's vital that you appreciate the similarities between men's and women's genitals, not only in form, but in function.

What You See

The **penis** is the cause of endless concern and speculation for more men than you'd imagine. In fact, the one thing all penises seem to have in common is the worry and concern that they command from their owners! Men may think their penises are too small, too thin, too thick; that they lean in the wrong direction or bend slightly in the wrong place. These comparisons can be made because penises are indeed different shapes and sizes, but the idea that one is better than another is an illusion created largely by pornographic portrayals of the "right stuff." Unfortunately, many men (and women) buy this illusion and subsequently feel that their penises (or their partners') don't live up to the fictional standards of perfection.

Fiction aside, the reality is that while there is a great deal of variability in the size of men's penises when they are soft (which is the perspective from which most men compare their penises to other men's), there are fewer differences in size when penises are hard or erect. That is, the smaller penis tends to expand more than the larger flaccid penis when it becomes erect. The end result is that when erect, most men's penises are about six inches long. And the bottom line of this great penis competition is that the size of the penis has virtually no physical effect whatsoever on sexual pleasure. What most men and women don't realize is that the nerve endings in the vagina are far more sensitive to the touch and the thrusting motion of the penis than they are to the pressure of a longer or thicker one. One old saying we have heard remains the truth: When it comes to the penis or any other sexual organ, *it's the magician, not the wand, that makes the magic*.

As seen in Figure 1, the penis itself consists of a shaft and

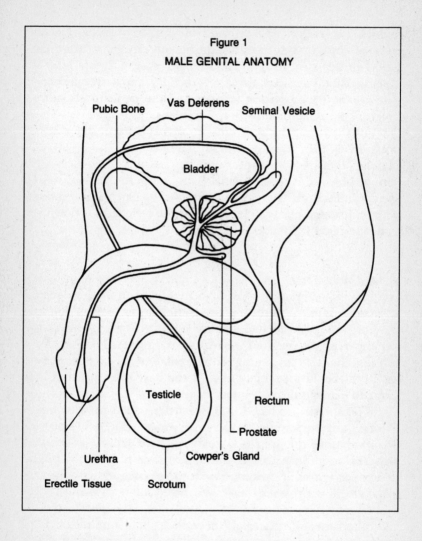

Figure 1
MALE GENITAL ANATOMY

a head. Since it contains more nerve endings, the head or tip of the penis tends to be the more sensitive part, especially around the coronal ridge, which connects the head to the shaft. The tip of the penis matches a woman's clitoris in structure, function, and origin. The skin on the shaft of the penis matches that of a woman's inner vaginal lips (see Figure 2). Underneath the skin of the penis are three cylinders of spongy tissue. Each of these spongy tissues has a tough fibrous covering. Many tiny blood vessels run through the spongy tissue. When a man becomes sexually excited, these vessels fill to capacity with blood, causing the spongy tissue to swell and the penis to get larger. There is no bone or muscle in the penis.

Also visible is the **scrotum**—a sac that contains the testicles or balls, as they're often called. The skin on the scrotal sac matches that of a woman's outer vaginal lips. Because sperm cannot be produced at normal body temperature, the scrotal sac contracts and stretches in response to changes in temperature and sexual excitement, keeping the testicles a little cooler than the rest of the body.

What You Don't See

Located inside the scrotum, the **testicles** produce sperm and the hormone testosterone. For the sake of comfort, one testicle usually hangs lower than the other inside the scrotal sac. During sex, the testicles get bigger and rotate up inside the scrotal sac until they are pressing against the base of the pelvic floor prior to ejaculation.

The sperm produced in the testicles makes up only about 5 percent of the seminal fluid men ejaculate. Immediately prior to ejaculation, the sperm mixes with fluid from the **seminal vesicles** and the **prostate gland**. Prostatic fluid and seminal vesicle secretions are responsible for the remainder of the total ejaculate. The prostatic fluid gives the ejaculate its whitish color and odor.

The **Cowper's gland** also secretes a small amount of clear, sticky liquid, which may or may not be visible on the tip of the penis *before* ejaculation. The Cowper's gland secretions make the urethra less acidic, which makes it safer for sperm to pass through the urethra. Because it often contains millions of sperm cells, the Cowper's gland secretion is one of the reasons the withdrawal method of birth control is so very unreliable.

The **vasa deferentia** are two firm tubes that run from the testicles to the prostate gland. Sperm is stored at the upper end until it mixes with the fluid from the seminal vesicles and prostate gland. When a man has a vasectomy, it is the vasa deferentia that are cut. Because most of the ejaculate is made up of fluids from the prostate and seminal vesicles, there is no noticeable difference in the amount of ejaculate after a man has a vasectomy. When a man reaches orgasm or "comes," he ejaculates the seminal fluid through the **urethra**, a tube that runs through one of the penis's spongy cylinders. Connected to the bladder, the urethra conducts both urine and semen, *but not at the same time*.

FEMALE SEXUAL ORGANS

What You See

As seen in Figure 2, the **clitoris** is a small protruding bit of tissue about the size of a large pea. The clitoris contains as many nerve endings as the head of a man's penis. It is extremely sensitive and reacts to stimulation in much the same way the penis does. However, unlike the penis, through which the man urinates and ejaculates, the clitoris has *only* one function: to provide pleasure. When a woman is sexually aroused, her clitoris enlarges or becomes erect, increasing in diameter and sometimes in length. Just before she reaches orgasm, the clitoris retracts under the **clitoral hood**. When a woman is not sexually excited, the hood covers the clitoris.

Because of its location—above the vaginal opening—the clitoris may not receive direct stimulation during intercourse. However, it does receive indirect stimulation from the thrusting of the penis against the inner vaginal lips, which are connected to the clitoral hood. In addition, a couple can position themselves with either partner on top, so that the clitoris receives more direct stimulation. To do this, the woman should part her inner lips so that the clitoris can receive stimulation from being pressed against her partner's pubic bone. Typically, though, during intercourse women receive only indirect stim-

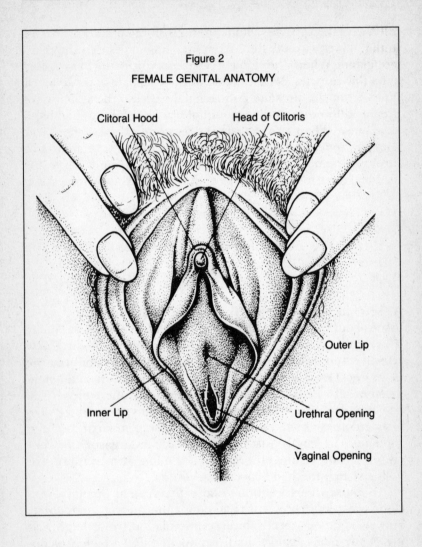

Figure 2

FEMALE GENITAL ANATOMY

Clitoral Hood   Head of Clitoris

Outer Lip

Inner Lip   Urethral Opening

Vaginal Opening

ulation to the most sensitive area of their sexual organs, while men receive direct stimulation to the most sensitive area of their sexual organs. It is only natural and normal, then, that many women require direct clitoral stimulation, in addition to indirect stimulation during intercourse, to reach orgasm. Some women believe something is wrong with them if they are unable to reach orgasm without their clitoris's receiving more direct stimulation, but there is not. It is a physiological reality that affects the vast majority of women and can be easily attended to during sex.

The **vaginal lips**, which normally cover the opening to the vagina, are composed of the outer lips (labia majora) and the inner lips (labia minora). Both the inner and outer vaginal lips are sensitive to touch. Like faces, the genitals of women (and men), while having the same parts, are all unique in their appearance. For example, some women have a lot of pubic hair; others have little. Some have hair on their outer lips and some don't. There is also a great deal of natural variability among women in the size of the inner and outer lips. It is important to remember that these differences in size, amount of hair, and positioning are natural and normal—not better or worse.

What You Don't See

The **vagina**, which is frequently and mistakenly thought of as a hole, is actually only a potential space. When a woman becomes sexually excited, the walls of the vagina balloon out. The rest of the time the vaginal walls are relaxed and touch each other. The outer third of the vagina contains the most nerve endings and for the majority of women is the most sensitive part.

Like the spongy tissue of the penis, the vaginal walls contain many tiny blood vessels that fill with blood when a woman is sexually excited. This causes the walls to balloon out. A process similar to sweating, called **lubrication**, causes fluid to seep through the vaginal tissue. This fluid lubricates the vagina, but may not lubricate the opening to the vagina. The only fluid produced on the outside of the vagina is emitted from **Bartholin's glands**. These glands are near the opening of the vagina, but produce only a small amount of fluid. Therefore, when a woman is sexually excited, she (or her partner) may need to use some of the vaginal lubrication to lubricate the vaginal opening. Saliva, K-Y jelly, and other non-petroleum-base lubricants can also be used for additional lubrication. (Caution: Petroleum-base lubricants should never be used for vaginal lubrication. These jellies are not water soluble and will eventually further inhibit lubrication by clogging up the pores of the vaginal walls.)

Although many women worry that some men may be "too big" for them, the vagina is remarkably elastic, expanding to fit snugly around any penis, large or small, as well as allowing a baby to pass through it during childbirth. The **pubococcygeal (PC) muscle** surrounds the vaginal opening and most experts believe that toning and strengthening this muscle can improve a woman's (and man's) ability to experience orgasms.

The **Grafenberg** or **G spot** gained notoriety several years ago. It is a small area of tissue—as small as a dime and usually no larger than a quarter—located on the vaginal wall midway between the cervix and the pubic bone. It can double in size during sexual activity and direct stimulation of this tissue is pleasurable for many women.

While this book has focused entirely on disorders of the desire phase, various sexual dysfunctions occur during the excitement and orgasm phases of human sexual response. Indeed, most of the popular literature on sexual problems has focused exclusively on excitement and orgasm phase disorders. If you suffer from any of those dysfunctions (e.g., impotence, premature or retarded ejaculation, anorgasmia) many of the books listed in the Bibliography may help you understand and resolve your difficulties.

Suggested Reading

SEXUAL ENHANCEMENT FOR WOMEN

Barbach, Lonnie. *For Yourself: The Fulfillment of Female Sexuality.* New York: Signet, 1975.

Heiman, Julia R., and LoPiccolo, Joseph. *Becoming Orgasmic: A Sexual Growth Program for Women.* New York: Prentice Hall Press, 1988.

SEXUAL ENHANCEMENT FOR MEN

Zilbergeld, Bernie. *Male Sexuality: A Guide to Sexual Fulfillment.* New York: Bantam, 1981.

SEXUAL ENHANCEMENT FOR COUPLES

Barbach, Lonnie. *For Each Other: Sharing Sexual Intimacy.* New York: Signet, 1984.

SEXUAL FANTASIES OF MEN

Friday, Nancy. *Men in Love.* New York: Dell Publishing Co., 1980.

SEXUAL FANTASIES OF WOMEN

Friday, Nancy. *Forbidden Flowers*. New York: Pocket Books, 1975.
Friday, Nancy. *My Secret Garden: Women's Sexual Fantasies*. New York: Pocket Books, 1973.

SEXUALLY TRANSMITTED DISEASES

Kaplan, Helen Singer. *The Real Truth About Women and AIDS: How to Eliminate the Risks Without Giving Up Love and Sex*. New York: Simon & Schuster, 1987.

RELATIONSHIPS IN GENERAL

Scarf, Maggie. *Intimate Partners*. New York: Random House, 1987.

DUAL-CAREER COUPLES

Bird, Caroline. *The Two Paycheck Marriage*. New York: Pocket Books, 1979.
Sekaran, Uma. *Dual-Career Families*. San Francisco: Jossey-Bass Publishers, 1986.

THE INFLUENCE OF ALCOHOLISM ON RELATIONSHIPS

Marlin, Emily. *Hope: New Choices and Recovery Strategies for Adult Children of Alcoholism*. New York: Harper & Row, 1987.
Wortitz, Janet Geringer. *Adult Children of Alcoholics*. Pompano Beach, Fla.: Health Communications, 1983.
Wortitz, Janet Geringer. *Marriage on the Rocks*. New York: Delacorte Press, 1979.

SURVIVORS OF SEXUAL ABUSE

Bass, Ellen, and Davis, Laura. *The Courage to Heal: A Guide for Women Survivors of Child Sexual Abuse.* New York: Harper & Row, 1988.

Brownmiller, Susan. *Against Our Will: Men, Women and Rape.* New York: Simon & Schuster, 1975.

Engel, Beverly. *The Right to Innocence: Healing the Tragedy of Childhood Sexual Abuse.* Los Angeles: Jeremy Tarcher, 1982.

LOSS OF RELATIONSHIPS

Colgrove, Melba; Bloomfield, Harold; and McWilliams, Peter. *How to Survive the Loss of a Love.* New York: Bantam Books, 1976.

Index

Index